I0095668

Konstantin Butz, Robert A. Winkler (eds.)
Hardcore Research

Culture & Theory | Volume 281

Konstantin Butz is an assistant professor at the Academy of Media Arts Cologne in Germany. He received his Ph.D. from the University of Cologne in 2012 with a dissertation on the subculture of skate punk.

Robert A. Winkler is an assistant professor at the Paris-Lodron-University Salzburg in Austria. He received his Ph.D. from the International Graduate Centre for the Study of Culture (GCSC) at Justus-Liebig-University Gießen in 2019 with a dissertation on race and gender in hardcore punk.

Konstantin Butz, Robert A. Winkler (eds.)

Hardcore Research

Punk, Practice, Politics

[transcript]

The publication of this book was generously supported by the Academy of Media Arts Cologne (Department of Art and Media Studies), the Paris Lodron University Salzburg (Department of English & American Studies), and the Association for the Promotion of Academic Research at the Paris Lodron University Salzburg (Förderverein zur wissenschaftlichen Forschung an der Paris-Lodron-Universität Salzburg).

PARIS
LODRON
UNIVERSITÄT
SALZBURG

Kunsthochschule für Medien Köln
Academy of Media Arts Cologne

Bibliographic information published by the Deutsche Nationalbibliothek
The Deutsche Nationalbibliothek lists this publication in the Deutsche Nationalbibliografie; detailed bibliographic data are available in the Internet at http://dnb.d-nb.de

Cover layout: Alexander Butz (hello@alxbtz.com)
Cover photograph: © Farrah Skeiky (farrahskeiky.com)

https://doi.org/10.14361/9783839464069
Print-ISBN 978-3-8376-6406-5
PDF-ISBN 978-3-8394-6406-9
ISSN of series: 2702-8968
eISSN of series: 2702-8976

Contents

Introduction

Konstantin Butz and Robert A. Winkler

Beyond *Hardcore '81*

We're a little late to the party. When the idea for this anthology arose during an American Studies conference that we both attended in the spring of 2019, we hoped to be able to publish it in 2021: exactly 40 years after Canadian punk band D.O.A. released their infamous album *Hardcore '81*. Since that record arguably introduced the term "hardcore" in the subcultural context of punk music for the first time,[1] and as numerous popular publications on punk and hardcore culture similarly locate the term's emergence around 1981 (cf. e.g. Blush; Cogan; Keithley; Markey and Schwartz), we thought 2021 would be the perfect year for a publication that looks back at the rich, diverse, and ambiguous events and developments that shaped this subcultural and musical phenomenon up to this very day. We were convinced that the 40th anniversary of hardcore should not pass unnoticed, and thus started brainstorming forms and formats for how to look from today's perspective at this impressive time span. If we were going to "celebrate" 40 years of hardcore, we thought that the most obvious headline for our birthday card could be a simple and yet suggestive homage to what, four decades ago, had been called *Hardcore '81*. We thus came up with the title *Hardcore '21*. Indeed, for the first few months that we began working on the book and reaching out to possible contributors, we were quite content with *Hardcore '21*, as it explicitly marked the contemporary point in time from which we hoped to establish new and critical approaches to hardcore while simultaneously evoking associations with the very first appearances of the term in the North American punk scenes of 1981.

---

1   The record was accompanied by a festival (and tour) called "Hardcore '81," which, alongside D.O.A., presented other influential bands such as California's Black Flag and Nevada's 7 Seconds. In 2021, D.O.A. embarked on a tour through Canada and the US in celebration of 40 years of *Hardcore '81*.

However, a certain pandemic massively interfered with—or better, screwed up—both our own schedules and the schedules of our contributors. Due to COVID-19, priorities were adjusted, deadlines had to be postponed, and some authors unfortunately were forced to cancel their contributions because of pandemic-inflicted obligations. It became very clear that *Hardcore '21* would definitely not be ready for publication in 2021, and, with the passing of time and eventually the beginning and progression of 2021 itself, we realized that this title would no longer work for our book. We did not like the idea of publishing an anthology called *Hardcore '21* in the year '22—let alone '23!— as that would effectively miss the point of alluding to the concrete occasion that inspired it in the first place. Nevertheless, even with an outdated working title and ever-growing delays in our production schedule, many authors remained aboard, first-draft essays went on their way, and we realized that—obviously—our interest in hardcore and its manifold influences was not dependent on a mere date or number anyway. After all, maybe our concentration on the years 1981/2021 and an alleged 40th anniversary had been a bit too obsessive: Why be so formal about a cultural formation whose core values seemed to be organized around questioning and rebelling against formalities and orthodoxies?

The last thing we wanted and want to do with our book is adhere to the contingent and often meaningless ritual of celebrating (sub-) cultural evolutions as fixed events within determined historicizations. Certainly, the year 1981 was decisive for the establishment of "hardcore" as a term that people started to understand within the specific context of punk culture. But who exactly could actually prove that this term had never before been used to articulate that culture's specificities—be it in music, style, or attitude? At least as a musical genre, the roots of hardcore seem to precede the term's popularization in 1981. For instance, in his article, "Rise of Suburban Punk Rock in Los Angeles," historian Dewar MacLeod mentions the extraordinary fastness and loudness of Orange County band The Middle Class on their seven-inch record *Out of Vogue*, and Hermosa Beach band Black Flag on their own seven-inch record *Nervous Breakdown*—both released in 1978—and states: "With these two singles, hardcore was born" (127).[2] From this point of view, we would have to add at least three more candles (and an altered date) to our cake that read *Hardcore '81*, and, still, we could not be sure if there was not yet an older

---

2   See also MacLeod's detailed study *Kids of the Black Hole: Punk Rock in Postsuburban California*.

record, another long-lost article in an overlooked fanzine, or just a forgotten conversation between a few young punks that—even earlier than the above examples—referred to hardcore as either an adjective or a noun with which to express a dedicated involvement in particular subcultural activities.[3] Scene member Steven Blush, in his much-cited book *American Hardcore*,[4] summarizes it this way: "Regardless of the precise origin, when Punks said, 'Hardcore,' other Punks knew what they meant. Hardcore expressed an extreme: the absolute most Punk" (16).[5]

Blush's shift from the "precise origin" of the term to its expressive meaning within the context of punk indicates that hardcore might best be understood as a rather flexible and processual concept that evolves discursively from the conversations and exchanges of its protagonists, instead of relying on a historically fixed definition. Whereas a record such as *Hardcore '81* can bear witness to the linguistic presence of a certain term at a certain time by putting a year on it, the "extreme" that fills the term with concrete meaning depends on the respective punks that enunciate it and actually say (and *live*): "hardcore!"

From *Hardcore California* to *Hardcore Research*

An insight into the diversity that might characterize such an understanding of hardcore as a sustained discourse and lived practice can be found in another very early source: a publication that actually uses the word in a book title for the first time and explicitly ties it to the evolution of punk cultures. In their 1983 *Hardcore California: A History of Punk and New Wave*, Peter Belsito

---

3   Marc Spitz and Brendan Mullen in the "This is Hardcore" chapter of their oral history *We Got the Neutron Bomb: The Untold Story of L.A. Punk*, for instance, classify hardcore as "[l]ouder, faster, angrier" and date it around the year 1979 (x). Similarly, George Hurchalla in *Going Underground: American Punk 1979–1992* and Tony Rettman in *Why be Something that You're Not: Detroit Hardcore 1979–1985* argue that the underground phenomenon of hardcore kicks off at the end of the 1970s.

4   Blush's account also serves as basis for Paul Rachman's 2006 documentary *American Hardcore: The History of American Punk Rock 1980–1986.*

5   Blush exemplarily highlights the close interconnections and ties between punk and hardcore and indicates that they are productively intertwined and related. Acknowledging this inextricable pairing, in this introduction, we chose to use the abbreviation "hardcore/punk" whenever we felt that a specific differentiation between the two was neither necessary nor possible. For the most part, the boundaries between punk and hardcore are fluid.

and Bob Davis present a comprehensive overview of early 1980s punk and hardcore scenes in the two cities of Los Angeles and San Francisco. "Everyone mentioned in this book," the two editors claim, "originated in the hardcore" (7). They continue by exemplarily specifying the term:

> Hardcore: a bleached-blonde defiant sixteen-year-old living alone in a downtown hotel; sleazy but on her own. Hardcore: the S.S.I. [supplemental security income] recipient being paid off by the government to stay out of trouble renting a rehearsal studio with his monthly check. Hardcore: the corporate flunky who quits his job to manage a band of acned adolescents. (ibid.)

With this descriptive introduction, Belsito and Davis evoke the varied cast of 1980s hardcore types that ranged from teenagers to adults, from poverty-stricken musicians to self-proclaimed band managers and way beyond, as the multitude of characters populating the photographs and texts of their book prove. What all of them have in common, the editors emphasize, is that these are "people who did it themselves" (ibid.), thereby anticipating the strong influence of autonomous do-it-yourself (DIY) ethics that shape hardcore cultures until today.[6] And although not everyone mentioned in *Hardcore California* "has continued in the hardcore," Belsito and Davis conclude that "they all know what it means" (ibid.). Thus, they parallel Blush's account of hardcore and the term's semantic reliance on shared knowledge among like-minded people who feel affiliated with punk culture.

Both sources—the books by Blush and Belsito/Davis—seem to conceive of hardcore as an epistemic concept that shapes its protagonists' way of producing meaning and knowledge within a certain local, temporal, and subcultural context. Belsito and Davis, at the end of their preface, gear their take on the fast pace of 1980s hardcore scenes in particular, and the future of hardcore in general:

---

6   For a comprehensive account of the emergence of DIY hardcore/punk record labels in the early 1980s, see Alan O'Connor's *Punk Record Labels and the Struggle for Autonomy: The Emergence of DIY*. Rebekah Cordova traces the educative aspect of hardcore/punk's DIY ethos in *DIY Punk as Education: From Mis-Education to Educative Healing*; Daniel Makagon takes a look at self-organized hardcore/punk concerts in *Underground: The Subterranean Culture of DIY Punk Shows*; and Paula Guerra and Pedro Quintela present nine essays on independent, autonomous, and improvised hardcore/punk publishing in their anthology *Punk, Fanzines and DIY Cultures in a Global World: Fast, Furious and Xerox*.

Every 18 to 24 months a new generation passes through the scene. There are bands discussed in this book that weren't even formed when we began compiling information in 1981. The people change, but the scene stays young. Later, even the title of the pop underground and its philosophy *will* change. Regardless of the name they choose, the hardcore are always the hardcore. (ibid.)[7]

Forty years after Belsito and Davis acknowledged hardcore as the "pop underground" and described its early adherents, hardcore and its philosophy has *indeed* changed, progressed, and eventually become the autonym of a subculture that—while fans and aficionados would certainly still claim that they "all know what it means"—has actually diversified into a whole variety of movements and subgroups.[8] From packs of privileged young white men who turn their suburban boredom into ultrafast and violent music performances, to ethically aware communities engaged in the peace movement, civil rights, anti-racism, and animal liberation; from kids who organize DIY concerts in countries all over the world to bands that relentlessly tour the globe and thus either rely on old or establish new networks for like-minded musicians; from punk rockers who turn to spirituality and preach abstinence from alcohol and drugs, to feminist and queer groups fighting patriarchal structures and undermining heteronormative sexuality: what unifies everyone who identifies with the term hardcore is an either self-proclaimed or imposed position outside of normative structures.[9] In this sense, "hardcore has always remained

---

7   Throughout this introduction and in the articles of our anthology, quotes in italics are emphasized in the original unless noted otherwise.

8   Beyond the various forms of the subculture of hardcore tied to punk that constitute the focus of this anthology, there are a number of other (sub-) cultural phenomena that make use of the same term, the most obvious ones being hardcore pornography (see e.g. Linda Williams) and hardcore techno and rave (see e.g. Jeremy Gilbert).

9   A list of publications that touches on all facets of hardcore can obviously not be exhaustive, and will always remain preliminary. In the following we make a few suggestions (beyond the works of the authors who contribute to this anthology) of where to start reading about the respective topics: For an extensive collection of primary and secondary sources documenting the nexus of hardcore/punk, race in general, and whiteness in particular, see Stephen Duncombe and Maxwell Tremblay's *White Riot: Punk Rock and the Politics of Race*; Jonathan Pieslak delves into the complex relation of hardcore/punk scenes and radical deep ecology groups in *Music and Radicalism: An Introduction to the Music Cultures of al-Qa'ida, Racist Skinheads, Christian-Affiliated Radicals, and Eco-Animal Rights Militants*; Phoenix X Eeyore provides insights into the history of earth

the hardcore" in providing the means for different manifestations of a critical subcultural avant-garde—be it aesthetically, ethically, or politically. As an emancipatory movement that set out to question, challenge, and alter the existing structures of both corporate and independent music scenes as well as particular social conditions and society at large, hardcore's main "political" claim was and still is to offer an alternative to what is perceived as the norm and the mainstream.

In the year 2023, there are still hardcore bands, hardcore shows, hardcore zines (both online and in print), and—just as Belsito and Davis with their 1983 publication—there are still people who write and compile books, essays, and texts that comment on, document, and analyze hardcore. And, in fact, with regard to the latter activity we have an actual (and pretty precise) anniversary to celebrate: While we missed the "birthday" of *Hardcore '81* and while it remains hard to really pinpoint when exactly hardcore emerged as a subcultural formation, it is pretty safe to say that *Hardcore California*, exactly 40 years ago, indeed constituted "the most complete document in existence dealing with this subject" as the editors themselves had rightly estimated (7). Thus, while we would (now) definitely refrain from framing our anthology as a booklet to accompany the 40th birthday ceremony of hardcore itself, we really like the idea of contextualizing it as an acknowledgement of 40 years of analytical and

---

and animal liberation in the US hardcore scene in *Total Revolution? An Outsider History of Hardline: From Vegan Straight Edge and Radical Animal Rights to Millenarian Mystical Muslims and Antifascist Fascism*; for accounts of the emergence, proliferation, politics, and contradictions of Straight Edge see Ross Haenfler's *Straight Edge: Clean-Living Youth, Hardcore Punk, and Social Change*, Gabriel Kuhn's two books *Sober Living for the Revolution: Hardcore Punk, Straight Edge, and Radical Politics* and *X: Straight Edge and Radical Sobriety*, Brian Peterson's *Burning Fight: The Nineties Hardcore Revolution in Ethics, Politics, Spirit, and Sound* as well as Robert T. Wood's *Straightedge: Complexity and Contradictions of a Subculture*; the history of homocore/queercore is covered by David Ciminelli and Ken Knox's *Homocore: The Loud and Raucous Rise of Queer Rock*; for our German-speaking readers we recommend the excellent *Homopunk History* by Philipp Meinert; Curran Nault analyzes the connection of queer theory/practice and hardcore/punk theory/practice with emphasis on queercore mediamaking in *Queercore: Queer Punk Media Subculture*; for decidedly feminist takes on hardcore/punk see e.g. Lauraine Leblanc's *Pretty in Punk: Girl's Gender Resistance in a Boys' Subculture*, Vivien Goldman's *Revenge of the She-Punks: A Feminist Music History From Poly Styrene to Pussy Riot*, and, for our German-speaking readers, *Our Piece of Punk: Ein queer_feministischer Blick auf den Kuchen*, edited by Barbara Lüdde and Judit Vetter, as well as *Punk as F*ck: Die Szene aus FLINTA-Perspektive*, edited by Diana Ringelsiep and Ronja Schwikowski.

documentary *writing* about hardcore and consequently: 40 years of *hardcore research*.[10]

Although the editors of *Hardcore California* themselves explained that the content of their book "didn't come from the record room at the library" as they drew "more on experience than on dry research" (ibid.), we still—and for that very reason—perceive them as pioneers and practitioners of doing active and concrete research on the specific subject matter of hardcore, who in doing so proved that it is not only possible but also extremely insightful and thought-provoking to publish a whole book on such an eclectic subcultural topic. With their work, Belsito and Davis paved the way for far-reaching and comprehensive approaches to hardcore and punk that have eventually materialized in the works and analyses of dedicated (academic) researchers—some of which we have the privilege of bringing together in this volume. They provide proof that while hardcore developed as a subcultural phenomenon over the last forty years, it simultaneously migrated into academic fields as a subject of diverse scholarly disciplines including anthropology, philosophy, American studies, Chicana/o Studies, cultural studies, musicology, political science, queer studies, sociology, history, and literature. It is from these discursive standpoints that the scholars in this anthology establish their analytic accounts of past and present hardcore/punk.[11]

Hardcore Researchers

As most academic authors working on hardcore/punk bring a decidedly personal interest to this cultural and musical phenomenon and many explicitly mention their own involvement in hardcore/punk scenes and networks,

---

10   Of course, there has been analytical writing about punk in general before Belsito and Davis used the specific title *Hardcore California* in 1983 and thereby introduced that particular term into the existing literature on punk. The most obvious example would certainly be Dick Hebdige's 1979 *Subculture: The Meaning of Style*, which still pops up in every introduction to books and essays on punk, hardcore, and alternative (youth) cultures. Interestingly, the word "hardcore" does appear at one point in Hebdige's book; however, he merely uses it to refer to members of the British subculture at hand, i.e. "hardcore members" who preferred the "derisory connotations" of the name "punk" as opposed to "the more neutral 'new wave'" (112). Thus, Hebdige does not implement the word as a specific subcultural term or autonym in itself.

11   See footnote 5 for a comment on the abbreviation "hardcore/punk."

this book delineates a scholarly field that is deeply embedded in self-reflexive subcultural engagement. In this sense, our anthology is both about hardcore/punk as a subcultural phenomenon and about ways of doing research that are literally *hardcore*—i.e., with the utmost dedication and emancipatory ideals. It introduces various academic perspectives that engage different methods of professional research to analyze and dissect the subcultural fringes and broader cultural interconnections in which hardcore/punk materializes. What we think of and tentatively frame as "hardcore research" with the title of our book fuses passionate interest, live and lived experience, and academic rigor. Our anthology thus brings together different notions of both subcultural and scholarly practice by interconnecting the authors' practical involvement in hardcore/punk contexts—ranging from musicianship to political activism to cultural and journalistic commentary—and their methodological expertise in different academic fields. From this angle, our contributors are "hardcore researchers." They work and teach in academia; most of them received doctoral degrees through directly working on hardcore/punk; and all of them have personal histories of active participation and passionate interest in hardcore/punk scenes around the globe.[12] Their personal and pro-

---

12   The contributions in this anthology mainly focus on the North American context, which is probably not too surprising given the fact that we both come from the field of American Studies, and thus have mainly approached the study of hardcore/punk from that specific angle. Consequently, in compiling this book, we reached out to authors who have been influential for our research and who work with a similar focus on North American hardcore/punk. However, we want to explicitly emphasize that the notion of "hardcore research" would by no means be complete by considering only North American scenes. In fact, there are countless studies that document and analyze hardcore/punk cultures all over the globe. For a first impression of the richness of "hardcore research" beyond North America, see for example: Russ Bestley, Mike Dines, Alastair Gordon, and Paula Guerra's two edited volumes *The Punk Reader: Research Transmissions from the Local and the Global* and *Trans-Global Punk Scenes: The Punk Reader. Volume 2*; Julian C H Lee and Marco Ferrarese's anthology *Punks, Monks, and Politics: Authenticity in Thailand, Indonesia and Malaysia*; Marquis H.K.'s *Thirty Years of Anger: One Man's Journey through the Australian Underground Hardcore Punk & Extreme Metal Scenes*; Deon Maas and Keith Jones' documentary *Punk in Africa*; Jennifer Milioto Matsue's *Making Music in Japan's Underground: The Underground Tokyo Hardcore Scene*; Olga Rodríguez-Ulloa, Rodrigo Quijano, and Shane Greene's *Punk!: Las Américas Edition*; Ingo Rohrer's *Cohesion and Dissolution: Friendship in the Globalized Punk and Hardcore Scene of Buenos Aires*; and Jian Xiao's *Punk Culture in Contemporary China*.

fessional biographies predestine them as experts who present insightful and critical examinations of both the rich and varied histories of this subcultural phenomenon, and its current reverberations at the intersection of cultural and academic practice.

While we might be among only a handful of academics who would have considered acknowledging (or commemorating) the occasion of an alleged 40th anniversary of hardcore and, even more specifically, the 40th anniversary of analytic *writing* about hardcore, we are by no means the first ones to think about the nexus of hardcore/punk and academia in general. In 2012, Zack Furness edited the volume *Punkademics: The Basement Show in the Ivory Tower*, stating that he did so because he was "intensely curious about the ways in which people reconciled their interests and understood the dynamics between [the] two very different 'scenes'" of punk and academia (8). In his book, Furness presents around a dozen essays that uniquely illustrate "what other people had to say about scholarship on punk" and "broadly speaking, [...] what kind of sense people made of their punk/academic situation" (ibid.). We understand the anthology *Hardcore Research* as a contribution to and perpetuation of the project that Furness initiated a decade ago with *Punkademics*, and we reinforce his contention that academic scholarship on hardcore/punk has not only contributed to rethinking punk history, re-conceptualizing its dynamics, challenging hegemonic narratives about punk and its politics, but also—most significantly—that it "expand[s] the parameters of research itself" (18). As the subtitle of *Hardcore Research* implies, we are interested in what kinds and interpretations of *punk*(s) pervade and underlie hardcore, what kinds of *practice*(s)—both cultural and academic—our authors find compelling, and what kinds of *politics* shape and drive the scenes, participants, and articulations of hardcore/punk. In nodding to the 40 years of writing about hardcore that we can look back at today, our book provides a heuristic presentation of contemporary perspectives that constantly foster that ongoing discourse and the accompanying dialog between hardcore/punk scenes and hardcore/punk research(ers). While far from being exhaustive, and indeed without any interest in claiming completeness, the selection of contributions that we chose to present in this anthology introduces sixteen individual takes on a flourishing subcultural phenomenon that continues to provoke extremely diverse analyses, reactions, reflections, and discussions. The different articles do not holistically define what hardcore research *is*, but they offer distinct insights into the richness of what it *can be*.

Cover and Concept

On the cover of this book, we are extremely pleased to feature a photograph by Farrah Skeiky, a well-known Arab-American photographer, creative director, and writer based in Washington, DC. In 2020 she self-published the book *Present Tense: DC Punk and DIY Right Now*, which she describes "as a response to those who might think that DC punk died out in the 90s, or speak to the creativity of this community in the past tense" (Skeiky). She conceives of her book as "an argument against nostalgia, against complacency. It is a celebration of one of the most revered traditions of modern music, in the context of today" (ibid.). In that sense, we consider Skeiky herself an actual hardcore researcher, as her photographic work documents a striving scene while being characterized by an extraordinary sense for those particular moments of physical and musical intensity that have always defined hardcore/punk performances. Her extraordinary shot of the crowd—or the "pit," as many hardcore/punk kids would call it—in interaction with musicians of the Baltimore hardcore band Turnstile not only perfectly captures such a moment but also features a contemporary band that, particularly with their 2021 album *Glow On*, proves that—more than 40 years into its existence—the genre of hardcore music can still bring forth highly innovative art and expression. In a sense, *Glow On* represents a popular and critically acclaimed version of what—to again invoke the draft title of our book—could in fact be regarded as Hardcore '21, which of course makes a photograph of Turnstile even more fitting for the cover of this anthology.[13] In addition to its remarkable account of present-day hardcore, the "pit" in Skeiky's photograph also parallels the way we look at the organization and presentation of the contributions in this book. It implies a concrete instruction for our readers:

---

13   Yes, we know that there is no accounting for musical taste and not everyone who follows contemporary hardcore might necessarily place Turnstile on the top of their record shelves (or streaming playlists for that matter) but a brief look at the video "Turnstile Love Connection" or their Tiny Desk appearance (you will find both on *YouTube*) indicates to what extent they exemplify a version of hardcore that goes beyond a thirty-second song of three distorted guitar chords—which, of course, would still be a perfectly fine and genre-defining way of playing hardcore as well. Personally, we love both. Regardless of Turnstile's position within the contemporary hardcore scene, we regard Skeiky's photo of them and their audience as an exemplary document of the participatory moments and openings that hardcore music can create for both musicians and audiences alike.

Just as the "pit" does not work according to a strictly choreographed arrangement and instead offers a multitude of opportunities to enter and to participate, we refrained from imposing a fixed sequence or chronology upon the different contributions that constitute *Hardcore Research*. Of course, it is possible to read this book from front to back, but we would rather invite you to approach the articles presented here similar to the setting of a hardcore show and just (stage-) dive right into it at your convenience. You might bump into a text that you will wholeheartedly disagree with; you might pogo along with authors and theories that you are familiar with and that you call friends; you might slam dance with contentions that you find either convincing or far-fetched: whatever you take away from *Hardcore Research*, it is our hope that you find it inspiring for further reflections on the complex facets of the topic at hand. The best-case scenario for us would, once again, be metaphorically linked to the setting depicted in Skeiky's cover photograph. In analogy to Turnstile's lead vocalist Brenden Yates, who screams out his version of hardcore directly from within the crowd, from within the individuals that carry him and make his performance possible, from within the different shouts and cheers that constitute the many-voiced pit that is hardcore, we encourage you to read *Hardcore Research* as an invitation to articulate and contribute your own voice: whether it is to shout back, sing along, or present your own individual lyrics.

Content and Contributors

To guide your choice of where to enter *Hardcore Research*, in the following, and in accordance with our table of contents, we alphabetically list our contributors and briefly introduce the titles and topics of their respective articles:

Gerfried Ambrosch uses his article "Changing Perspectives: From Participation to Observation (Autoethnography of a Punk Researcher)" to consider the change in perspective that accompanies a switch from participating as an active member of the hardcore/punk scene to observing it as researcher. He undergirds his reflections with references to his own experiences as a touring hardcore musician.

Ellen Bernhard, in "Milo Goes to College, Ellen Goes to Grad School: The Series of Events that Turned an Afterschool Hobby into a Hardcore Pursuit of Punk Rock" takes us on her journey from high school to grad school and the academic interest she develops in the hardcore/punk scenes and music that shaped her youth. She writes from the perspective of a generation that grew up with (and learned about hardcore/punk from) the internet, and considers the relevance of the punk rock ethos for her teaching activities in the field of digital communication.

In "A Network of Hardcore Researchers: Punk Studies, Punk Scholarship, Punk Pedagogy," **Russ Bestley**, **Mike Dines**, and **Francis Stewart** provide an overview of punk scholarship with a particular focus on the Punk Scholars Network (PSN) and the history of changing methodological approaches towards the subject of hardcore/punk. The many works they reference in their bibliography provide an excellent starting point for further reading into the academic study of punk and hardcore.

Marcus Clayton, in "'Dancing on the Corpses' Ashes': On Post-Hardcore Performance and Erased Nonwhite Bodies," engages the punk ethos to highlight the underestimated survival of nonwhite, Afrolatinx, and queer bodies through the power of performance. He presents a close analysis of hardcore/punk videos with a particular focus on the work of El Paso's late 1990s post-hardcore band At The Drive-In.

Brian Cogan, who published the comprehensive *Encyclopedia of Punk Music and Culture*, and **Kevin Dunn**, author of *Global Punk: Resistance and Rebellion in Everyday Life*, seized the occasion of our anthology to converse about their careers writing about hardcore/punk. Representing very different academic trajectories, in their contribution "Hardcore, Punk, and Academia" they discuss their involvement within punk scenes, how their personal experiences and interests have led them to the similar task of writing punk scholarship, and what it means to be a "hardcore academic" from their individual perspectives.

Sean Cullen, in "'Survival of the Streets': Krishna Consciousness and Religion in Hardcore Punk at the End of the Cold War," discusses conceptions of the hardcore subgenre of Straight Edge, as well as the notions of the sacred and the secular within hardcore/punk, by looking at the influences of Krishna spirituality on the American punk scene in general and on hardcore vocalist Ray Cappo and his bands Youth of Today and Shelter in particular.

Recalling Canadian hardcore punk band D.O.A.'s debut album (the predecessor to *Hardcore '81*) in the title of his contribution "*Something Better Change*: Hardcore and the Promise of a Liberating Punk Education," **David Ensminger** reflects on hardcore punk praxis in the context of a pedagogy that helps students to empower and emancipate themselves from existing power structures. In doing so, he includes considerations of the chances and challenges of contemporary internet phenomena and online education.

Shayna Maskell looks at the construction of race within hardcore/punk by reconsidering the narratives associated with the seminal all-black hardcore band Bad Brains. In "'There is no hope for the USA': Bad Brains and The Sounds of Race in DC Hardcore," she analyzes the band's history and their performances of multiple racial identities in view of the complicated aesthetics of racialized sound, the reinterpretation of rock 'n' roll, the lyrical parallels to folk music, and the inclusion of reggae.

With our contribution "Ms. Bob Davis and *Hardcore California*: A Conversation About a Forty-Year-Old Document of Hardcore Research" we come full circle and include an exclusive interview with one of the editors of *Hardcore California: A History of Punk and New Wave*. In addition to recalling the genealogy of her and Belsito's 1983 book, **Ms. Bob Davis** touches on early punk and art scenes around the famous DIY venue Valencia Tool & Die in San Francisco and her unique career as a musician, academic, and transgender activist.

In their article "Writing *from* Hardcore: Interwoven Lines of Becoming," **Alain Müller** and **Marion Schulze** explore heuristic potentialities to capture hardcore as a constructive force by referring to the conceptual apparatus of Gilles Deleuze and Félix Guattari. In doing so, they reflect on the intimate relationship between hardcore and their own research as academics.

Alan Parkes' comprehensive account "White Punks in the Chocolate City: Hardcore and Local History in Washington, DC" provides a detailed insight into youth cultures in late twentieth-century DC by showing that the history of hardcore stands not only to expose the significance of the subculture, but also the histories and deep-seated political and social realities which influenced its members.

David Pearson offers a rare musicological approach to hardcore in his article "The Musical Aesthetics of Hardcore: Straightforward, Strident, and Antagonistic." While offering analytical accounts of hardcore style and rhetoric through readings of exemplary songs and their notations, Pearson articulates a straightforward critique of postmodern theory, which we encourage to read in fruitful and productive contrast to Daniel S. Traber's rather postmodern contribution to this anthology.

In her article "Adventures of a DIY Oral Historian: How the Hardcore Punk Rock Scene of the 1980s Continues to Influence My Life as a Writer," **Stacy Russo**, author of the book *We Were Going to Change the World: Interviews with Women from the 1970s & 1980s Southern California Punk Rock Scene*, offers a very personal reflection on her writerly practice and its interconnections to her experiences in the early California hardcore scene.

Daniel S. Traber, in "Whose Loud Fast Rules? – Always Already Post-Hardcore," presents a unique look back at the last (almost) 40 years of his preoccupation with punk and hardcore by establishing an incomplete and random list of what he labels as post-hardcore precursors. Traber engages and relies on postmodern thought and theory, which we encourage reading in fruitful and productive contrast to the straightforward critique of postmodernism that David Pearson articulates in his contribution.

With his article "'Have You Never Been Mellow?' – Joy and Ugliness in Punk and Hardcore Aesthetics," **Maxwell Tremblay** presents a very pointed and witty commentary on the singular aesthetics of punk and hardcore by discussing it within the scope of personal observations and accompanying philosophical and cultural implications.

Extending and recapitulating the findings of her highly comprehensive book *Queer-Feminist Punk: An Anti-Social History*, **Katharina Wiedlack**, in her contribution "Queer-feminist Hardcore/Punk: Academic Research and Community Support in the Age of the Pandemic," maps out how queer-feminist hardcore/punk answers to the contemporary moment. She considers the backlash against queers, trans* and non-normatively gender individuals, and women* spearheaded by the Trump administration, the interconnections between queer-feminist hardcore/punks and the Black Lives Matter movement, and the ramifications of—and subcultural reactions to—the COVID-19 pandemic.

Last but not least, we would like to point to the "Contributors" section with author biographies at the end of this book. Besides short CVs, it includes a questionnaire for every contributor listing up to three of their most important publications on hardcore/punk, three records that shaped their interest in hardcore/punk, three theoretical books that are important for them, and the first hardcore/punk show as well as the first academic conference they attended. We regard this information as providing not only interesting insights into the personal and academic backgrounds of our authors, but also inspiration for further reading, hearing, and looking into the subcultural and academic discourses that underlie and pervade the articles in *Hardcore Research*.

References and Further Reading

American Hardcore: The History of American Punk Rock 1980-1986. Written by Steven Blush, directed by Paul Rachman, Sony Pictures, 2006.

Belsito, Peter, and Bob Davis (eds.). *Hardcore California: A History of Punk and New Wave*. 1983. The Last Gasp of San Francisco, [8th printing] 2004.

Bestley, Russ, Dines, Michael, Gordon, Alastair, and Paula Guerra (eds.). *The Punk Reader: Research Transmissions from the Local and the Global*. Intellect, 2019.

Bestley, Russ, Dines, Michael, Gordon, Alastair, and Paula Guerra (eds.). *Trans-Global Punk Scenes: The Punk Reader. Volume 2*. Intellect, 2021.

Blush, Steven. *American Hardcore*. Feral House, 2001.

Ciminelli, David, and Ken Knox. *Homocore: The Loud and Raucous Rise of Queer Rock*. Alyson Publications, 2005.

Cogan, Brian *The Encyclopedia of Punk*. Sterling Publishing, 2008.

Cordova, Rebekah. *DIY Punk as Education: From Mis-Education to Educative Healing*. Information Age Publishing, 2017.

Duncombe, Stephen, and Maxwell Tremblay (eds.). *White Riot: Punk Rock and the Politics of Race*. Verso, 2011.

Eeyore, Phoenix X. *Total Revolution? An Outsider History of Hardline: From Vegan Straight Edge and Radical Animal Rights to Millenarian Mystical Muslims and Antifascist Fascism*. Warcry Communications, 2022.

Furness, Zack. *Punkademics: The Basement Show in the Ivory Tower*. Minor Compositions & Autonomedia, 2012.

Gilbert, Jeremy. "The Hardcore Continuum? – A Report on the 'The Hardcore Continuum?' Symposium Held at the University of East London, April 29th 2009." *Dancecult: Journal of Electronic Dance Music Culture*, 1.1, 2009, pp. 118–22.

Goldman, Vivien. *Revenge of the She-Punks: A Feminist Music History from Poly Styrene to Pussy Riot*. University of Texas Press, 2019.

Guerra, Paula, and Pedro Quintela (eds.). *Punk, Fanzines and DIY Cultures in a Global World: Fast, Furious and Xerox*. Palgrave Macmillan, 2020.

Haenfler, Ross. *Straight Edge: Clean-Living Youth, Hardcore Punk, and Social Change*. Rutgers University Press, 2006.

Hebdige, Dick. *Subculture – The Meaning of Style*. 1979. Routledge, 2006.

H.K., Marquis. *Thirty Years of Anger: One Man's Journey through the Australian Underground Hardcore Punk & Extreme Metal Scenes*. Boolarong Press, 2016.

Hurchalla, George. *Going Underground: American Punk 1979-1992*. AK Press, 2005.

Keithley, Joe. *Talk – Action = 0 – An Illustrated History of D.O.A.* Arsenal Pulp Press, 2011.

Kuhn, Gabriel. *Sober Living for the Revolution: Hardcore Punk, Straight Edge, and Radical Politics*. PM Press, 2010.

Kuhn, Gabriel. *X: Straight Edge and Radical Sobriety*. PM Press, 2019.

Leblanc, Lauraine. *Pretty in Punk: Girl's Gender Resistance in a Boys' Subculture*. Rutgers University Press, 1999.

Lee, Julian CH, and Marco Ferrarese. *Punks, Monks and Politics: Authenticity in Thailand, Indonesia and Malaysia*. Rowman & Littlefield International, 2018.

Lüdde, Barbara, and Judit Vetter (eds.). *Our Piece of Punk: Ein queer_feministischer Blick auf den Kuchen*. Ventil, 2018.

MacLeod, Dewar. *Kids of the Black Hole: Punk Rock in Postsuburban California*. University of Oklahoma Press, 2010.

MacLeod, Dewar. "'Social Distortion' – The Rise of Suburban Punk Rock in Los Angeles." *America Under Construction – Boundaries and Identities in Popular Culture*, edited by Kristi S. Long and Matthew Nadelhaft, Garland Publishing, 1997, pp. 123–48.

Makagon, Daniel. *Underground: The Subterranean World of DIY Punk Shows*. Microcosm Publishing, 2015.

Markey, David and Jordan Schwartz. *We Got Power! – Hardcore Punk Scenes from 1980s Southern California*. Bazillion Points, 2012.

Matsue, Jennifer Milioto. *Making Music in Japan's Underground: The Underground Tokyo Hardcore Scene*. Routledge, 2009.

Meinert, Philipp. *Homopunk History*. Ventil, 2018.

Nault, Curran. *Queercore: Queer Punk Media Subculture*. Routledge, 2018.

O'Connor, Alan. *Punk Record Labels and the Struggle for Autonomy: The Emergence of DIY*. Lexington Books, 2008.

Peterson, Brian. *Burning Fight: The Nineties Hardcore Revolution in Ethics, Politics, Spirit, and Sound*. Revelation Records, 2009.

Pieslak, Jonathan. *Music and Radicalism: An Introduction to the Music Cultures of al-Qa'ida, Racist Skinheads, Christian-Affiliated Radicals, and Eco-Animal Rights Militants*. University Press of New England, 2015.

Punk in Africa: Three Chords, Three Countries, One Revolution. Directed by Deon Maas and Keith Jones; produced by Keith Jones and Jeffrey Brown, 2012.

Rettman, Tony. *Why be Something that You're Not: Detroit Hardcore 1979-1985*. Revelation Records, 2010.

Ringelsiep, Diana, and Ronja Schwikowski (eds.). *Punk as F*ck: Die Szene aus FLINTA-Perspektive*. Ventil, 2022.

Rodríguez-Ulloa, Olga, Quijano, Rodrigo, and Shane Greene (eds.). *Punk!: Las Américas Edition*. Intellect, 2021.

Rohrer, Ingo. *Cohesion and Dissolution: Friendship in the Globalized Punk and Hardcore Scene of Buenos Aires*. Springer, 2014.

Skeiky, Farrah. farrahskeiky.com. Accessed 11 Aug. 2022.

Spitz, Mark, and Brendan Mullen. *We Got the Neutron Bomb – The Untold Story of L.A. Punk*. Three Rivers Press, 2001.

Williams, Linda. *Hard Core: Power, Pleasure, and the "Frenzy of the Visible."* University of California Press, 1989.

Wood, Robert T. *Straightedge Youth: Complexity and Contradictions of a Subculture*. Syracuse University Press, 2006.

Xiao, Jian. *Punk Culture in Contemporary China*. Palgrave Macmillan, 2018.

Changing Perspectives: From Participation to Observation (Autoethnography of a Punk Researcher)

Gerfried Ambrosch

When I interviewed Greg Bennick, singer for the straight edge hardcore punk band Trial from Seattle, I asked him what other aspects of his life, besides his musical activities, were influenced by hardcore. "Everything!" he replied. "It influences everything. My life revolves around hardcore" (Bennick 166). The same used to apply to me. In fact, it was the reason I decided to become a punk researcher. However, doing so entailed a change in perspective, from participation to observation, from subjective involvement to objective scholarly analysis. Though I do not consider these two approaches mutually exclusive, academic rigor can have the effect of shattering idealized perceptions. But challenging narratives and orthodoxies has always been part of punk culture.[1] This attitude lends itself to punk research as well. According to Bad Religion singer Greg Graffin, who is an evolutionary biologist, "Punk rock, at its best, embraces an openness to experience, a reliance on reason and evidence, and a questioning of received wisdom" (Graffin and Olson 6). In Graffin's opinion, this pertains to punk as well as to science, which "also is about questioning and not settling for dogma" (6). At its worst, however, punk creates ideological echo chambers: the antithesis of intellectual openness and a hindrance to free and critical inquiry. As early as 1981, this tendency prompted the Dead Kennedys to proclaim, "Punk ain't no religious cult / Punk means thinking for yourself" (Dead Kennedys). These lyrics from their song "Nazi Punks Fuck Off" reflect an area of tension within punk culture, between tribalistic dog-

---

1 For simplicity's sake, I use the term *punk* to refer to both punk rock and hardcore (unless a distinction is required).

matism and independent thought, which is both fascinating to investigate and (potentially) difficult for punk researchers to navigate.

One thing punk researchers tend to have in common is that most of us used to be—or still are—actively involved in punk communities. This, I believe, is a valid generalization, for the simple reason that active participation in the scene—as opposed to mere spectatorship of the kind associated with mass entertainment—is part and parcel of what it means to be a punk rocker or hardcore *kid* as well as an important source of empowerment. Arguably, such participation is almost a prerequisite for becoming a punk researcher. Punk, with its long and rich histories, is simply too complex and multifaceted a subject to be explored and understood from the sidelines. Therefore, when it comes to punk research and scholarship, active involvement in the scene should not be regarded as a cause for concern (bias) but, instead, as a valuable asset. Take my own biography. As a touring musician, I have been able to collect intimate insights into international DIY punk communities, from Vancouver to London to Istanbul. Spanning more than half of my life—and more than half of punk history—my decades-long involvement in the DIY punk scene has undoubtedly benefitted my research. Published in 2018, my monograph, *The Poetry of Punk: The Meaning behind Punk Rock and Hardcore Lyrics*, would not have been possible without it. Ultimately, however, punk researchers who are, or used to be, involved in punk must learn to see punk culture—*their* culture—with new, disinterested eyes. When subjected to critical scrutiny, many of the customs, values, and beliefs one has shared for many years suddenly appear in a different light. This may elicit a sense of schizophrenia, especially in those who, like this researcher, never fully retired from punk.[2] As difficult as such a change of perspective may be, it is exactly what is required in order to make one's research accessible to scholars who have no, or extremely limited, knowledge of the goings-on in punk communities. Thus, the punk researcher acts as a link and mediator between punk culture and academia. The goal of punk research and scholarship, in my opinion, should be to promote a better understanding of this fascinating culture, which, for all its flaws, has played a key role in many people's lives as well as in the development of popular culture more broadly. This influence is by no means limited to music or the ivory towers of academia. The fact that US presidential candidate Beto O'Rourke cited Ian MacKaye of Minor Threat and Fugazi as a major inspiration in his life—"I have so much reverence for

---

2   Prior to the Covid-19 pandemic, my bands used to tour on a semi-regular basis.

him and he means so much to me in my life" (O'Rourke)—illustrates punk's influence on wider society. Punk research is a way of making sense of this phenomenon.

Situated at the crossroads of Literary and Cultural Studies, my own research has primarily focused on punk lyrics, both as a form of poetry and as vectors of meaning within punk communities. They are an ideal means by which to trace the developments and explain the conflicts and schisms that have shaped—and *continue* to shape—punk culture. I had the opportunity to ask a number of influential punk lyricists, including Ian MacKaye, Jello Biafra, Ray Cappo, and Henry Rollins, about their different approaches to songwriting and the role and significance of the lyrics in punk. Though their answers varied considerably, most of my interviewees agreed that the lyrics occupied a special place in the construction of a punk song. Perhaps more so than in other genres, it is the interplay of music and lyrics, of sound and sense, that determines the impact and meaning of punk rock and hardcore songs. One peculiarity of punk, in particular hardcore punk, is that the high-octane delivery of the lyrics often makes punk vocalists difficult to understand. Indeed, seemingly inarticulate vocal styles, such as shouting and screaming, appear to be especially prevalent in underground punk scenes that set great store on lyrical expression, often as a means of conveying political messages.[3] Though extreme vocalization has largely lost its shock value, this tendency is rooted in punk's rejection of societal norms and expectations, as Brian D., the singer of the anarchist hardcore band Catharsis, explains:

> [T]hat's one of the aspects in which punk is a really fundamental refusal of the way that human beings are constructed in this society. Punk fashion is about looking unemployable. Punk politics are about refusing to play the game, and even punk vocalisation is about incomprehensibility, is about becoming wild, and that creates a situation in which the lyrics are not important in the way that they are in conventional acoustic guitar folk music. (Brian D. 100)

This raises the question: in what ways *are* the lyrics important? "[W]e need to know that the lyrics are there, that there's substance in the words behind what's happening musically," argues Greg Bennick (150). Hardcore, he continues, is "music that is played passionately as an expression of truth, and

---

3   My favorite example of this approach is the song "Arsonist's Prayer" by Catharsis (Catharsis; see Ambrosch 163–173).

the lyrics augment that passion and specify that truth. ... it's passionate music and lyrics" (152). However, at the same time, the meaning of punk songs is, to a large extent, context-dependent: "I don't hear your band while walking through a shopping mall," explains Bennick; "I hear your band in a broken house in Vancouver, BC.[4] So, from the context, I can draw that we share some ideas in common, so I can appreciate what's happening" (152). This idea of a community based on shared beliefs, a shared ethos, is central to many people's conception of what punk is or should be. As the band Gorilla Biscuits put it in 1989, "We believed the same things" (Gorilla Biscuits). The song that contains this lyric, "New Direction," is dismissive of career-oriented bands that pursue a new, more commercial musical direction and thus demonstrate that they no longer share the same values and ideas as their former peers from the hardcore scene. This both agrees and conflicts with Ian MacKaye's definition of punk and "what people call hardcore" (MacKaye 185). For MacKaye, punk "is a place where new ideas can be presented without bowing to, or being pushed along by, profit motives." Indeed, "what [punk] is most interested in is new ideas and giving a place for people to present those ideas" (185).

Punk's anti-commercialism, however, is embedded in an ideological framework which can function as a filter for unwelcome ideas and viewpoints. This creates echo chambers, especially in underground punk communities, where certain political opinions are held as axiomatic and, therefore, are seldom challenged. For instance, the narrative that Western society and its institutions are inherently oppressive and exploitative—which ignores the enormous increase in human freedom and well-being that has been achieved through political and economic democratization—appears to be immune to falsification. Ideas that easily attach to this worldview, however, are often readily absorbed into punk culture.

Perhaps one of the most peculiar developments in the history of punk has been the influx of religious groups, which provoked a strong immune reaction in large pockets of the scene. Punk, after all, had always rejected (organized) religion. This trend, and the surrounding controversy, which led to heated debates between those who insisted that religion had no place in punk and those who argued that, if punk was serious in its critique of Western society's culture of materialism, it should be open to 'spiritual' messages, culminated in the 1990s when bands like Shelter—Youth of Today singer Ray Cappo's massively popular Krishnacore outfit—introduced Krishnaism to the

---

4   Bennick is referring to my band's performance a few nights earlier.

(straight edge) hardcore scene. Other denominations, in particular Christianity and Islam, also gained considerable influence in the 1990s and early 2000s and were met with similar hostility from atheist and agnostic punks. The crux of this conflict was whether punk, as a broadly progressive movement that prides itself in tolerance and open-mindedness, should tolerate tendencies that many participants regarded as reactionary. Brian D., a dyed-in-the-wool anarchist, strongly objects to the idea that punk and religion go together:

> Part of the vitality of the hardcore scene was the constant debates about what should or shouldn't have a place in it. So on the one hand, I guess I can't complain about spirituality in hardcore, when I wanted so much for it to be a space for radical organizing and resistance; on the other hand, I feel that hardcore has always been at its best as a place of rejection of the status quo, and fucking religion is part of the status quo. (qtd. in Peterson 110)

While I am partial to the view that punk and religion do *not* go together, I was eager to hear the other side of the argument, which is why I chose to interview punk legend Ray "Raghunath" Cappo, a Hare Krishna devotee and the author of songs such as "In Defense of Reality," which may best be described as an attack on the scientific worldview: "Today's modern science is your modern religion. ... blind faith in their decision" (Shelter).[5] His remarks, however, confirmed that faith-based spirituality is in conflict with punk's "reliance on reason and evidence" (to repeat Greg Graffin's sentiment). Here is a short excerpt from the interview:

> The theories of evolution are theories. They're mere theories. And it's guesswork taught as fact. It's not fact. They're theories. We're teaching our children to memorize theories and we accept and teach them as fact, but there are many holes in them. There are communities with different paradigms. So, that's a religion in itself. It's guesswork taught as fact. (Cappo 254)

Here, Cappo draws a false equivalence between science and religion, discrediting science as just another religion while rejecting the theory of evolution as "guesswork taught as fact." Science, however, relies on experiment and the method of falsification, whereas religion revolves around spiritual revelation and makes unfalsifiable claims about the nature of the universe. Epistemologically, religious communities are not merely "communities with different paradigms;" they are fundamentally different from the scientific community.

---

5   For an analysis of the song, see Ambrosch 72–73.

It is simply wrong to suggest, as Cappo does, that science discourages skepticism—on the contrary, science is all about challenging received wisdom. When Cappo claims that "[t]here have been many people that had mystical experiences in all different traditions, and we write them all off" (255) because "they can't fit within our paradigm of a scientific method" (254), he makes the mistake of confusing scientific efforts to understand such experiences—for example, in the context of (evolutionary) psychology and neuroscience—with an attempt to invalidate them. This distinction is also relevant for punk researchers, who investigate, and try to make sense of, a socio-cultural phenomenon that offers experiences resembling religio-spiritual experiences. As I write in *The Poetry of Punk*,

> [...] it could be argued that punk itself has some of the characteristics of a secular religion. Around the globe, punks recognize each other as members of the same 'tribe,' the same 'family,' and engage in bizarre group rituals and rites of passage (such as slam-dancing and body modification). It is no coincidence that punk bands that are defined by their political agenda are often labeled as 'preachy' or are accused of 'preaching to the converted.' Moreover, punk concerts can be said to resemble religious ceremonies. There is ecstasy and a sense of letting go; there are sermons and confessions of faith; there are preachers and there is a congregation: the mosh pit, the lyrics, the sing-alongs, the singer, and the audience. (Ambrosch 67)

The lyrics, my main field of research, function like mantras, "something that's just in very few words that you can carry with you and see everywhere you go" (Bennick 149). "It's amazing how these mantras actually create your own consciousness, create the consciousness that people who hear them repeat them. There is potency that hearing things changes the mind" (Cappo 251). These experiences are familiar to punk researchers whose initial motivation to explore punk in a scholarly manner—which, in my opinion, requires a skeptical and disinterested approach to the values and traditions of punk culture—sprang from their passionate involvement and participation in that culture. While this may not apply to all punk researchers,[6] it was my fascination with all things punk, and my love for punk rock and hardcore music, that set me on

---

6   Dick Hebdige, author of the ubiquitously cited *Subculture: The Meaning of Style* (1979), was never a punk, for example. Yet he is considered one of the originators of the field of punk research.

this path; that and my friend and mentor Hugo Keiper (1955-2019), whose research[7] and lectures on pop and rock lyrics had a profound impact on my academic work. Knowing first-hand what an important role punk songs play in the lives of those involved in the scene—many of whom end up carrying punk values out into the world—I am convinced that there is value in bringing these songs (and other aspects of punk culture) to the attention of an academic audience. Studying punk can teach us a great deal about the meaning of community, rebellion, and creative expression in the modern—or, rather, postmodern—world. Punk, at its core, is a way of dealing with the human condition, of taking Heidegger's "thrownness" (*Geworfenheit*) and turning it into something positive and meaningful: an empowered life. This sentiment is best captured in the final lines of the Trial song "Reflections," originally released in 1999: "'we are the tortured and insane, disillusioned and mundane, unknown and unnamed, desperate and enslaved and we want something more'" (Trial).[8]

References

Ambrosch, Gerfried. *The Poetry of Punk: The Meaning behind Punk Rock and Hardcore Lyrics*. Routledge, 2018.

Bennick, Greg. "Greg Bennick." Interview by Gerfried Ambrosch. *Punk Matters: Interviews with Punk Artists and Activists*, Active, 2019, pp. 147–79.

Brian D. "Brian D." Interview by Gerfried Ambrosch. *Punk Matters: Interviews with Punk Artists and Activists*, Active, 2019, pp. 92–109.

Cappo, Ray. "Ray 'Raghunath' Cappo." Interview by Gerfried Ambrosch. *Punk Matters: Interviews with Punk Artists and Activists*, Active, 2019, pp. 250–6.

Catharsis. "Arsonist's Prayer." *Scorched Earth Policy*, 2001.

Dead Kennedys. "Nazi Punks Fuck Off." *In God We Trust, Inc.* Alternative Tentacles, 1981.

Gorilla Biscuits. "New Direction." *Start Today*. Revelation, 1989.

Graffin, Greg, and Steve Olson. *Anarchy Evolution: Faith, Science, and Bad Religion in a World without God*. Harper Collins, 2010.

Hebdige, Dick. *Subculture: The Meaning of Style*. Routledge, 1979.

---

7   See, for example, Keiper's "'The Windmills of Your Mind'" and "Of Hooks, Earworms, and Other Fishing Tackle."

8   A particularly intense rendition of the song, performed at Trial's 2005 reunion show in Seattle, can be found on *YouTube* ("TRIAL").

Keiper, Hugo. "Of Hooks, Earworms, and Other Fishing Tackle: Observations on the Structure, Impact, and Reading of Pop / Rock Songs." *Moderne Sprachen* 61.2, 2017, pp. 149–89.

Keiper, Hugo. "'The Windmills of Your Mind': Notes Towards an Aesthetic of the Pop Song." *Symphony and Song: The Intersection of Words and Music*, edited by Victor Kennedy and Michelle Gadpaille, Cambridge Scholars Publishing, 2016, pp. 15–50.

MacKaye, Ian. "Ian MacKaye." Interview by Gerfried Ambrosch. *Punk Matters: Interviews with Punk Artists and Activists*, Active, 2019, pp. 183–99.

O'Rourke, Beto. "Beto O'Rourke: 'I'm Just Born to Be in It.'" Interview by Joe Hagan. *Vanity Fair*. 13 March 2019, vanityfair.com/news/2019/03/beto-orourke-cover-story. Accessed 19 May 2022.

Peterson, Brian. *Burning Fight: The Nineties Hardcore Revolution in Ethics, Politics, and Sound*. Revelation, 2009.

Shelter. "In Defense of Reality." *Quest for Certainty*. Equal Vision, 1992.

Trial. "Reflections." *Are These Our Lives?* Panic, 2009.

"TRIAL - Reflections - Reunion Retrospective (Live in Seattle 2005)." *YouTube*, uploaded by Rafael Stringasci, 19 April 2011, https://www.youtube.com/watch?v=cR_5i-uLcyo.

Milo Goes to College, Ellen Goes to Grad School: The Series of Events that Turned an Afterschool Hobby into a Hardcore Pursuit of Punk Rock

Ellen Bernhard

My punk rock introduction came from the likeliest (and arguably least punk) of sources: the internet. I didn't have a cool, older sibling to introduce me to some obscure band's discography from the 80s, nor did I live anywhere near a major city like New York or Los Angeles with easy access to concerts and people who could provide me with that introduction. I was also not around for those early explosions of punk into the public's consciousness during the 70s and 80s, and if we're being honest, I was too young to appreciate the pop punk wave that followed grunge during the mid-90s.

What I did have access to, rather, was television and the internet. My own introduction to punk emerged with help from shows like VH1's *Pop-Up Video* and early morning music video rotations on MTV. It was there that I was introduced to bands like blink-182 and Sum 41, whose videos were repeated ad nauseum on music video countdown shows like *Total Request Live*. While critics may argue that these bands aren't remotely punk, they were my first exposure to this style of music. It was fast, loud, and dare I say, relatable. Sure, these bands were kind of cheesy, but their emergence into the mainstream in the late 90s and early 2000s was clearly a case of my being in the right place at the right time—a perfect storm facilitated by teenage angst and access to the internet. These pop punk bands were amusing—they didn't take themselves seriously, and the topics sung about in their music resonated to a 13-year-old living in the suburbs. I'd watch Sum 41's music videos on MTV, videos that were filled with your run-of-the-mill teenage antics. They'd race shopping carts through stores and subject unsuspecting passerby to a Super Soaker ambush. In a similar fashion, bands like New Found Glory sang about unrequited love from the garage of a house in the suburbs. I'll be the first to admit it wasn't the most unique or even the most fascinating punk rock introduction story, but without these bands, I don't know if I would have ever developed an interest in the genre at all.

The popular bands I saw on MTV became the gateway to what would become a hardcore pursuit of punk rock. With my free time after school on the weekends, I went in search of the other bands that existed in the punk rock universe. Obviously, these mainstream bands were influenced and inspired by the ones that came before them, so this was the music that I needed to learn more about. If bands like Sum 41, Green Day, and the Offspring were played on repeat on MTV and the radio, there had to be others that were also worth discovering. As a kid who didn't play sports, join clubs, or really get involved with anything academically, music (and the tireless pursuit to find it) became my hobby. Using the bands I was familiar with from MTV as a starting point, I researched their record labels, tracked down their prior discographies, and tried as best I could to put together a collection of bands whose albums I would purchase at Best Buy. All of this research was done prior to YouTube and Spotify, prior to the algorithms that cater to every click, search engine input, and swipe. Late nights were spent cataloging these songs and bands, and unbeknownst to me at the time, this diligent quest was a foreshadow of the academic research to come.

In the late 90s and into the 2000s, I spent my afternoons on the family computer scouring the internet in search of the punk bands MTV wasn't playing, cataloging all kinds of (often incorrectly labeled) songs to burn onto CDs that I traded with my friends. Tracks from Osker, Bad Religion, the Mighty Mighty Bosstones, the Descendents and other bands from the Epitaph and Fat Wreck Chords rosters filled those playlists. I also experimented with other punk-adjacent genres, finding interest in the emo-inspired and pop punk bands from Drive-Thru Records as well as a couple ska bands here and there. These bands were an important transition from the mainstream pop punk that was on the radio—while bands like the Descendents and Osker had the pop punk sound, they became the introduction to the remainder of the punk rock genre that wasn't making it to MTV. In reflecting on this time, I can still remember the specific songs I put on some of those mix CDs, and at times of boredom (and often procrastination), I'll head over to YouTube to travel down the rabbit hole in search of such songs that I haven't heard since middle school.

As a band that had thirteen studio albums by the mid-2000s, the law of averages suggests that Bad Religion's music would frequently make an appearance in my CD searches online and in-store. Perhaps it was the fast and aggressive nature of their music, or Greg Graffin's penchant for big words that made Bad Religion stand out from the rest, but the political and intellectual nature of their music resonated in ways that the early 2000s radio-friendly pop punk did not. I first heard Bad Religion's "I Want to Conquer the World" in 2002, and after seeing them perform at the 2004 Warped Tour following the release of *The Empire Strikes First*, I realized that this was the punk rock message that resonated most strongly with me. *The Empire Strikes First* was my first encounter with a more nuanced message than the one I frequently heard from the MTV-friendly pop punk bands. It opened my eyes to the ways punk rock aligned with many of the beliefs and views I had already held, and these beliefs were reaffirmed in the lyrics and music of Bad Religion.

Bad Religion was the gateway not just to punk rock, but to the notion that punk rock could be more than just a goofy expression of adolescent angst. Their songs criticized decades of political wrongs and social injustices, and all of this was done with lightning speed and three-part harmonies. Their discography was expansive—each album offering scathing commentary of the issues of the time, providing me with references to issues I could pursue further with my own research. In discussing Bad Religion with friends, we all thought it was unusual that Greg Graffin had a Ph.D.—a literal doctor who was also the face of one of the most well-known punk bands at the time. The two concepts—higher education and punk rock, seemed juxtaposed—at that time, education (high school, more specifically) conflicted with my then-expanding perspectives on the antiauthoritarian ethos of punk rock, and I didn't understand how these seemingly incompatible paradigms could align. But like Greg Graffin's doctoral research on evolutionary biology, it wasn't until I pursued my own Ph.D. that the evolution of my own perspectives on punk rock and higher education began to take shape.

And like Bad Religion's Greg Graffin and the Descendents' Milo Aukerman, whose tenure in higher education was honored in the title of their 1982 album *Milo Goes to College*, I was off to grad school. I didn't go to grad school to research punk rock. At that point, I didn't even think that was feasible. Showing up at Drexel University in the fall of 2011, I had little understanding of what I would need to do to get a Ph.D., and even less about what I wanted to research while I was there. Was I supposed to leave Drexel having spent several years investigating something obscure, niche, and integral to the larger understanding of communication and media studies? I gave little thought to academic pursuit of punk—it remained an extracurricular activity that I always hoped would not be interrupted by night classes, paper deadlines, and other grad school obligations.

During that first year of grad school, I learned about a popular culture conference being held in Boston that spring. While scrolling through the conference's website, I stumbled upon a panel dedicated exclusively to punk rock—contributions on punk culture, the music, scene participation and punk history were all encouraged. It was at this point that it finally clicked—punk rock and higher education are actually excellent partners. Both institutions are grounded in the hardcore pursuit of questioning the world around us, and while the former is often embodied in a hardcore sound, the latter offers a space for hardcore investigation. In this case, a hardcore investigation of punk rock. So, with my desire to participate in the conference, and having no other expertise to my name, I proposed an abstract.

I applied for the Punk Studies panel of the conference, ready to research political imagery in punk music videos, specifically from bands on the *Rock Against Bush* compilations that were released by Fat Wreck Chords in 2004. Sitting behind my laptop, I showed examples and made my argument about the post-9/11 visual message presented in music videos from bands like Rise Against, Strike Anywhere, and Green Day. Content with the completion of my first conference presentation, I waited for questions from those in the audience. The first "not really a question, but more of a comment" came from the back of the room:

Those bands aren't punk.

I didn't really have a response to the person who asked the "not really a question, but more of a comment." The idea that these bands weren't punk caught me completely off guard. To me, these bands *were* punk—they were my version of punk. These were the bands that I learned about through my searches on poorly constructed blogs, learned about by following the breadcrumbs in the liner notes and thank you lists of some of the most popular bands in the genre. They had become the cornerstone of what I knew to be punk rock—and while they might not be the most obscure or relevant bands in the genre, or even the best ones for that matter, they had played an important part in introducing me to the music, and ultimately an ethos, that I felt important enough to pursue as an academic. My exposure to punk rock emerged around the time of 9/11—and while bands like blink-182 and Sum 41 were an important part of that introduction, it was the politically-minded bands like Bad Religion, Rise Against, and Anti-Flag that shaped my own awareness of injustices and inequality that existed around the world. Their post-9/11 albums helped me appreciate both punk rock's hardcore sound and the genre's hardcore determination to pursue wrongdoings and prejudices that exist in the world today.

Following that conference, I knew I had found my academic niche. The conference presentation was more than enough incentive needed to prove to others that these bands, and the more recent activity taking place within punk scenes everywhere, were worth investigating. I felt it necessary to share these stories and to continue to learn more about the evolving ways punk fans both identified with the music and defined the genre for themselves. I wanted to use my time in grad school to demonstrate that punk was still evolving, and that there were many others out there who found their way to punk rock through the same mainstream routes I did, but through years of exploration, found a message within the punk rock ethos that resonated with them today. More than that, I wanted to prove that although punk meant different things to different people, this involvement was often more than just a passing hobby or a weekend activity—that even today there were scores of fans and musicians who dedicated their time, money, and efforts to creating thriving punk scenes around the world.

My dissertation research, like my own introduction to punk rock, was expansive and random. I dove into the early literature on music subcultures and punk rock's early connection to male, working class communities in the UK. This literature argued for reactionary, class-based participation which was often labeled as "deviant" by outsiders (Debies-Carl 115). Early subcultural research (specifically the Birmingham School and the Centre for Contemporary Cultural Studies) argued for an all-or-nothing approach to one's involvement in a subculture with a focus on class, fashion, and gender (Torkelson). While these features exist in today's punk spaces, I discovered that investigating today's punk scenes through this perspective seemed inadequate. Because of this, I found the lens of post-subcultural theory to align with the more fluid and abstract associations that many participants in contemporary subcultures identified. Rather than viewing punk as a space where one's commitment and fashion choices equated to a punk identity, post-subcultural theory viewed involvement as a "dynamic and participatory process," left to the individual to define (Bennett 28). Today's punk scenes are more dynamic than early subcultural research suggests—subcultures do not exist in insular spaces where external societal factors fail to make an impact. Rather, subcultures are highly influenced by the many cultural forces that exist in and around such communities. While such literature understood mass media as a detriment to a subculture, later research identified the beneficial relationship that could exist between mass media and subcultures (Thornton). Thinking about my own exposure to punk rock through these various mass media outlets, this idea became an overarching theme to pursue in my dissertation research.

I composed two studies for my dissertation, conducting interviews with current fans and musicians who saw themselves as active participants within their own scenes today. Though not recruited purposefully, most of my fifteen interview participants were millennials—the majority of whom learned about punk rock during those critical teenage years which took place at the turn of the millennium. An introduction facilitated by pop culture, mass consumerism, and technology, I heard stories of how participants learned about punk from MTV's *Headbanger's Ball* or from browsing the t-shirt and vinyl collections at Hot Topic. And much like my own introduction, many of my participants credited bands like blink-182, Green Day, and the Offspring as being the first bands they considered to be part of their early exposure to punk rock. While this introduction was often enabled by these mainstream avenues, those who identified with the punk scene today were able to offer a more nuanced understanding of their continued involvement, adopting practices that often led to a participation including more DIY, autonomous contributions one might not initially expect from an introduction so heavily influenced by commercial popular culture.

Those I spoke to acknowledged their arguably "not-punk" introductions to the genre through mainstream means. My participants never expressed ill-will or embarrassment in crediting MTV and Hot Topic for providing the resources to not only gain access to new music, but eventually to a network of other likeminded individuals who saw such exposure as a gateway into less popular bands. This conclusion has become the impetus for much of my ongoing research: one of the first questions I generally ask interview participants is about their introduction to punk rock. And quite often, that introduction involves some facilitation by technology, pop culture, or mass media, often combined with the help of friends and/or older siblings.

After conducting my interviews and reviewing the transcripts, it was obvious that punk rock was more than just a passing phase or weekend hobby for my participants. The hardcore dedication was not necessarily evident in a commitment to the punk "look," for example—rather, the dedication existed in the ideological determination to make punk scenes more inclusive communities. Participants stressed the importance of inclusion, and the significance of creating spaces that welcomed those who aligned with the values of diversity and acceptance. My interviews also showed that participants recognized the sustained work that needed to be done to ensure that today's punk scenes have difficult and much-needed discussions about intersectionality and diversity, with efforts to make the scene a safer place for all. In this commitment to the punk ethos, we see the dedication and hopefulness of a more inclusive space in the future (Bernhard, *Contemporary Punk Rock Communities*).

Currently, my intent is to focus on what is going on in today's scene, exploring the issues that generate the most conversations on social media, the site where many of these discussions are held. As punk rock's subjective qualities are often the topic of much debate, I have witnessed many such exchanges unfold in various digital spaces, often in real time. Through a mix of in-depth interviews, textual analysis, and social media analysis, my goal is to understand how contemporary punk rock is impacted by the large societal forces that co-exist around today's punk scene. The impact of these forces on both fans and the genre needs to be considered. While it might be easy to roll our eyes and scoff at a platform like Facebook, there is no doubt the punk scene is alive and well in this digital space. Today's punk bands often take to social media to announce tour dates and new merchandise, and in the era of Covid and limited social gatherings, bands even used platforms such as Instagram and Twitch to bring livestream performances to their fans (Rendell). These technologies facilitate networking and allow for connections in a subculture that operates translocally. Such communities "transcend the need for face-to-face interaction" (Peterson & Bennett 9), and through social media groups, comment sections and group chats, it is possible to see how such networks facilitate the preservation of a contemporary punk scene.

If I have learned anything from my time as a punk scholar, it is that there is no true, definitive way to categorize the music or those who listen to it. As a result, I am continually questioning the true meaning of punk rock. What does it mean to be, listen to, or consider oneself a part of a punk rock scene? For some, punk represents an optimistic look toward the future, where the issues surrounding punk's controversial and at times, exclusionary history are tackled with promises to do better. For others, punk rock represents a burn-it-to-the-ground, nothing-is-off-limits attitude, with those of this mind using this stance to offend or justify questionable behavior. This dichotomy, I found, became evident when I researched the public apology on social media from the band NOFX after controversial comments were made about mass shootings during their set at the Las Vegas Punk Rock Bowling music festival in

2018 (Bernhard, "'I thought it was a very punk rock thing to say'"). NOFX was met with immediate backlash from both fans and sponsors and the band was forced to make a public apology on their social media accounts to address their comments. The post received thousands of responses from fans and became a de facto discussion board for followers to debate their own interpretations on what it means to "be" punk today. Many commenters offered insight inspired by their own positive and negative experiences in various punk scenes, and others suggested, at times very aggressively, that it doesn't matter who was offended by NOFX's comments. For these commenters, NOFX's act of causing controversy and offending many was entirely justified as a "punk" act, and the repercussions against the band were unwarranted—a display of "political correctness" at a time when punk rock and NOFX were viewed as the latest victims of cancel culture. In the end, it is clear that those who love the music are most passionate about its message—and while this message may not be uniform for all fans, the commitment and dedication to a punk rock ethos remains evident in the ways fans continue to interact and engage with other punks in these digital spaces.

The response to my research from the scene has been largely positive. Many people are excited to talk to me, and to share their stories and experiences in their respective punk communities. A recent recruitment post for participants interested in discussing the soundtracks of the video game series *Tony Hawk's Pro Skater* and Epitaph Records' *Punk-O-Rama* compilations yielded such an enthusiastic response that I spent two hours responding to emails after posting a recruitment flyer on social media. I was able to interview over thirty people who excitedly shared stories about their early memories of playing the video games or finding the comps for $5 at the local CD store. When I tell acquaintances about this research, their faces light up in recollection of hearing Goldfinger's "Superman" and Dead Kennedys' "Police Truck" in the video game for the first time. At present, my research has focused on Bad Religion—with their 2018 release of *The Age of Unreason* and its brutal reproach of Donald Trump and the repercussions of his election win in 2016. I am drawn to the album's rhetorical strategies in offering a no holds barred response to the growing threat of conspiracy theories, anti-intellectualism, and xenophobia in American culture. My hope is to continue to locate those important moments in today's punk rock scene, as I consider both past and present influences to create a different kind of DIY mixtape of punk experiences from fans around the world.

The "not really a question, but more of a comment" from my first conference presentation in Boston was enough motivation to turn my lifelong personal interest in the genre into a hardcore pursuit to demonstrate that punk rock was a topic worthy of investigation. I am fortunate to have learned a great deal from fellow punk rock colleagues around the world who have their own unique perspectives on punk, all of them driven by their passion and love of the music and community it creates. We can learn so much when talking to one another about a music genre that espouses a strong belief in unity—becoming more involved with the Punk Scholars Network[1] has introduced me to people from all generations, geographic locations, and academic fields who have the same passion for a style of music that transcends language and cultural barriers.

While students might not have any interest in hearing my thoughts on the best Bad Religion album (it's *Suffer*), I think the punk rock ethos is something that can be relevant to every subject I teach in the digital communication field—as a music genre with its ethos rooted in tolerance and acceptance, punk rock is one that advocates for diverse and welcoming spaces for people from all backgrounds, cultures, and lifestyles. Punk rock continues to be a place of growth, and at times controversy, but I believe its hardcore devotees strive to create a scene that makes a positive impact on the world. Some might not think such optimism is very punk rock, but isn't that the point?

References

Bennett, Andy. "The Continuing Importance of the 'Cultural' in the Study of Youth." *Youth Studies Australia* 30.3, 2011, pp. 27–33.

Bernhard, Ellen. *Contemporary Punk Rock Communities: Scenes of Inclusion and Dedication.* Lexington Books, 2019.

Bernhard, Ellen. "'I thought it was a very punk rock thing to say': NOFX's (sort-of) public apology and (in)civility in defining contemporary punk rock in online spaces." *Punk & Post-Punk* 9.1, 2020, pp 7–22.

Debies-Carl, Jeffrey S. "Are the Kids Alright? A Critique and Agenda for Taking Youth Cultures Seriously." *Social Science Information* 52.1, 2013, pp. 110–33.

---

1   Cf. the article by Bestley, Dines, and Stewart in this book [the editors].

Peterson, Richard A., and Andy Bennett. "Introducing Music Scenes." *Music Scenes: Local, Translocal, and Virtual*, edited by Andy Bennett and Richard A. Peterson, Vanderbilt University Press, 2004, pp. 1–15.

Rendell, James. "Staying In, Rocking Out: Online Live Music Portal Shows During the Coronavirus Pandemic." *Convergence* 27.4, 2021. journals.sagepub.com/doi/10.1177/1354856520976451. Accessed 1 June 2022.

Thornton, Sarah. *Club Cultures: Music, Media, and Subcultural Capital*. Blackwell Publishers, 1995.

Torkelson, Jason. "Life After (Straightedge) Subculture." *Qualitative Sociology* 33.3, 2010, pp. 257–74.

A Network of Hardcore Researchers: Punk Studies, Punk Scholarship, Punk Pedagogy

Russ Bestley, Mike Dines, Francis Stewart

We have come a long way since the term 'punk' achieved a kind of public no-toriety in the late 1970s, and the academic study of punk—what we might call broadly 'punk scholarship'—has evolved in a disparate number of directions. Since punk (as an umbrella term encapsulating a music-based youth subcul-ture and parallel movements in fashion, design, the arts, lifestyle and politics) first gained a media presence, observers and commentators have documented its development and reflected on its meaning(s). Over the years, many active participants have adopted a kind of insider position as critical commentators, keepers of the flame, archivists and narrators (and tastemakers) whose per-sonal responsibility is to uphold what they see as the spirit and legacy of a significant socio-cultural movement.

By its very nature punk history, and especially anything that suggests a coherent 'punk philosophy' is contested and difficult to define. Given the widespread rhetoric of independence and individuality associated with punk attitudes and lifestyles (do-it-yourself, anyone can do it, agency and auton-omy), the knowledge, expertise and authority that affords a critical position on the part of the observer (or scholar) is often tied up with notions of authen-ticity. The passionate fan or collector might then assume a level of expertise that could be used to push back against unwanted intrusion in the subcul-ture by dowdy academics. This schism is further complicated by the growth in number of punk scholars coming from within the scene; active punk partici-pants who have moved into an academic environment as teachers, researchers or academic managers, as both 'fans' and 'scholars.' These individuals walk a tightrope between both sides of a perceived divide, trying to remain true to their own interpretation of the 'punk cause' while facing questions about the legitimacy of their chosen field of study from within the walls of the academy.

This article, therefore, seeks to provide a brief overview of punk scholarship within the framework of the Punk Scholars Network (PSN) and the emergence of new methodological approaches towards the subject.[1] It begins by looking at 'punk studies' as means of interrogating the complexities of identity, style and 'self,' and how these characteristics were brought forward with the formation of the PSN in 2012. The second part of this work turns to an examination of newly emerging methodologies when dealing with punk, in particular in its various iterations such as hardcore punk, straight edge and anarcho-punk. These include accounts of punk through the lens of religion, aesthetics, LGBT, gender and queer studies, disability and ableism, pedagogy and ageing. While this chapter offers a mere glimpse into a complex and ever-broadening area of study, the authors hope that it might act as a valuable resource for those looking for further reading.

Shot By Both Sides: The Unlikely Emergence of Punk Studies

One could argue that Dick Hebdige set a benchmark for punk-as-scholarly-subject in the field of cultural studies as far back as 1979 with his seminal *Subculture: The Meaning of Style*, while Dave Laing's *One Chord Wonders* (1985) developed methodological approaches to punk music, lyrics and expression six years later. Popular punk histories followed, often reflecting 'landmark' anniversaries and benefitting from critical hindsight and an audience with a keen interest in reflecting on very recent history, much of it personal. The personal nature of these histories often highlighted the importance of the specific period or type of punk, such as hardcore, for individual authors and readers. Roger Sabin's *Punk Rock: So What?* (1999b) subsequently attempted a broader analytical critique that encompassed the emerging and diverging themes of the discipline over the previous twenty years. Even so, by the advent of the millennium punk in all its iterations was a (more or less) legitimate object of study, although 'punk scholarship' was still largely left to historians and cultural theorists rather than, for instance, ethnographers or sociologists.

---

1   Given the nature of this article as an extensive overview and for reasons of readability, we have decided to deviate from the MLA style used in the rest of the book and provide the year of publication and not the entire title when enumerating and citing from various sources [the editors].

Change was afoot, however, in part inspired by several authors and commentators who wanted to delve further into the 'meaning' of punk. Craig O'Hara's *The Philosophy of Punk: More Than Noise!* kickstarted the debate in 1999, with Lars J. Kristiansen's *Screaming For Change: Articulating a Unifying Philosophy of Punk Rock* and *The Truth of Revolution, Brother: The Philosophies of Punk*, a series of interviews compiled by Robin Ryde, Lucy Sofianos, and Charlie Waterhouse, following on in 2012 and 2014 respectively. Around the same time, US academic Zack Furness compiled a book of essays by self-styled punk teachers and academics, *Punkademics* (2012), which tried to identify the impact of punk attitudes and ideologies within the classroom; followed soon after by David Beer's *Punk Sociology* (2014), a book that looked to embed the creativity and spontaneity of punk within the discipline of sociology.

Russ Bestley reflected on this development in an article in the academic journal *Punk & Post-Punk* in 2015, "(I want some) demystification: Deconstructing punk," looking back at the journey taken by the journal over the previous four years along with the ideals and direction of the (at that point unrelated) Punk Scholars Network that had formed around a year after the journal first launched in 2012. This was a period of critical self-reflection for some academics involved in the study of punk—questions were being openly debated regarding the purpose and legitimacy of our research, the goals of our collective endeavor and the nature of 'punk' itself as a subject, a set of values or an approach. Indeed, as the scope, definition and purpose of punk scholarship widened, debates arose about the legitimacy of a kind of philosophical 'punk approach' to study, rather than the study of punk. If the notion of 'punk studies' extends beyond the study of 'punk' to encompass a loose description of a mode of study—a lens through which to observe, analyze, and comment on the wider world—then a 'punk attitude' might be seen as legitimizing both good and bad extensions to the academic pursuit of knowledge. In short, if 'punk studies' embraces a broad range of do-it-yourself, individualistic, amateur, or untrained attitudes toward traditional forms of scholarly activity, then don't we run the gauntlet of excusing bad practice in the name of an unsubstantiated, 'radical' form of opposition?

It was against this backdrop that the Punk Scholars Network emerged in 2012. As yet, the only historical overview of the network resides as an Afterword in Mike Dines and Laura Way's *Postgraduate Voices in Punk Studies: Your Wisdom, Our Youth* (157–62). As Dines states, the PSN emerged from a call for chapters for what would eventually become the co-edited *The Aesthetic of our*

Anger: Anarcho-Punk, Politics, Music (2016), a volume that interrogates the emergence of the UK-based anarcho-punk scene of the 1980s. Dines notes,

> I sent out a Call for Chapters and soon heard back from a number of academics. Matt Worley from Reading University was one of the first, and then came Russ Bestley, Ana Raposo, Matt Grimes and Pete Dale: all punk scholars in their own right, working on wide ranging debates and ideas around punk. Bestley and Raposo were looking at graphic design, the image of subversion that can be found on the records of Crass and their colleagues. Grimes was studying anarcho-punk and memory, whilst Pete Dale was working on his *Anyone Can Do-It*, a volume that uncovers the intricacies of the DIY scene. (Dines 2017: 159–60)

Pete Dale suggested that Dines contact Alastair 'Gords' Gordon, an academic who had previously self-published his undergraduate dissertation *Throwing the Punk Rock Baby Out With the Dirty Bath Water: Crass and Punk Rock, An Appraisal* (1996): a work which still remains relevant today and has since been reissued under the title of *Crass Reflections* (2016) by Itchy Monkey Press. Gords' enthusiasm for punk scholarship sat alongside a healthy distrust for academia that, he believed, viewed his activities "with suspicion" (qtd. in Dines 2017: 160). In other words, Gords felt that the

> camaraderie [he had] previously experienced in the DIY punk scene was missing in the academia" and, thinking of the CCCS and other research networks, therefore had the idea of the PSN: "I thought, why not start a network of my own? Reach out to others in the field and in true DIY spirit drag the thing into existence. (ibid.)

From a few initial meetings between Gords and Dines, the first network meeting was held on Saturday 24th November 2012 at De Montfort University in Leicester, where discussions arose around setting up communication channels, supporting each other in academia and the organization of the first 'official' PSN event at the University of Reading.

From here, the Punk Scholars Network quickly grew. Dines started the PSN Facebook page and, after meeting Laura Way at De Montfort University (where he and Gords were interviewing Penny Rimbaud from the anarcho-punk band Crass), working with her to set up the first Annual Punk Scholars Conference and Postgraduate Symposium at Leicester University, where Way was finishing her PhD. Further developments followed, including the first of the *Punk Reader* books (2019), an attempt to map the global contemporary punk scene, and the formalization of a link with Intellect Publishing and what would eventually become the Global Punk book series. In effect, the latter took the idea of *The Punk Reader* a step further, mapping a global punk trajectory and encompassing a diverse range of interrelated histories and approaches to our subject. In the meantime, international interest grew, with PSN branches sprouting in all parts of the world, including Indonesia, Canada and Greece. Alongside this expansion the PSN actively engaged to support new and expanding research, mirroring a long-standing commitment towards those studying undergraduate and postgraduate degrees. This also reflected the desire of those involved to break down academic 'snobbishness' and to encourage a wider participation in punk studies both within and beyond academia.

In many regards, the development of the PSN and its works has mirrored the development of 'newer' versions or iterations of punk itself. Hardcore punk, which started as an offshoot from punk and new wave, sought to return the subculture to what its proponents saw as its primary purpose of refuting musical pomposity and rejecting the selling out of the scene to commercial interests. It did this through less opaque lyrics, straightforward chord progression and tonal structures and downtuned instruments, along with a return to smaller spaces in which the audience and the band are often on the same ground. Of course, it did not remain as such as hardcore grew in popularity and larger venues were needed to accommodate the number of fans and band members became more proficient in their musical skills. What, arguably, has not changed is the purpose of hardcore, much like the purpose of the PSN and punk academic writing and scholarship, best summed in the annual conference's motto in Porto organized by Paula Guerra and Andy Bennett: "Keep It Simple, Make It Fast."

Dines' overview of the PSN is useful, in that he situates the current state of punk scholarship within a framework of Furness' *Punkademics* (2012) and the radical pedagogy of Paulo Freire. "Studying is a difficult task," writes Freire. "[It] requires a systematic critical attitude and intellectual discipline acquired only through practice" (1985: 2). And, drawing upon ideas earlier embraced in *Pedagogy of the Oppressed* (1972), he notes how

> this critical attitude is precisely what "banking education" does not engender. Quite the contrary, its focus is fundamentally to kill our curiosity, our inquisitive spirit, and our creativity. A student's discipline becomes a discipline for ingenuity in relation to the text, rather than an essential critique

of it ... what is required of readers, in essence, is not comprehension of content but memorization. Instead of understanding the text, the challenge becomes its memorization and if readers can do this, they will have responded to the challenge. (Freire 1985: 2)

Importantly, the initial Punk Scholars Postgraduate Symposium at Leicester University in 2014 became an important springboard for the next seven years (as noted below, 2020 saw a virtual, online global conference that spanned a week of events, talks and live bands, etc.), alongside events in Reading, Oxford, Leicester, London, Birmingham, Northampton, Bolton, Lincoln, Newcastle and Los Angeles. These disparate events reflected a broad range of critical themes including global, historical, and contemporary punk scenes such as hardcore, straight edge hardcore, queercore and Afro-punk, punk pedagogy, DIY, punk and spirituality, identities and sexualities, punk art and aesthetics, curatorial practices and the social and political legacy of the 1980s anarcho-punk movement.

Evolution, Diversification, and Confrontation

From the heady days of Hebdige, therefore, and his work with the Centre for Contemporary Cultural Studies (CCCS), punk scholarship has grown in multiple ways in recent years, in no small part due to the rigorous standards and various interests of the *Punk & Post-Punk* journal and the solidification and growth of the Punk Scholars Network. Another factor that has significantly influenced the growth of the scholarship has been the diverse array of academic fields represented within the network, both within our studentship and amongst colleagues. Punk is being given serious consideration and attention within fields as diverse as graphic design, art history, education studies, teacher training, sociology, anthropology, music studies, musicology, history, politics, gender studies, cultural studies, communication studies, Latinx studies, and religious studies. This brings with it a range of methods and methodologies, while also offering new insights through the individual lenses applied to the study of punk as a concept, punk as community, punk as praxis and punk as people.

Geographically, more regions are being documented, helping to move away from the earlier UK/European/North American-centric accounts of punk and instead bringing insights from China (Xiao 2016), Turkey (Way and

Wallace 2016), Malta (Giappone 2018) Australia (Sharp 2019), Mexico (Poma and Gravante 2017), Iran (Martin-Iverson 2017) and Malaysia (Ferrarese 2017). Thematically, a range of different concerns have emerged, in part reflecting the ways in which scholars wanted a more critical engagement with punk, both conceptually and in terms of method. This has brought to the fore key themes such as LGBT and gender concerns (LeBlanc 1999; Ambrosch 2016; Nault 2018; Carella and Wymer 2019; Brown 2020); race and racism (Sabin 1999a; Duncombe and Tremblay 2011; Davila 2019; Woods 2020); disability and ableism (Mogk 2013; McKay 2014; Stewart 2019); and women within punk (Reddington 2007; Strahan 2016; Rouse 2019; Way 2020), alongside the widening of punk research into ageing, religion, art and design, fashion and pedagogy.

This scholarship and critical engagement further builds upon and/or fundamentally shifts away from earlier writings on punk which, though vital, focused on specific elements around subcultural definitions and praxis. The scholarship emerging today is far more in tune with Ellen Bernhard's[2] assertion that punk and punks are,

> [...] more than just music and mohawks—they operate as sites of autonomous practice and networked communities where a tireless pursuit for social action is amplified by the platforms and forces that exist within the scene today ... [and whilst] self-sufficiency is preferred, scene-related practices are influenced and affected by the larger forces that exist within society today. (3)

Contemporary research, then, has built upon the class-conscious, predominantly sociology-based analyses of the Birmingham School to further examine larger socially constructed issues such as racism, sexism, homophobia, transphobia, ableism, colonialism, migration, pedagogy, and religion alongside more established analyses of class and style; driven in part by the impetus behind different academic disciplines, and individual reasons for entering those fields.

In terms of religion, for instance, one need only turn to the writing of Francis Stewart (2015, 2017), Mike Dines (2015, 2021), Ibrahim Abraham (2020), as well as Mike Dines and Matt Grimes (2021). Here, religion and spirituality are used as a way in which to unpack new ideas and findings around subcultural entry, commitment, and identity. For instance, Stewart looks at

---

2   Cf. the article by Bernhard in this book [the editors].

hardcore punk through Edward Bailey's notion of Implicit Religion, and the "occulture" of Christopher Partridge, exploring ways in which straight edge punk, in particular, can be a means of investigating "the interaction between popular culture, theological discourse and religious identity" (Stewart 2015: 3). On the other hand, Dines (2015) looks at the formation and evolution of Krishnacore[3] (a hybrid subgenre influenced by the Hare Krishna movement) via the lens of Indian aesthetics, comparing whether the devotion within the punk styles of bands such as 108, Prema and Shelter is as "applicable to the punk rock aesthetic as it is to the [devotional music of the] bhajan or kirtan of the Indian musical tradition" (Dines 2015: 148). In addition, Abraham's fascinating and insightful edited collection on punk and Christianity compares "the compatibility of punk's expressive, do-it-yourself (DIY) ethic with the youthful energy of evangelicalism" (2), focusing on the tensions between Christianity and the wider punk scene.

Similarly, punk's musical, stylistic and visual aesthetics can be placed under scrutiny, the canon of 'punk style' brought into question both historically and culturally. Russ Bestley (2011, 2015, 2020a, 2021) has developed a body of research into the evolution of punk, post-punk, and new wave graphic design with a particular emphasis on the punk diaspora: the shift from major metropolitan centers to the provinces in the United Kingdom, for instance, led to localized interpretations of punk's visual canon and a range of novel typo/graphic conventions. At the same time, the mythology of 'DIY' production and punk's natural voice of 'opposition' can be critically interrogated in relation to a much broader range of artefacts from around the world (Bestley and Ogg 2012; Bestley 2018, 2020b). Alongside Bestley, researchers including Becky Binns (Bestley and Binns 2018), Ana Raposo (Raposo and Bestley 2020), and Ian Trowell (2020) have explored the relationship between punk visual aesthetics and anarchism, neo-fascism and art history respectively, while Monica Sklar (2014) and Nathaniel Weiner (2018) have undertaken detailed research on punk fashion, style, and dress.

Of course, there is still value in celebrating and examining punk of the 1970s, not least in examining the roots of punk and notions of ageing and nostalgia. Personal accounts of punk are essential for our understanding of those roots and mirror the eclectic methodologies within punk scholarship. Here, alongside traditional archival research, auto-ethnography, oral histories and fandom are essential to the unpacking of punk's contextual history

---

3   Cf. the article by Cullen in this book [the editors].

since the 1970s. Matthew Worley's *No Future: Punk, Politics and British Youth Culture, 1976-1984* (2017) is central to this discourse, along with the work of The Subcultures Network (2015, 2018, 2020). Moreover, one need only turn to the excellent exhibitions that focus on specific time periods from the history of punk, for example *Punk Lust* at the Museum of Sex, New York in 2019 which explored the way changes in relation to sexuality influenced first wave punk, and *Photo-Punk*, curated by Ian Dickson and Kevin Cummins in 2017 at Brighton Museum in commemoration of 40 years of punk.

Similarly, new methodologies and new ways of 'seeing' mean that those who were less visible are coming to the fore. For instance, a focus on the role of women or punks of color can highlight the structural inequalities rendered by the perception (and for some the insistence) of punk as the purview of the white working class (male). A whitewashing of the history of the subculture is ubiquitous within memorial events, biographies, autobiographies, memoirs and photo books. For example, Malott and Peña's (2004) survey of US punk recordings from 1980–1997 failed to even look for women of color, with the categories of performer broken into white males, non-white males (an additional centering of whiteness) and white females.

Roger Sabin (1999a) criticized punk's assumption of being anti-racist because of its connection with Rock Against Racism and reggae, whilst ignoring how it perpetuated or failed to respond to racist attacks on members of Asian and Middle Eastern communities, especially in the UK. He noted the significance of the combination of punk mythmaking and the over-assumption of participants in being able to overcome the societal forces that it emerged from. Elizabeth Stinson (2012) recalibrated punk genealogies by examining punk performances through a black feminist lens. She notes that punk's lineage with race and colonial histories entwine across the Atlantic between the US and the UK in an exchange of influences, familiarity, and style, which confirms Nyong'o's observation that 'race' is produced out of an ongoing process of reconstruction following the work of black abolitionists (2005, 2010). Nguyen noted already in 1998 in *Punk Planet* that whilst punk has been able to mount finessed critiques and opposition to foreign policy, apartheid, and the Gulf War it has singularly failed to turn that lens upon itself and the "straightwhiteboy" hegemony (2011; Hanson 2017).

Parameters shape the choices that are available to people, but they are also made by choice. While it is difficult to outline the areas where punk has failed to hold itself to account, particularly where it has allowed itself to continue to reinforce structural oppressions, we have to acknowledge the role that punk scholarship has had in that. However, if we take seriously questions around the negative and capricious capacity of art, the broader imagination that bringing in analysis and critical scrutiny from marginalized communities and scholars—especially from those within fields that have not traditionally engaged with punk but have spent decades pushing back—suggests positive signs that the future direction of punk studies will encompass, learn from, and engage with a much wider range of critical scholarship.

Perhaps the most successful event that the Punk Scholars Network has organized, thus far, was the 2020 Global Punk annual conference. Forced by the coronavirus pandemic to hold an online conference, the PSN conference committee decided to seize the opportunity to go big in a truly global sense and organized, in conjunction with other branches a seven-day conference that spanned the globe. Each regional branch had its own day, within its own time zone, ran their schedule as they wanted to, in their language of choice, and gave access online to anyone who wanted it. Instead of hearing from Western academics about punk in Indonesia, the punks of Indonesia shared their lived experiences, their academic or otherwise engagement with punk and local bands performed. The same was true of Australia and New Zealand, Iberia, Colombia, the USA, and the UK.

Contemporary scholarship of punk, therefore, continues to build upon a rich diversity of subcultural analyses, not least in deconstructing notions of authenticity, of asserting that punk is and can only be about a certain time frame or iteration. The notion of authenticity around punk is a deep rooted and problematic one. The desire for and the control of authenticity has been with punk from its earliest forms, from accusations of being a sell-out to not being as 'committed' in self-presentational styles (particularly pronounced as an accusation against women) or not knowing the minute detail of a band or their lyrics whilst professing to be a fan. Its presence within punk scholarship should therefore be no surprise; it was at the core of the CCCS approach to subcultural studies. Alastair Gordon (2014) notes,

> broadly the CCCS offered a model of subcultures as coherent blocs, doing sartorial battle with other subcultures or trying to weed out inauthentic "poseurs" through predictable disciplinary channels of commodification and ideological control. (184)

This CCCS approach ignores the significance of discourse and gestures of authenticity that are necessary navigations within punk both as a subcultural identity/experience and as a punk scholar. Authenticity is therefore always in flux; it is always a negotiation and scholarship needs to account for the power differential and interplays at hand between those who get to determine authentic 'punkness' and those who must conform or reach for it (and the tacit approval of the gatekeeper). This is a future direction for punk scholarship, but it must be approached carefully. Not only is the scholar, especially the punk practitioner scholar, required to be attuned to power dynamics, but they must also be reflexive on their own privilege and position and sensitive to the continual stretching of punk as a concept to avoid it becoming 'over-stretched' to the point of meaninglessness.

Conclusion

Punk scholarship has come a long way over the past four decades. Interest in the field has grown exponentially over the past ten years, leading to a critical mass of multidisciplinary research spanning the arts, humanities and social sciences. The Punk Scholars Network has taken the lead in establishing connections, developing communication channels and supporting a diverse range of contributors pursuing equally varied and disparate lines of enquiry. Some of the research into 'punk' involves looking back, re-evaluating the past, and reflecting on alternative and unwritten histories beyond accepted and well-travelled stereotypes. For other punk scholars, interest lies in the 'now'—in punk scenes around the world, their views, their values and their aspirations. New critical lenses are applied to our subject and, at times, the aims and objectives—some might say the 'philosophy'—of punk participants informs the development of our methodologies, our critical frames of reference and our approach to our subject. This fluidity and flexibility provides us with an opportunity to continue to grow and diversify, while always building on common ground.

References

Abraham, Ibrahim, editor. *Christian Punk: Identity and Performance*. Bloomsbury, 2020.

Ambrosch, Gerfried. "'Refusing to be a man': Gender, feminism and queer identity in the punk culture." *Punk & Post-Punk* 5.3, 2016, pp. 247–64.

Beer, David. *Punk Sociology*. Palgrave Macmillan, 2012.

Bernhard, Ellen. *Contemporary Punk Rock Communities: Scenes of Inclusion and Dedication*. Lexington Books, 2019.

Bestley, Russ. "Design it yourself? Punk's division of labour." *Punk & Post-Punk* 7.1, 2018, pp. 7–24.

Bestley, Russ. "From 'London's Burning' to 'Sten Guns in Sunderland.'" *Punk & Post-Punk* 1.1, 2011, pp. 41–70.

Bestley, Russ. "(I want some) demystification: Deconstructing punk." *Punk & Post-Punk* 4.2-3, 2015, pp. 117–27.

Bestley, Russ. "Kicks in Style – A Punk Design Aesthetic." *The Oxford Handbook of Punk Rock*, edited by George McKay and Gina Arnold, Oxford Handbooks, 2021.

Bestley, Russ. "Punk Rock!! So What? – Negotiating an Exhibition of Punk Art and Design." *Punk Now!! Contemporary Perspectives on Punk*, edited by Matt Grimes and Mike Dines, Intellect Books, 2020a, pp. 204–19.

Bestley, Russ. "Punk Uncovered: An Unofficial History of Provincial Opposition." *Too Fast To Live, Too Young To Die: Punk and Post-Punk Graphic Design*, edited by Andrew Krivine, Pavilion, 2020b.

Bestley, Russ, and Rebecca Binns. "The Evolution of an Anarcho-Punk Narrative (1978-84)." *Ripped, Torn and Cut: Pop, Politics and Punk Fanzines from 1976*, edited by The Subcultures Network, Manchester University Press, 2018, pp. 129–49.

Bestley, Russ, and Alex Ogg. *The Art of Punk*. Omnibus, 2012.

Brown, Peter Robert. "The Screamers: Pop ambition, punk nihilism, and queer futurities." *Canadian Review of American Studies* 50.3, 2020, pp. 428–52.

Carella, Kirsten, and Kathryn Wymer. "You want me to surrender my identity? Laura Jane Grace, transition and selling out." *Punk & Post-Punk* 8.2, 2019, pp. 193–207.

Davila, Richard Cruz. "See no colour, hear no colour, speak no colour: Problematizing colourblindness in Los Angeles punk historiography." *Punk & Post-Punk* 8.1, 2019, pp. 89–104.

Dines, Mike. "Afterword: Academia as Subversion: The Birth of the Punk Scholars Network." *Postgraduate Voices in Punk Studies: Your Wisdom, Our Youth*, edited by Mike Dines and Laura Way, Cambridge Scholars Press, 2017, pp. 157–62.

Dines, Mike. "From Punk Rock to Prabhupāda: Locating the Musical, Philosophical and Spiritual Journey of Contemporary Krishnacore." *Trans-Global Punk Scenes: The Punk Reader Vol.2*, edited by Russ Bestley, Mike

Dines, Paula Guerra, and Alastair Gordon, Intellect Books, 2021, pp. 237–54.

Dines, Mike. "The Sacralization of Straightedge Punk: Nada Brahma and the Divine Received: Embodiment of Krishnacore." *Musicological Annual* 50.2, 2015, pp. 147–56.

Dines, Mike, and Matt Grimes. "'Message from Thee Temple': Magick, Occultism, Mysticism, and Psychic TV." *Exploring the Spiritual in Popular Music: Beatified Beats*, edited by Mike Dines and Georgina Gregory, Bloomsbury, 2021, pp. 193–208.

Dines, Mike, and Laura Way, editors. *Postgraduate Voices in Punk Studies: Your Wisdom, Our Youth*. Cambridge Scholars Press, 2017.

Dines, Mike, and Matthew Worley, editors. *The Aesthetic of Our Anger: Anarcho-Punk, Politics and Music*. Minor Compositions, 2016.

Dines, Mike, Gordon, Alastair, Guerra, Paula, and Russ Bestley, editors. *The Punk Reader: Research Transmissions from the Local and the Global*. Intellect Books, 2019.

Duncombe, Stephen, and Maxwell Tremblay, editors. *White Riot: Punk Rock and the Politics of Race*. Verso, 2011.

Ferrarese, Marco. "A Profane Existence: DIY Culture, Sonic Extremism and Punk Identity in 21st Century Malaysia." *The Punk Reader: Research Transmissions from the Local and the Global*, edited by Mike Dines, Alastair Gordon, Paula Guerra and Russ Bestley, Intellect, 2017, pp. 271–92.

Freire, Paulo. *Pedagogy of the Oppressed*. Penguin, 1972.

Freire, Paulo. *The Politics of Education: Culture, Power and Liberation*. Bergin & Garvey, 1985.

Furness, Zack, editor. *Punkademics*. Minor Compositions, 2012.

Giappone, K. "It's about being true to yourself: an interview with Miguel 'Kinnie' Debattista, from Batteries not included." *Punk & Post-Punk* 7.3, 2018, pp. 433–45.

Gordon, Alastair. *Crass Reflections*. Itchy Monkey Press, 2016.

Gordon, Alastair. "Distinctions of Identity and the Everyday Punk Self." *Punk & Post-Punk* 3.3, 2014, pp. 183–202.

Gordon, Alastair. *Throwing The Punk Rock Baby Out With The Dirty Bath Water: Crass and Punk Rock, A Critical Appraisal*. Self-Published, 1996.

Hanson, Karis. "'Whitestraightboy' Hegemony in Punk Rock: Exploring Practices Within a Purportedly Progressive Subculture." *Postgraduate Voices in Punk Studies: Your Wisdom, Our Youth*, edited by Mike Dines and Laura Way, Cambridge Scholars Publishing, 2017, pp. 117–32.

Kristiansen, Lars J. *Screaming For Change: Articulating a Unifying Philosophy of Punk Rock*. Lexington Books, 2012.

Laing, Dave. *One Chord Wonders: Power and Meaning in Punk Rock*. Open University Press, 1985.

LeBlanc, Lauraine. *Pretty in Punk: Girls' Gender Resistance in a Boy's Subculture*. Rutgers University Press, 1999.

Malott, Curry, and Milagros Peña. *Punk Rockers' Revolution: A Pedagogy of Race, Class, and Gender*. Peter Lang, 2004.

Martin-Iverson, Sean. "DIY or DIE: Do It Yourself Production and the Struggle for an Autonomous Community in the Bandung Hardcore Punk Scene." *The Punk Reader: Research Transmissions from the Local and the Global*, edited by Mike Dines, Alastair Gordon, Paula Guerra and Russ Bestley, Intellect, 2017, pp. 249–69.

McKay, George. *Cripping Subculture: Punk Rock and Disability*. UEAEPrints, 2014.

Mogk, Marja Evelyn. *Different Bodies: Essays on Disability in Film and Television*. McFarland & Co., 2013.

Nault, Curran. *Queercore: Queer Punk Media Subculture*. Routledge, 2018.

Nguyen, Mimi. "It's (Not) a White World: Looking for Race in Punk." *White Riot: Punk Rock and the Politics of Race*, edited by Stephen Duncombe and Maxwell Tremblay, Verso, 2011, pp. 256–68.

Nyong'o, Tavia. "Brown Punk: Kalup Linzy's Musical Anticipations." *TDR: The Drama Review* 54.3, 2010, pp. 71–86.

Nyong'o, Tavia. "Punk'd Theory." *Social Text* 84-85, 2005, pp. 19–34.

O'Hara, Craig. *The Philosophy of Punk: More Than Noise!*. AK Press, 1999.

Poma, Alice, and Tommaso Gravante. "Crack in the System: A Bottom-Up Analysis of the Anarcho-Punk Movement in Mexico." *The Punk Reader: Research Transmissions from the Local and the Global*, edited by Mike Dines, Alastair Gordon, Paula Guerra and Russ Bestley, Intellect, 2017, pp. 97–113.

Raposo, Ana, and Russ Bestley. "Designing fascism: The evolution of a neo-Nazi punk aesthetic." *Punk & Post-Punk* 9.3, 2020, pp. 467–98.

Reddington, Helen. *The Lost Women of Rock Music: Female Musicians of the Punk Era*. Ashgate, 2007.

Rouse, Jennah. "Punks are not girls: Exploring Discrimination and Empowerment through the experiences of punk and alt-rock musicians in Leeds." *Punk & Post-Punk* 8.1, 2019, pp. 73–88.

Ryde, Robin, Sofianos, Lucy, and Charlie Waterhouse, editors. *The Truth of Revolution, Brother: The Philosophies of Punk*. Situation Press, 2014.

Sabin, Roger. "'I won't let that dago by': Rethinking Punk and Racism." *Punk Rock: So What? The Cultural Legacy of Punk*, edited by Roger Sabin, Routledge, 1999a, pp. 199–218.

Sabin, Roger. *Punk Rock: So What? The Cultural Legacy of Punk*. Routledge, 1999b.

Sharp, Megan. "Hypervisibility in Australian Punk Scenes: Queer experiences of spatial logics of gender and sexuality." *Punk & Post-Punk* 8.3, 2019, pp. 363–78.

Sklar, Monica. *Punk Style*. Bloomsbury, 2014.

Stewart, Francis. "No more heroes anymore: Marginalized identities in punk memorialization and curation." *Punk & Post-Punk* 8.2, 2019, pp. 209–26.

Stewart, Francis. *Punk Rock Is My Religion: Straight Edge Punk and "Religious" Identity*. Routledge, 2017.

Stewart, Francis. "The Anarchist, the Punk Rocker and the Buddha Walk into a Bar(n): Dharma Punx and Rebel Dharma." Punk & Post-Punk 4.4, 2015, pp. 71–89.

Stinson, Elizabeth. "Means of Detection: A Critical Archiving of Black Feminism and Punk Performance." *Women & Performance: a journal of feminist theory* 22.2-3, 2012, pp. 275–311.

Strahan, Lucinda. "I don't wanna walk around with you: Routes, roots and composing the grrrl geography of rebellion in Stephanie Kuehnert's *I Wanna Be Your Joey Ramone*." *Punk & Post-Punk* 5.3, 2016, pp. 265–80.

Subcultures Network, The. *Fight Back: Punk, Politics and Resistance*. Manchester University Press, 2015.

Subcultures Network, The. *Hebdige and Subculture in the Twenty-First Century: Through the Subcultural Lens*. Manchester University Press, 2020.

Subcultures Network, The. *Ripped, Torn and Cut: Pop, Politics and Punk Fanzines from 1976*. Manchester University Press, 2018.

Trowell, Ian. "Counter-realities and conflicted place: Gee Vaucher's *The Feeding of the Five Thousand* in the punk art tradition." *Punk & Post-Punk* 9.3, 2020, pp. 397–424.

Way, Laura. *Punk, Gender and Ageing: Just Typical Girls?* Emerald Publishing, 2020.

Way, Lyndon C.S., and Dylan Wallace. "The punks, the web, local concerns and global appeal: cultural hybridity in Turkish hardcore punk." *Punk & Post-Punk* 5.2, 2016, pp. 111–29.

Weiner, Nathaniel. "'Put on your boots and Harrington!': The ordinariness of 1970s UK punk dress." *Punk & Post-Punk* 7.2, 2018, pp. 181–202.

Woods, Maxwell. "Decolonization, decolonial excess, and punk: Reflections on the cultural politics of race and coloniality in North Atlantic punk." *Cultural Studies* 34.6, 2020, pp. 519–42.

Worley, Matthew. *No Future: Punk, Politics and British Youth Culture, 1976-1984.* Cambridge University Press, 2017.

Xiao, Jian. "Striving for Authenticity: Punk in China." *Punk & Post-Punk* 5.1, 2016, pp. 67–81.

"Dancing on the Corpses' Ashes": On Post-Hardcore Performance and Erased Nonwhite Bodies

Marcus Clayton

People underestimate the survival of nonwhite bodies through the power of performance. This is especially true of punk performances, which are meant to actively destroy white supremacy and all its branches, simultaneously reanimating representations of marginalized bodies within punk's ethos—within this text, hereby personally defined as an ethos that seeks community within the margins, seeks constant safety for said community, and utilizes different forms of noise and/or distortion to seek visibility despite dominantly white patriarchal systems. Within punk comes an inherent pledge toward visibility in the name of social justice, a pledge of cacophonous noise to disrupt white patriarchal forces from eradicating othered existences. While some could say this pledge became lost among the advent of hardcore in the early 1980s, marginalized communities still used hardcore scenes to ignite articulations of political discourse through performance; this expression doubled down with the later conception of post-hardcore, where the emotional weight of visibility became much more tangible in the hands of othered bodies. This evolution of hardcore, this melding of quiet meditation on emotion with the bombastic hostility of punk rock, allowed an avenue for inclusion that gave both the listener and musician a sense of catharsis some would say was missing from the punk scenes. A catharsis excavated from Guy Picciotto's wails in Rites of Spring's "For Want Of" when he yells, "I believed / that in forgetting I might set myself free / but I woke up this morning / with a piece of past caught in my throat / and then I chocked," declaring this layer of punk rock a safe haven for bodies to reflect and revisit, to let ghosts walk among the Earth to reclaim agency over their final words.

This ethos of reclamation in post-hardcore music, especially within the hands of marginalized bands, harnesses what critic José Esteban Muñoz calls "feeling brown" in an effort to unify marginalized communities in their shared despair and eventual victories. He emphasizes how, "it nonetheless captures a certain political utopian aspiration that does not cleanse the stain of feeling like a problem in the manner in which the cultural detergent of weak multi-culturalism does ... Feeling Brown is *feeling together in difference*" ("'Chico, What Does It Feel Like to Be a Problem?'" 39; my emphasis). This is especially evident when he looks at how the "sorrow songs" from negro spirituals did work in uplifting marginalized voices, and how similar work is done through theme songs celebrating brown bodies despite those same bodies' perpetual other-ing on mainstream television. While the historical burdens of these songs are obviously very different, this does unify music and noise as a factor in disrupting erasure—the very hardships that encumbers othered bodies, that transform their lives into static for white ears, instead become artistic modes of communication and togetherness that keep marginalized histories alive. With this in mind, I wish to engage punk from various angles to emphasize how "feeling brown" not only unifies, but repairs marginalized communities: from literary restructuring of undocumented histories in "punk" literature, to the queer and Afrolatinx bodies in drag among 80s hardcore scenes, to the noise of brown post-hardcore resurrecting the slain through music. The punk ethos, however expressed or performed by a body of color, is a necessity to combat erasure and de-emphasize complacency within the larger construct of society. Whether or not music is playing, the punk ethos lives on within post-hardcore after "feeling brown" evolves.

The Audacity of Visibility

To fully understand how the ethos of punk embraces survival, it is imperative that one looks outside of music to see its reach in different communities. Consider the 2020 book, *The Undocumented Americans* by Karla Cornejo-Villavicencio. The text hybridizes memoir and journalism to dive into the lives of undocumented immigrants trying their best to live in America without allowing skewed notions of their existence dictate how they function. This book focuses on the idea of "feeling brown" with punk contours in that the text concerns itself with preservation and visibility for a community Cornejo-Villavicencio holds dear, one that is often discarded and considered unbefitting for society. As a whole, the book refuses to shy away from the more heinous events of the selected individuals' lives, including the desperation of contractors, ICE raids, the effects of having little to no medical resources, the effects of 9/11, and the guilt of having privilege when those in the community suffer.

Cornejo-Villavicencio's ability to humanize these tragic events performs the work of visibility within the written word in a way that illuminates the punk ethos. Community becomes a harbinger for survival in the narrative, distilling the long-standing history of punk with the Latinx culture's need to unify among scenes of motion. Cornejo-Villavicencio crafts her narratives to give these forgotten lives a voice, taking their existence out of the pitying stare of the white gaze and letting them flourish with their own gesticulations speaking for their histories. In an interview, the author herself signifies *The Undocumented Americans* as her "punk rock manifesto," noting its disavowal from liberal cooption of undocumented life as an object of political pathos, and amplifying its need to reach a wider community of undocumented people to know they are not invisible; they do, indeed, exist and matter.

> I want kids to know that they can just take from history and they can just take from our traditions and just fuck shit up. I want them to stay in school, I want them to be creative, I want them to think of ways to express them-selves and expel their demons in ways that do not perpetuate intergener-ational trauma. I want them to say, "This ends with me." I want them to not romanticize their parents, please. I'm not fucking around when I say I want you to think of this book as permission to be punk … just gather the rawest supplies you have—your memories, your feelings, your traumas, ev-erything—and make something out of it that's just truly your own and that's going to cause some people in suits to look at you twice. Put some bobby pins in it. (Cornejo-Villavicencio qtd. in Lozada)

The tone of the novel stays consistently accessible, also, to honor the continued struggle of undocumented people within and just outside of the country. In writing this manuscript, Cornejo-Villavicencio has admitted to carrying an immense weight of survivor's guilt that could only be alleviated from allowing other undocumented lives to live on in the pages of her book. This is evident in the dedication to Claudia Gomez Gonzalez, a Guatemalan woman shot dead by Texas Border Patrol just after crossing into the United States. Her inclusion was a necessity for Cornejo-Villavicencio in rounding out the book, stating,

I remember feeling so heartbroken by her death, as if I had betrayed her. She was this very young woman, had these very big dreams. In these pictures you see of her, she had such a look of determination and seriousness on her face. And then, she was murdered for having this dream. I felt like I had blood on my hands ... I am such a good poster child for those kinds of opportunities. I wish I could have protected her, and I didn't. (qtd. in Gonzalez-Ramirez).

The simple act of including Gomez-Gonzalez in the book, giving the woman her own page, forces readers to spend time with her lost existence and allows her to breathe even if only in the minds of the reader. She can no longer be forgotten by the status quo; she can no longer be erased as Cornejo-Villavicencio's punk ethos galvanized the lost life like a marble statue.

Cornejo-Villavicencio takes Muñoz's notion of "feeling brown" and amplifies the positive connotation lost in its translation, searing the punk ethos into brownness where it was meant to exist and evolve. The "sorrows" sung into the ether by marginalized bodies keep them from erasure, even when whiteness and patriarchy try to exacerbate said sorrows. This can be further articulated diving into Muñoz's acclaimed *Disidentifications* essay, "'The White to Be Angry': Vaginal Crème Davis's Terrorist Drag," where he pays special attention toward the 1980's punk rock and hardcore scenes in Los Angeles, noting the essentiality of the scene in aiding marginalized Angelenos in finding space and visibility. While the scene in his view thrives on ethos over aesthetic, he does not see white punk as abetting said marginalized visibility as needed. He swiftly points out that, "the LA punk scene worked very hard to whitewash and straighten its image. Although many people of color and queers were part of this cultural movement, they often remained closeted in the scene's early days" ("'The White to Be Angry'" 95). Muñoz then points towards LA punk band X as such an example of whiteness when trying its "best" but still faltering at being an ally: their songs dive into the dark underbelly of LA life, lambasting sexual assault and racism through lyrics that are steeped in sarcasm and parody, embodying the very evils they attempt to critique. Their song, "Los Angeles," especially takes shots at racism, although the way it utilizes slurs in the lyrics, such as the opening verse, "She had to leave Los Angeles / All her toys wore out in black and her boys had too / She started to hate every n****r and Jew / Every Mexican that gave her a lotta shit / Every homosexual and the idle rich," runs a risk of emboldening white supremacy that made "Nazi Punks" feel welcomed into the scenes, further alienating marginalized individuals.

Admittedly, X's song does well to paint the Los Angeles landscape as one ravaged by economic strife via white flight, but the voices are still steeped in privileges that the city's denizens were often denied. This is the ongoing frustrations punk communities face when trying to retrieve histories propelling marginalized voices. Punk is seen as white because the vitriolic lyricism of the music speaks to the white's absolution from injustices rather than the creation of space for nonwhite, non-hetero punks. The ethos is relegated toward the aggressive and sardonic modes of the genre, creating narratives too abstract to define inclusive cultural relevancy. Being that the 1980s saw unrest due to Reaganomics, AIDS, and the War on Drugs, it reads as preposterous to think marginalized communities who were most affected by these legislative acts would not be able to speak on their own behalf with authentic narratives that do not, in any way, sympathize with oppressors. Hardcore punk managed to focus attention on the collective dissatisfaction with the Reagan administration, especially true with the Dead Kennedys' pervasive usage of overt political commentary in their songs—"We've Got Bigger Problems Now" being a prime example of outlining a dystopian American life with Reagan at the helm that cannot be confused as ideal. However, unfortunately, this did little to change how white punk communities often failed (and still fail) to see strife beyond their own boredom, hearing the political messaging as white noise for slam dancing.

What's more, pertaining to the Dead Kennedys, when asked for diversity, many white punks center the band (fronted by white singer, Jello Biafra), as an "Afropunk" band due to the presence of DH Peligro on drums. While this acknowledgment is no doubt a boon for marginalized visibility in hardcore scenes, one cannot help but still starve for more respect and visibility in hardcore punk scenes. This is why Muñoz's writing on Vaginal Davis—an originator of the homo-core punk movement and a gender-queer art-music icon—proves a necessary piece to understanding visibility in punk that Cornejo-Villavicencio harnesses for her own writing; in this writing we see nonwhite punk undoing white stagnation, we see punk stretched beyond music and into social justice the way it was always meant to do.

Punk Ethos in Practice

Vaginal Davis' very existence is punk in ethos—existing despite social norms, creating noise to announce the presence of ignored cultures. As a hardcore punk performer and a Drag Queen, she crafted her identity to fit into the mold of the Los Angeles punk scene while *not* disowning the complexities of her blackness, brownness, or queerness. Musically, her ability to synthesize punk aesthetics with the cultural work of Afrolatinadad spoke to the punk ethos of preservation and survival, which is especially notable in her experience with names. Her various hardcore bands went by titles such as The Afro Sisters, Black Fag, and ¡Cholita! The Female Menudo, all of which introduced elements of "feeling brown" through the mere actualization of naming. This control over character subverts the crises of the Afrolatinx identity:

> [I]n seeking to find a place in US culture and society, there is at work in the experience of many Afro-Latinos a pull in two directions at once ... there is an extensive history to this drama of re-placement ... as manifest in the language, religion, musical and artistic expressivity, and of course in the role of Black Latin Americans in the political and social history of the hemisphere[.] (Flores 327)

Davis' exploration of her identities within each of her listed band names does not simply create an "eye catching" moniker to be remembered for their audaciousness; it speaks her lived experiences into existence without the need for a white voice, it unifies the musicality of hardcore punk with the cultural resistance to erasure often forgotten in white punk. Davis' implementation of her multiracial identity, synthesized with her queerness, worked to reconstruct punk to be more inclusive to bodies that matched her own—bodies that felt displaced in a dominantly heteronormative and violent musical scene—allowing a cultural vocabulary to be inserted into the lexicon of punk in harmony with the genre's typically violent stance against conformity. Looking at her name alone—a play on political activist, Angela Davis—one sees her inclusion of militant "Black power" ideals permeating her identity within her drag and punk performances. Her academic background merged with her love of performance, and some of her punk shows saw her and two white bandmates (both donning white afro wigs) fornicate with effigies of white businessmen by placing large dildos in the rectums of said effigies. To her admission, "it really freaked out a lot of the middle-class post-punk crowd—they didn't get the campy element of it, but I didn't really care" (Davis qtd in Muñoz "'The White to Be Angry'" 84). Being that this level of performance is usually reserved for drag shows made appearances in straight punk clubs thoroughly revitalizing for the hardcore scene, injecting experimentation and hybridity to allow for punks just outside the social norm of "conventional punk rock" to find inclusion. Muñoz goes on to praise this fortuitous audacity, stating, "[...] the punk rock drag diva elucidates a stage or temporal space where the person of color's consciousness turns to her or his community after an immersion in white culture and education. The ultra-militant phase that Davis describes is a powerful counteridentification with the dominant culture" ("'The White to Be Angry'" 98). Through these actions, Davis' performance becomes her rhetoric and vice versa; when exclusion becomes an obstacle within an identity held dear, the perpetuation of the self within that circle makes one loud, colorful, impossible to erase. Muñoz highlights these characteristics of Davis' proximity to punk in an effort to not only signal a disruption of the overwhelming presence of white punks in hardcore scenes, but to fortify the work nonwhite punk does for cultures outside of the local hardcore scene.

Remedies for Erasure in the Mainstream

This cultural work was emboldened in the late 1990's when Latinx fronted, El Paso Post-hardcore outlet, At The Drive-In, reached a modest yet unprecedented level of mainstream success. Following in the footsteps of Vaginal Davis, At The Drive-In dedicated much of their energy to performances entrenched in cultural reverence and aggressive visibility. Gone were mohawks and dog collars that punctuated white punk in the 1980s, favoring tattered t-shirts flaunting their brown skin and textured hair that exemplified their ancestry. At The Drive-In made sure their shows were inviting to hardcore kids from marginalized communities, women, and even white punks learning from other cultures. The two primary songwriters of the group, singer Cedric Bixler-Zavala and guitarist Omar Rodriguez-Lopez, were aesthetically essential to the devaluing of white punk fashion in the mainstream. Both musicians sported large afros, ratty skinny jeans borrowed from female elders, and tattoos they reported to have received by friends in their El Paso circles. Much like Davis, they levied their names in the public eye to galvanize their detachment from whiteness, intentionally hyphenating last names to honor their familial ties to brownness. During live performances, their chaotic energy saw the gyrations from *every* member utilize salsa and cumbia dance moves to match the rhythm of the hardcore sounds. This allowed the audience to absorb their performances and internalize their movements as an art form, to witness their movements as an expression of their upbringing despite the supposed whiteness of punk rock. The members hung flags of

Puerto Rico, Mexico, Lebanon, and Texas over their instruments as representation and meditation on their various cultures. The "violence" onstage as they played loud guitar music and sang venomous lyrics lambasting patriarchy and racism allowed them to siphon injury from the crowd—asking the crowd to dance instead of "mosh" and using space between songs to check on the safety of the audience. This approach to performing music is a reflection of their upbringing in a community ravaged by economic strife and racial tensions, where punk rock scenes were utilized to combat confrontation with inclusivity and care through any means made available to them.

As noted in Michelle Habell-Pallán's work on Chicana punk, this attracted punks of color because, "the DIY (do-it-yourself) sensibility at the core of punk musical subcultures found resonance with the practice of rasquache, a Chicana/o cultural practice of 'making do' with limited resources; and punk's critique of the status quo-of poverty, sexuality, class inequality, and war spoke directly to working-class [marginalized] youth" (163). Furthermore, the punk ethos dislodged capitalistic gains from their cultural perspectives, as the embrace of the DIY ethic "disavows materialism and consumerism and the individualist fame of rock stars ... [while also reflecting] the fact that Latino punks are marginalized economically and have limited access to production and distribution facilities" (Zavella 29). This should not be confused for misfortune. The continuation of culture work, despite resources afforded to affluent white populations being absent in marginalized communities, strengthens the visibility of the punk ethos for Latinx acts and other punks of color, fortifying vitality for survival.

At The Drive-In's contemporaries at the time, including acts such as Green Day, blink-182, The Offspring, and others, found themselves far more concerned with the fashionable aspects of punk rock among an ever-increasing attention to glamor and individual survival within mainstream popular culture. To compare, for example, The Offspring released the music video for "Original Prankster" (2000) the same year At The Drive-In released their mainstream breakout record, *Relationship of Command*. The song is largely comedic, depicting the consequences of pulling pranks, set to music that synthesizes punk rock, hip-hop, and Latin influenced rhythms. While this sounds progressive on paper, the video sets out to alienate the punk ethos by using various images of hubris and misogyny. The setting takes place at a beach area with a plethora of black and brown women in revealing bikinis lining the background shots. Cholos fill out the background as well, sporting Pendleton shirts and bandanas, ogling women, fishing off the Piers, and driving lowrider cars

(The Offspring 0:21-0:32). A brown actor only speaks to sing the "you can do it" line in the song, modeled after actor Rob Schneider's poor imitation of an immigrant's accent originating from the 1998 film *The Water Boy*. At the forefront of the lighthearted video, The Offspring's band members play their instruments in sunglasses and smiles, the aforementioned marginalized bodies acting as a moat to their punk castle. The band's goatees and bleached blonde hair crystalize white male fashion of the late 1990's and early 2000s, and they use this video to propel a marketable brand of punk rock to the masses. There is a point in the video as well where the young boy (as a prank) sets fire to his Lab teacher during Chemistry class as the Lab teacher tried to look up a student's skirt. Both the young boy and the Lab teacher leave the scene unharmed, and the young woman is completely forgotten (1:31-2:02). The song charted high on the Billboards, and the music video received heavy airplay on MTV in 2000: a palatable punk rock for the masses that placed white bodies in front—prosperous and ebullient—and everyone else on the margins.

Ghosts of Juarez Making Noise

The attractive punk rock of the time strayed from ideas related to social justice and visibility for the other in order to lean into problematic ideals for the sake of capitalism. By the time At The Drive-In released the single for their song, "Invalid Litter Dept.," their entire aesthetic got ignored for not adhering to the canonical punk other white bands delivered. As guitarist Rodriguez-Lopez succinctly said, "[in the early 2000s] it was cool to be stupid and misogynist [in the mainstream punk scene because] that was the trend" (qtd. in Bakare). Despite mainstream attention calling for all musical acts to follow the same route as The Offspring, no matter how niche the act, At The Drive-In adhered to their own learned ethos. They basked in their post-hardcore aesthetic, opting to use their wider platform for the voiceless within their community. This is exemplified with the music video release of "Invalid Litter Dept."

At The Drive-In's clip aligned with the song's lyrical content revolving around the countless murders of women in Ciudad Juarez—the Mexican city directly neighboring their hometown of El Paso, Texas. The song itself brings visibility to a catastrophe close to their community (both in physical and cultural proximity) in a manner that was politically scarce in punk and hardcore scenes at the time; almost loathed considering the openly misogynistic attitudes of white punks of the early 2000s that would spill into the mid-2000s emo and post-hardcore scenes. Nonetheless, the song brought the murders to the attention of their fanbase, as well as a new audience discovering the band through mainstream outlets. This exposure did the work of bringing visibility to crimes that damaged what the punk ethos tried to build. It brought the rampant violence and misogyny within the Mexican government to light, almost as though presenting the murders as a slippery slope for the increasingly aggressive patriarchy of the late 90s and early 2000s American mainstream culture. When one looks at the motives behind the violence within the Mexican government, one sees how At The Drive-In's video connects what appeals to mainstream audiences with the on-going male-controlled vice-grip on society; how erasure is not just a mode of forgetting, but an attempt to hide patriarchal inferiority concurrent with non-white and non-male success:

> Observers point to a set of economic, social, political, and cultural factors that include (a) rapid population growth in a frontier city, (b) a transient population of economic immigrants and the breakdown of community ties, (c) low salaries and poor working conditions in the maquilas, and (d) weak or corrupt government, police, and judicial institutions. All of these are postulated to create an environment in which criminal violence is likely to become widespread. But most observers emphasize cultural factors for both the violence against women and the impunity that accompanies it ... the economic empowerment of women produced a violent backlash by men in a classically machista society. (Ensalaco 420)

The video itself took this discourse surrounding women's visibility a step further, being comprised entirely of documentary style footage of the city of Juarez filmed in muted colors or black and white. Much of the video spends time cutting between shots of a bustling Mexican street, Juarez landmarks, the US/Mexico border, dirt floors pockmarked in loose clothing, unmarked graves and painted crosses, newspaper reels, and flowers. While the band appears in the video alongside these images, they are stoic for the entirety of the song. They take up as little space as possible while factual texts about the murders are displayed on screen throughout the video. Each member wears darkened street clothes, possibly representing the mourning for the women while city life in Juarez is forced to continue uninterrupted. Not a single word is mouthed, nor an instrument played, as the time is reserved to propel the city and the lives of the women into households of the mainstream music listener. Conventional flash and special effects are swapped for objective information, bringing every detail of the murders to the forefront of the music video, crafting a narrative of remembrance for the slain women over the punk music. The text is purposeful, placed around shots aligned with either mirrored lyrical content or an establishing shot within the video. For example, one text reads, "*Maquiladoras*, meaning 'twin plants,' are American-owned factories based in Mexico. These factories use cheap labor and avoid tariffs" (At The Drive-In 1:43-1:54), as said factories are shown from the inside, machinery working at full tilt, and women working tirelessly through sped up footage of backbreaking labor. Among these shots, the spliced in newspaper reels reveal quick headlines with "murder," "rape," "slayings," and full articles reading "desaparece otra adolescente" alongside displayed photos of the women in question with names and ages underneath as evidence of existence (2:35-3:06). Another shot does similar work, quickly hanging on a "Missing Persons" poster adhered to the base of a utility pole. The woman on the poster is named Elizabeth Nuñez Gomez, aged 16 years at the time of disappearance, with her face on full display—alive and well within the picture (1:35-1:36). This action further galvanizes the pathos of the song, begging the listener and viewer to acknowledge the missing women as human beings trying their best to live without constant fear of death, only to be reduced to a photograph or box of text in a newspaper for the simple "crime" of being a woman at the wrong hour of the day. Broad shots of empty holes prepared to be graves, missing clothes, and horizons covered in bouquets and crosses as grave markers extend this urgency (2:39-2:43 and 5:31-5:51), showing the viewer that the consistent death toll has and will continue to affect scores of women if attention is not paid to these atrocities.

The song itself is a relatively unique one for At The Drive-In's discography, trading shouts for spoken word during the verses, trading screams for catchy hooks in the chorus to aid the listener in remembering the song's thesis. The music, while decidedly more mid-tempo and contemplative than their other work, still retains the punk ethos in its message and its artistic flourishes. The music alters its aural duties not to conform to the punk status quo, but to act as a defining eulogy that honors the lost while indicting the corrupt. This is most prominent in lyrics such as, "In the company of wolves / was a stretcher made of cobblestone curfews / as the federales performed their custodial customs / quite well / dancing on the corpses' ashes." Here, singer Bixler-Zavala explicitly puts blame on the Mexican government for enabling their dominantly machista culture to allow the women's lives to disappear into the ether, treating their slain bodies like garbage polluting their streets. The line "dancing on the corpses' ashes" is repeated a multitude of times through-out the song, but is especially pertinent here as it highlights how the gov-ernment does not protect its citizens. Instead, the government mirrors the murderers (the "wolves") as it chooses to celebrate its own lack of compassion for the slain.

In the final moments of the song, in hopes to emulate the social change the lyrics and video cry for, the rhythm changes. The music gets heavier and Bixler-Zavala's vocal melodies become harsher and more pointed. The video transitions with the chilling message of, "to date (2000), approximately 570 women have been murdered ... all of the cases remain unsolved" and more footage of bouquets strewn over graves are shown alongside more headlines (4:41-4:47). However, these headlines begin to read, "accuses [bus] driver," "Women demand deaths be solved," and "women protest Juarez killings," signaling action against the atrocities by way of the women in question. While a positive message to end the dispiriting tune, this does not erase the missteps taken that cost these women their lives (4:53-5:17). As time tells, the murders continued, albeit occasionally tempered with action from Amnesty International, the Inter-American Commission, FEDEFAM, the Casa Amiga Crisis Center, and some necessary vigilantism. As of 2020, even during a global pandemic, homicides are still rampant in Ciudad Juarez, numbering in the thousands.

At The Drive-In end the song with Bixler-Zavala shouting the lines, "cal-lous heels / numbed in travel / endless maps made by their scalpels," painting a picture of the women who traveled (either to and from work, or journey-ing through life) and destroyed the feeling in their feet from the necessities and invisibilities of working in factories, while also utilizing their destroyed bodies as markers of where they can be found after the vicious murders, ab-staining from erasure even after death. These lines are punctuated by Bixler-Zavala's final repetition of "scalpels," a sharpened weapon used in stabbings and mutilations of these women, as he lets out four guttural, blood-curdling screams to end the songs' vocals. Fred Moten notes the power of the female voice when he says, "the interinanimation of the maternal and the material that is iconically manifest in the female voice is irreducible to meaning" (216). Bixler-Zavala's performance is reminiscent of Moten's statement as he uses this portion of the song to abandon his own narrative in an attempt to let the spirit of the lost female lives embody the ferocity of the words. The screams are desperate and viciously loud, coming from the gut as though stabbed in that very body part, tearing the throat as though trying one last time to transfer these women's pain to the listener who may be ignorant of their suffering. Much like At The Drive-In's decreased visibility in the music video in favor of spotlighting Juarez, Bixler-Zavala personifies the pain within the scream to the point of letting the perspective of his voice transform into that of the women who died alone and forgotten, using the sonic force of punk to let their stories be told and escape erasure once and for all.

Unlike The Offspring's "Original Prankster," "Invalid Litter Dept." did not make it to the Billboard charts, and the music video received exceptionally little airplay on music video stations across the country. This lack of focus, even or especially in the mainstream, is symptomatic of nonwhite punk and the punk ethos' non-survival within the white canon. At The Drive-In's mission yearned to fortify voices of color just as much as dismantling white ones, bolstering the ideals of critic Achille Mbembe when he pleaded, "the demythologizing of certain versions of history must go hand in hand with the demythologizing of whiteness ... whiteness is about entrapment ... It is the most corrosive and the most lethal when it makes us believe that it is everywhere; that everything originates from it and it has no outside." Still, as decades moved on from the early 2000s and At the Drive-In's mainstream peak, post-hardcore acts of color would pick up this slack and disseminate punk from marginalized hands regardless of mainstream "appeal." Voices at work are still voices, and they can communicate clearly if given the chance to learn the languages necessary to speak to ghosts—the women of Juarez would not be denied their true final say.

Punk Rock Ethos Afterlives

The reach of post-hardcore's quiet aggressiveness survives for a reason: the eradication of violence in favor of meditation utilizes punk ethos to return lost spirits to the body. After the disillusion of At The Drive-In, members split off into different musical acts that continued to carry the punk ethos on their back: Bixler-Zavala and Rodriguez-Lopez created The Mars Volta, a progressive punk band that doubled down on embracing their Latinx heritage in the name of visibility, while the remaining members formed Sparta in order to continue on with a more recognizable post-hardcore sound. Nonetheless, more punk and hardcore bands of color came to At The Drive-In's stead to further progress nonwhite voices in punk. In the 2010s, specifically, post-hardcore outfit The World Is a Beautiful Place and I Am No Longer Afraid to Die, directly carried At the Drive-In's lyrical sway into their music as time and situations evolved. Hereby known as The World Is..., the post-hardcore act already bends the conventions of punk by housing an average of eight or nine members, some instruments including keyboards and cellos, as well as unconventional song structures that stretch the contours of punk music: ten-plus minutes songs, multiple changes, acoustics, all while still playing to the punk aesthetic of loud guitars and furious rhythms.

What remains funnels through punk veins in singer Dave Bello who is of Puerto Rican heritage and uses his platform to sing lost lives back to life. While this is evident in songs such as "Marin Tiger," which speaks critically of the mistreatment of undocumented Puerto Ricans by American officials in the 1940s, their song "January 10th, 2014" acts as a direct descendent of At The Drive-In's "Invalid Litter Dept." as well as it speaks to the punk ethos sowed in Cornejo-Villavicencio's The Undocumented Americans. The subject continues where "Invalid Litter Dept." left off, singing of the Juarez killings with a voice the victims could have used to prevent more deaths. However, rather than lament the powerlessness of the women's bodies, the song amplifies their strengths, documenting real life female vigilantes taking the lives of the murderers.

The release of The World Is...'s video for "January 10th, 2014" did similar work to continue At the Drive-In's message, albeit with more cinematic flair and somewhat less of an audience. Released on YouTube in 2015, long after MTV diverted attention from music in favor of reality television, the narrative is told unencumbered by executive power. The band, instead, released a visceral retelling of a kidnapping and murder within Juarez Mexico, using the actor's performances to convey the story instead of dialogue or written words. All nine or so members of the band are missing from the video, opting to focus on the bodies acting as avatars for the lost brown women; the story itself, while rife with metaphor and allusions to Roman mythology, becomes a relatively cohesive story of war against a man and his abuse of power, thereby conveying violence in a manner that strays from the needless angst of white men and focuses on reclamation often sought after within the ethos of punk rock. This should take nothing away from Cornejo-Villavicencio, At the Drive-In, or Muñoz's respective abilities to utilize a punk ethos to excavate forgotten lives, but The World Is...'s music video offers yet another angle for these stories to be told to audiences blinded by mainstream static. Akin to Bixler-Zavala's screams acting as a conduit for the fallen women's pain, The World Is... balances Bello's vocals with keyboardist Katie Dvorak in order to create an interplay between a domineering male voice losing its power over an empowered female voice. This is best on display with the words, "Are you Diana, the hunter? / *Are you afraid of me now?* / Well, yeah, shouldn't I be?" signifying a real-life vigilante—known to news outlets as "Diana, the hunter"—who killed two bus drivers in an act of revenge against the decades long killing of women in Juarez, Mexico. Further, with the lines "I am an instrument / I am revenge / I am several women," sung by Dvorak, we see a fortified connection with the lives of the lost and the ancestors trying to reclaim their lives. This manages to reshape the real-life events of Diana's killings, restructuring news reports away from vigilantism and toward justice for murder and silenced sexual assault victims.

The images within the video galvanize the song's thesis, beginning with a single arrow lit on fire, wielded by a female archer, and fired into the sky before the narrative proper begins. As the story revolving around a man kidnapping a female hitchhiker progresses, we return to the arrow mid-song; the ablaze arrow lands in an open field, creating a flaming Wiccan symbol as a group of Roman Goddesses descend into the scene for attack (The World Is 3:15-3:41). The slow visuals allow the viewer to properly synthesize the symbolism with the post-hardcore tune, understanding how the Wiccan symbol further separates these bodies from white patriarchal systems—the illumination of alternative belief systems that deviate from organized religion, the literal reignition of pagan worship that saw many female lives destroyed over centuries due to accusations and gaslighting in the name of organized religion. The last third of the video sees the women take their revenge on the man, leaving an arrow in his back while his "spirit" stands in front of his dead body, watching his literal fall from grace as his body falls dead (4:01-5:37).

This video spiritually concludes At The Drive-In's single in terms of resurrection through song: using punk ethos to communicate among communities, to translate for the dead in hopes to attain justice through the distorted noise of hardcore. What's more, having the singers of color belt out these stories of revenge without the urge for monetary gain and with the acknowledgement of platform, they simultaneously aide these lost lives while unearthing Vaginal Davis' work toward marginalized visibility in hardcore circles. All the violence is aimed at tearing down oppressive structures, while whiteness remains away from the spotlight. These voices remain forever locked inside the wax of these songs, singing eulogies for forgotten lives ad nauseum. When they dance, it is with purpose while crafting universal languages. In the hands of marginalized punks, the music of post-hardcore amplifies the notion of "feeling brown" in a manner that is welcoming, diminishing subjugation from white punks and creating spaces for marginalized folk finding their groove in the mosh pits. Through these avenues of performance, punk bleeds into the lives of those who do not necessarily listen to the music, but believe in and need its messages—the undocumented, the stolen and slain, the ashes that deserve a second chance to speak.

References

At The Drive-In. "Invalid Litter Dept." *Relationship of Command*. Fearless Records / Grand Royal Records, https://www.youtube.com/watch?v=TLpJ9gFdaww&list=LL&index=4. 2000.

Bakare, Lanre. "'It was cool to be misogynist': At the Drive-In on fights, drugs and the dark days of nu-metal." *The Guardian*. 9 Nov. 2017, https://www.theguardian.com/music/2017/nov/09/it-was-cool-to-be-misogynist-at-the-drive-in-on-fights-drugs-and-the-dark-days-of-nu-metal. Accessed 10 June 2022.

Cornejo-Villavicencio, Karla. *The Undocumented Americans*. One World, 2020.

Ensalaco, Mark. "Murder in Ciudad Juárez: A Parable of Women's Struggle for Human Rights." *Violence Against Women*12.5, May 2006, pp. 417–40.

Flores, Román. "Triple-Consciousness? Approaches to Afro-Latino Culture in the United States." *Latin American and Caribbean Ethnic Studies* 4.3, Nov. 2009, pp. 319–28.

Gonzalez-Ramirez, Andrea. "'The Undocumented Americans' Is the Immigration Punk Manifesto We Need Today." *GEN by Medium*. 22 Mar. 2020, gen.medium.com/the-undocumented-americans-is-the-immigration-punk-manifesto-we-need-today-f09e01636952. Accessed 10 June 2022.

Habell-Pallán, Michelle. "'Soy Punkera. ¿y Qué?': Sexuality, Translocality, and Punk in Los Angeles and Beyond." *Rockin Las Americas: The Global Politics Of Rock In Latin/o America*, edited by Deborah Pacini Hernandez et al., University of Pittsburgh Press, 2004, pp. 160–78.

Lozada, Lucas I. "Karla Cornejo Villavicencio: DREAMer memoirs have their purpose. But that's not what I set out to write." *Guernica*. 10 June 2020, guernicamag.com/karla-cornejo-villavicencio-dreamer-memoirs-have-their-purpose-but-thats-not-what-i-set-out-to-write/. Accessed 10 June 2022.

Mbembe, Achille. "Decolonizing Knowledge and the Question of the Archive." *Atavist*. 14 May 2015, africaisacountry.atavist.com/decolonizing-knowledge-and-the-question-of-the-archive. Accessed 10 June 2022.

Moten, Fred. *In the Break: The Aesthetics of the Black Radical Tradition*. University of Minnesota Press, 2003.

Muñoz, José Esteban. "'Chico, What Does It Feel Like to Be a Problem?': The Transmission of Brownness." *The Sense of Brown*, edited by Joshua Chambers-Letson and Tavia Nyong'o, Duke University Press, 2020, pp. 36–46.

Muñoz, José Esteban. "'The White to be Angry': Vaginal Crème Davis's Terrorist Drag." *Disidentifications: Queers of Color and the Performance of Politics*, University of Minnesota Press, 1999, pp. 93–115.

The Offspring. "Original Prankster." *Conspiracy of One*. Columbia Records, youtube.com/watch?v=Qp6Qn8IwPf8. 2000.

The World Is a Beautiful Place & I am No Longer Afraid to Die. "January 10th, 2014." *Harmlessness*. Epitaph Records, https://www.youtube.com/watch?v=mVgolBtzgQQ. 2015.

Zavella, Patricia. "Beyond the Screams: Latino Punkeros Contest Nativist Discourses." *Latin American Perspectives* 39.2, 2012, pp. 27–41.

Hardcore, Punk, and Academia: A Conversation between Brian Cogan and Kevin Dunn

Brian Cogan and Kevin Dunn

For this volume, Brian Cogan (author of *The Encyclopedia of Punk*) and Kevin Dunn (author of *Global Punk: Resistance and Rebellion in Everyday Life*) sat down to have a conversation about their careers writing about punk. Representing very different academic trajectories, they discuss their involvement within punk scenes and how their personal experiences and interests have led them to the similar task of writing punk scholarship. Operating in quite different academic fields, they discuss how their work both reflects their academic training and challenges the disciplinary assumptions and structures. Throughout the conversation they illustrate what it means to be a "hardcore academic" from their own perspectives.

Brian: At the age of 16 I went to see so many hardcore bands. My grades were good, my parents said, "As long as your grades keep up you can go to these punk shows." That was an amazing leap of faith for a boy from conservative Staten Island. It probably helped that there were three boys in my family. If I was a girl, I'm sure I would never have gotten permission to do that. I started seeing all these different bands for five dollars, which I could make on my paper route. It was an education. It was building up a knowledge base that eventually led to my research. One thing builds on another: First you know about this band, then you know about these other bands, then you know: "This is punk." And hardcore was a huge part of that scene in the '80s. First, I didn't even differentiate between punk and hardcore. I just realized some bands were playing faster. I don't recall hearing the term that much until '80-'81. Then someone asked, "Have you checked out the *Hardcore '81* record by D.O.A.?" This was in the mid-80s, during the Reagan presidency. My favorite thing was how people used flyers with that shot from (the film) The Killers with Reagan holding out the gun, or Reagan with a mohawk. He was good fodder for flyers and zines back in those days. At first, I didn't realize that there was a political agenda behind a lot of bands. In heavy metal, which a lot of my friends were into, the agenda just seemed to be "party." But I realized that the punk scene aligned with a lot of the values I had, and a lot of the values I was developing. I became a punk without knowing it. I knew I was listening to this music but I didn't know I was becoming one of these people. And then, suddenly, I was one of those people. A hardcore matinee every week will do that!

Kevin: Definitely! That was also true for me. Though I can't, in hindsight, separate the way in which punk and my politics were feeding into each other. I was clearly attracted to some of the punk stuff, whether it was The Exploited or The Clash, with the clear political message that I found appealing. I remember listening to The Clash's London Calling, hearing "Spanish Bombs" and wondering what the hell this was about. So, I started reading about the Spanish Civil War and then reading about the politics of Central America because Joe Strummer yells "Sandinista!" Of course, I also read the biography of Montgomery Clift because they're singing about him on "The Right Profile." Interestingly, this was the same moment that hip hop was coming up, and there was some crossover. I started reading Malcolm X and Stokely Carmichael because I was getting turned on to that kind of political edgy hip hop that overlapped into punk spheres. When it comes to hardcore, on the one hand, the scenes were often so small that we weren't delineating between subgenres. I was playing in a band and we'd play with whoever. There wasn't a big enough scene where you could have a full hardcore show or a full ska show. I remember opening up for heavy metal bands. Subgenres just got blurred, at least until I moved to Boston where the scene was much bigger. Thus, I didn't have a clear delineation of hardcore. On the other hand, people who claimed to be hardcore were often just saying: "I'm hardcore because I play punk faster." There wasn't a definition of that subgenre except that the people who identified as hardcore in my local scene were the hyper-masculine meatheads who claimed, "I'm more punk than you, I'm more physically aggressive than you, so I'm hardcore." It wasn't until much later, in the late 1980s, that I saw why people were starting to delineate the subgenre of hardcore. What was hardcore for you? How did you understand it?

Brian: There was almost no hardcore on Staten Island where I grew up. A lot of bands were playing what we would call "seventies" punk. I think hardcore came slowly into the scene because we were on the most isolated borough. New developments were hard to get into quickly. I'd go to the city to see bands. New York had that whole "aggro" feel. It was like a van full of sweaty skinheads. A lot of homo-eroticism that they weren't even aware of in their sweaty crowd. All those guys would stare you down. They were like, "I'm more punk than you." And I was wondering, "Why? Cause you work out?" I didn't even know what a gym was or who went to gyms back in the early- and mid-80s. The New York scene was very angry and aggressive. Still, I love a lot of the bands from back then. There was so much to get into: Cro-Mags put out a few great records, the first Agnostic Front record is good, Murphy's Law was always fun. Then we discovered the whole L.A. scene and bands like the Descendents, Adolescents, and Bad Religion. They proved that you can do melodic hardcore. There is no reason why you can't do it with harmonies. Descendents and Bad Religion would always both surprise me and educate me, too. Bad Religion had those multisyllabic songs and when I was reading the lyric sheets to their songs I thought, "I need a dictionary." Hardcore doesn't have to be one specific thing. It can and should be much more diverse. I liked the direction that bands like Minutemen and Hüsker Dü were taking hardcore. Back then, I wasn't using the term hardcore as much as I do today. I would just think, "I like the direction punk is going." I like the hip hop influence, too. It seemed to me, at least from the '80s onwards, that hardcore was moving in a direction where it was going to become more adventurous. What were your thoughts on hardcore in terms of the aggressiveness?

Kevin: Even today, years later, it's hard for me to pull away from those early associations of hyper-masculinity with hardcore. I found the misogyny of the people who were self-identifying as hardcore repulsive. One of the things I was finding comfortable about punk was that it could be a space that was supportive of women and marginalized groups, where gender norms were being pushed as much as possible. That wasn't on the agenda for people around me identifying with hardcore. But later I started to recognize what hardcore was bringing to the table. People started to identify bands as hardcore that I had just regarded as punk. I started to recognize that the stripped-down focus of the music was intentional, with this really concise and focused lyrical delivery. I got that. If punk was a little bit more experimental, and ska was going this way, and psychopunk was going that way, hardcore had this focus. It was not because people only know three chords, it was because there was an urgency that they were trying to convey with hardcore. I was able to understand that a band like Minutemen can be regarded as a hardcore band while pushing the boundaries of what is considered hardcore. I thought that was liberating.

Brian: Switching to the academy—how did your academic journey begin?

Kevin: I went to college with an interest in politics. The questions that were driving me and that I was finding attractive in punk were driven by a political engagement. I majored in political science as an undergraduate and then continued on into graduate school. I got a master's degree and then went on to get my PhD. When I was an undergraduate, I was very much involved in the anti-apartheid movement. I came from this racist, white, supremacist, conservative town and I tried to figure my way out. Through that anti-apartheid activism, I developed a strong interest in Africa. I was specifically looking at international relations and Africa. It had nothing to do with punk, even though I was still active in the scene. Whether it was in college or graduate school, I was playing in bands, putting on shows, eventually running a record label. But that was separate from what I was doing academically. I should point out that American political science is a very deeply conservative academic discipline. American political science in the 1960s and '70s focused on behaviorism and positivism, and the rise of rational choice methodology. There was a privileging of using quantitative data and precisely formulated theories to statistical relations between independent and dependent variables. Though there were plenty of exceptions, American political science during the mid- to late-20th century was characterized by a conservative focus that reflected the interest and maintenance of state power. This was true for the related field of international relations which, in the US, emerged within a Cold War context. The larger international relations discipline is grounded in imperialism and colonialism. All of this is to say that it's a weird place for me in terms of my orientation and my interests. But punk definitely shaped what I was doing and how I was thinking. My understanding of what counts as political is much more broadly conceived than that of my contemporaries because of my experience in punk. Examining the lyrics of a song by The Exploited or analyzing a zine or the way someone dresses or the way that scenes are being organized—for me those are all sites of resistance. That is political. But that's not how politics are usually understood within my discipline. I had no illusions when I went into the fields of political science and international relations. My primary regional interest was Africa, which has long been marginalized in both fields. Moreover, my intellectual orientation was towards feminism, post-colonialism, and post-structuralism. I've always operated at the margins of the discipline even before I started writing about punk. What about you? How did you go from being a kid listening to punk rock in Staten Island to the academy?

Brian: I never thought I was going to get a master's degree or a PhD. It never occurred to me after college. I thought I was going to work in film and trying to get in the film industry. I was working at NYU, giving out video equipment and teaching people how to use it. Then someone said, "You know, you can get tuition remission and essentially get a free degree." I was thinking, "No one told me that, but OK!" The decision was that glib. Then I got involved with the media ecology department. Neil Postman was the chair. He wrote the book *Amusing Ourselves to Death: Public Discourse in the Age of Show Business* (1985). Neil was a great guy, a real mentor, a good friend. After talking to him, I was like, "Wait, you're saying that media is not entirely positive? That mass media turns serious topics into entertainment and distracts us from what's real? Wait a second. That's kind of punk rock." When I was done with the master's, I thought, "This was such a great experience." The advisor I had said, "Why don't you apply to the PhD program?" Although I was thinking it's a one-in-a-thousand chance to get in, I did apply. I had some residual goodwill from a bunch of the faculty who ran the committee and got in. But I did not do anything on punk because they shot down popular culture on the first day of the seminar: "You do not write about things such as 'punk rock.'"

Kevin: What discipline was that?

Brian: Media studies would be the easiest way to frame it. British Cultural Studies was mixed in with that as well. And Marshall McLuhan's approach of the medium is the message; the Toronto School, as we called it. This was back in the '90s, so there was no real talk of studying big data, or social networks, or anything of that nature. TV was the dominant medium at that point, and movies. Video games were just becoming a dominant medium.

Kevin: And they shut down your popular culture ideas?

Brian: They shut it down on day one. Instead, my dissertation was on how newspapers covered the personal computer, the Internet, and how they framed it as a positive thing. I was planning on turning the dissertation to a book but that never happened. It became a journal article. But then I saw a call for papers, looking for someone to edit an encyclopedia on punk. My wife said, "Well, you should write it." I contacted the editor and said, "I can do this. This is stuff I was born to do." I showed the editor at the press the one article I had done on punk so far and he said, "You seem to be the person for the job." Next thing, I am taking two years to write this thing. Of course, it was incomplete. The first version was an academic book and it did not turn out that good. I did not know about so many different aspects of punk that I had to figure out. I had to learn more about queercore fast. I had to learn more about all these sub-submovements fast. I filled in the gaps in my record collection and bought all that stuff, too. I learned more and more. Then I said, "OK, this is what I want to write about. I don't want to go back to traditional academic articles anymore." I've done a few academic articles since then but tailored more to hardcore and punk. I wrote an academic article on sports zines, an academic article on Crass, and an academic article on feminism and punk. I realized that you can do academic stuff on punk if you find the right niche journals or right places to do it. You can work it into presentations here and there. It's definitely not a huge topic at international conferences though. I am still on the margins with that. But now I'm too old to care what people say. If I am the fourth presenter on Sunday morning at eight o'clock, I can live with that. That's cool. When did you decide you're going to start writing about punk?

Kevin: As a rising young academic, I would regularly attend academic conferences and was invited to give talks across North America, Europe and Africa. Wherever I travelled, I got into the habit of going to local punk shows and making contacts with members of the local scenes. Scenes are maintained by personal connections and you can always find a way in if you know what to look for. You know the process: You go to the bar that looks like it might book punk shows, you go to the independent record store, you look for flyers on the wall, you try to find zines. After a few years, I realized that I was in the privileged position of accessing a wide range of local scenes and meeting a variety of amazing punks and scene-builders. I began taking notes and even scheduling formal interviews that I started getting published in *Maximum Rocknroll* and *Razorcake*, two of the most influential punk zines in North America and beyond. Then two events happened. After the birth of my second child, I was doing fieldwork in northern Uganda and eastern Democratic Republic of Congo. Though I had been doing work in both of these conflict zones for years, the emotional cost of doing so was now far more pronounced on both myself and my family back home. I realized that I could not be going into distant conflict zones anymore. I had to come up with a scholarly trajectory that was a little bit safer. The second event occurred at an academic conference in Portland, Oregon on the eve of the American invasion of Iraq (in 2003). Despite the fact that it was an international studies conference, fucking no one was talking about the war. I co-organized an anti-war protest there at the conference, because no one was talking about it, no one was doing anything. Here's an academic discipline that's focusing on global affairs and it's like, "Holy shit! We're about to go to war and no one's talking about it." It was clear that my academic discipline was of marginal importance to most people's lived experience. This was underscored when I went to a memorial punk show for Joe Strummer (who had passed away a few months earlier) held at a dive bar a few blocks from the academic conference. It was an amazing show. In between the songs, there was this banter and engagement about America's buildup to the war and I realized, "Holy fuck! My academic discipline is either unable or unwilling to talk about this oncoming war. But the punks here, they're on it. They're engaging, they're thinking about it, they're thinking about strategies for resistance." That's how I realized that I've got to start writing about punk. I already had access to this huge international network and I just started to write. A lot of that work informed my book *Global Punk: Resistance and Rebellion in Everyday Life* (2016) but I had also written some other scholarly articles about punk, anarcho-punk, zines, and Riot Grrrl. One of my articles on punk was published by a relatively mainstream international relations journal out of the UK and I understood that it caused a big deal with some of the editors because it contained several F-bombs. That raises a question that I continue to struggle with—and I'm going to throw this to you, Brian—the question of who am I writing for? I'm in a discipline that marginalizes me in general, which is fine. I'm writing about punk and the people in my discipline don't know what the hell to do with that. My colleagues wonder, "How does this fit into political science? How does this fit into international relations?" I am not trying to convince academia in general or political science specifically to take punk seriously because I really don't give a fuck what they think. But the intended audience that I have with my punk scholarship has always been a struggle. What about you? Who is your intended audience when you are writing about punk?

Brian: It's a limited audience. Probably, the only thing that got the second version of my punk encyclopedia out was that Barnes & Noble bought the rights—a big corporation. Now, regardless of what they're doing to independent bookstores, they asked me to rewrite the encyclopedia as a coffee table book, so

I did. It probably is the most well-known publication I've done just because it was in stores all over the country and people could buy it as a Christmas present. It's the only thing I ever made more than two dollars on in my academic career. But I never stopped writing for zines as well. I never stopped playing in my band, I never stopped trying to put out records. I never stopped networking, I never stopped meeting newer people and trying to talk about punk. All of that is connected to what Pierre Bourdieu calls "cultural capital." The idea that there are cultural signifiers of a shared community. If I saw someone with a The Clash T-shirt in college, I knew that was a friend right there. I knew every punk on my college campus, every single one of them. There was about 10 of us at most but I knew them all. I was lucky to say that after tenure, I was not going to write about anything that wouldn't make me happy. I do think writing is about getting the message out there. We want new people. A lot of my research involves who owns what forms of media, and who owns which companies. I try to tell my students about DIY and that you can do things independently. You can make your own product, you can do your own website, you can do a zine. I'm lucky enough to teach about subcultures in a lot of classes and I always bring punk and hardcore into that. To me the core values are still there, and I still want to hear more punks. I still want to see more marginalized people in punk. I want to try and live a life according to the values that I learned when I first started listening to The Clash, etc. I want to maintain that ideal. It makes me happier if I'm talking about this stuff. If I can get to talk about hardcore to some kids from Long Island who've never heard of it, to me that's a win.

Kevin: Which raises the question that I think is central to this anthology: What does it mean to be a "hardcore academic"?

Brian: I think hardcore academia has a positive and negative version. The negative version is the person who is cranking up random publications all the time and doing the same conference thing time and again, only updating it slightly. They are hardcore because they're ubiquitous. That's the negative version of it. The positive version is all about doing service to the field and helping people out. I used to be an awards coordinator for an organization, and I was particularly interested in the younger people who were working on their master's or PhD and who did not win the award. I encouraged them to still work on their projects. Encouraging younger people, to me that's "academic hardcore." Trying to give back. Does it mean the same thing for you?

Kevin: When Robert and Konstantin approached me with the idea for this anthology, I was thinking about how hardcore and punk inform my scholarship. I think there's two strands, one of which you've already talked about, which is, trying and using the tools at my disposal to share information, and if that means publishing in a zine, making my own zines, putting stuff out, that's it. I've been really fortunate, for example, to have a great working relationship with Razorcake magazine. They asked me, "Hey, you write about African politics, would you write something for our audience about African politics or climate change?" So, I've been able to take these academic, intellectual conversations that I've been having in my scholarship and in my classrooms, and say, "OK, I'm going to write a couple of thousand words for a general punk audience." Then it goes to thousands of people out there. That also relates to my earlier question about our intended audiences. I feel being a "hardcore academic" is being able to utilize these DIY, nontraditional avenues to get our ideas out there. The other way I think about being a "hardcore academic" gets back to conceptualizing hardcore as a stripped-down, focused, really intent, concise, musical intervention. Dr. Know of the Bad Brains, for example, can play guitar exquisitely, but he often chooses to hit you with some power chords—"Boom, boom, boom, boom"—to get his point across. So, for me, that second strand of being a "hardcore academic" in my discipline is about mastering the tools of my trade but employing them in nontraditional ways. Yes, I can talk your talk, I can walk your walk, but you know what? I'm going to take those tools of the trade and I'm going to use them in ways that you're not going to recognize as traditional or even legitimate. I'm going to use those tools to speak with intensity and focus on matters of extreme importance to me and my community. That, for me, is how I try to embody being a "hardcore academic."

Brian: And what about hardcore today? I think it is more fascinating today than ever. There are so many fascinating hardcore bands. Of course, you can't just keep singing about "the kids, the scene, and unity" almost 40 years later. You need more. You need to express what's going on in your country. What's going on in your city. What's going on in your town. You need to be cognizant that you're sending a message out there and that your message is consistent. There's so many people that say, "Punk ended in hardcore," or, "Hardcore is over." Well, it ended for you. You stopped. You walked away. That's fine. There's nothing wrong with that. But don't say that it's over. It's not. I'm guessing that someone in Malaysia is putting a great band together today that's going to write about what's going on there. I'm going to be blown away by it.

Kevin: This week has been fascinating for me. We're having this conversation in early February 2021 with a military coup recently occurring in Myanmar. I've always been fascinated by the Myanmar punk scene. It was an active punk scene that resisted the military regime before democratization a decade ago. It's been active in terms of human rights issues, religious freedom, and the plight of the Rohingya people. This week, the punks have been at the forefront of protesting the military coup. So, when I hear someone talk about punk in purely historic terms, my response is always: Don't tell me punk's dead or punk's not doing important work. It might not be doing important work for you, or in your local scene right now. But it's doing important work around the globe. It has also been great to see the ways in which, just in the past few years, punk has been responsive to issues around trans rights and trans issues that I feel other spaces in society have not been. It's rewarding to hear people say how they find punk a safe and supportive space. I don't want to be pollyannaish at all. I know there's so much more work to do. I don't want to create a false image, but I think that people can find the tools from punk and hardcore scenes to engage in self-empowerment and start changing the world around them.

Brian: I have a great example for that: I live in in Brooklyn and a woman in my building organized a Black Lives Matter protest right there. For almost every night for months, people in the building and then people from other buildings took out signs and went to occupy the street, occupy the area and held up signs and tried to get people to honk their car horns in solidarity. This small protest eventually became several hundred people. One day, out of nowhere, this woman who is 80 years old, came running in with her Black Lives Matter poster. That was just wonderful! I think such movements reflect core values of the punk scene, like organizing things yourself. Don't rely on someone else to organize protests. Keep trying to do something. Keep it going and keep showing up. Even if it is just a little protest, it's still going to send some kind of message. To me, that's positive. That's punk rock. That's hardcore right there.

References

Cogan, Brian. *The Encyclopedia of Punk Music and Culture*. Sterling, 2006.

Dunn, Kevin. *Global Punk: Resistance and Rebellion in Everyday Life*. Bloomsbury Academic, 2016.

Postman, Neil. *Amusing Ourselves to Death: Public Discourse in the Age of Show Business*. Viking, 1985.

"Survival of the Streets": Krishna Consciousness and Religion in Hardcore Punk at the End of the Cold War

Shaun Cullen

In 1989, at the very moment conservative political philosopher Francis Fukuyama famously called "the end of history," the lead singer of a band called Youth of Today was having a spiritual crisis. Youth of Today was founded in 1985 in New York City by Connecticut punk rocker Ray Cappo. Almost from the start, the band was controversial. Drawing on the influence of earlier Straight Edge punk bands like Minor Threat, SSD, and 7 Seconds, Cappo, his bandmates, and their compatriots in the New York hardcore scene transformed Straight Edge from an uplifting if overly restrictive life philosophy into a militant moral code resembling an actual social movement (Haenfler 58-80).[1] At least one contemporary observer, Sam McPheeters, singer in Born Against, another late 1980s New York hardcore band, has argued that Cappo's stance in Youth of Today was pseudo-fascistic. As McPheeters would have it, when Cappo started his next band Shelter, things were only going to get worse (130-35).

As a result of his spiritual crisis, Cappo traveled to India. As he would later explain in interviews, he had recently lost his father to a sudden illness and was undergoing the normal stress and self-doubt that comes with rock 'n' roll

---

1   Throughout this essay I use the term "Straight Edge" to describe the subgenre of Straight Edge hardcore punk, as well as the fashion and clothing style associated with that subgenre. The ins and outs of the Straight Edge punk subgenre are discussed extensively in Haenfler; Rettman, *Straight Edge*; and Wood. As discussed later in the essay, the subgenre of Straight Edge was inspired directly by the Minor Threat song with that name. The music in the subgenre promotes a moral code that stipulates abstinence from alcohol and drugs, and in some cases animal products, promiscuous sex, and/or sex outside committed relationships.

semi-stardom. Cappo's music with Youth of Today already inspired an almost religious devotion on the part of some fans; the New York hardcore scene was becoming increasingly violent; and Cappo was running the record label Revelation that released his and other Straight Edge bands' records—all of these factors probably increased his stress and encouraged his spiritual conversion. On Cappo's trip to India, he began to discover that nation's religious traditions and gradually made the conversion to an Americanized evangelical offshoot of traditional Hinduism that is popularly called "Hare Krishna."[2]

Within the context of late 1980s hardcore music, Cappo's conversion to Hare Krishna was surprising. As McPheeters disparagingly puts it, Cappo was promoting a "cult" (134).[3] There were precedents for his spirituality within hardcore, but the embrace of Krishna Consciousness was, for some in the scene, a bridge too far. Most notably, the band that many listeners consider the greatest New York hardcore band, the Cro-Mags, were Krishna devotees when they recorded their masterwork *The Age of Quarrel*. Also, elements of a more spiritual approach to hardcore were implicit in the genre from its founding, especially in the work of one of the genre's first most important bands Bad Brains. Indeed, in her book *Punk Rock Is My Religion*, religious scholar Francis Stewart has tracked a spiritual and religious tendency within punk rock more generally since its first emergence. Nevertheless, there was something particularly incongruent about Cappo's new beliefs (not to mention his style of dress) within the New York hardcore scene and specifically the Straight Edge subgroup he had helped found, a scene that was notable for its grittiness and what one might call its "social realism." Lyrically, Youth of Today was dedicated to depicting the Straight Edge lifestyle as it was lived with little rhetorical flourish. For instance, the end of one of Cappo's last songs with Youth of Today, "No More," a painfully earnest plea on behalf of vegetarianism, finds the singer nearly weeping on behalf of "a more conscious society." And this was before he embraced Krishna Consciousness. As McPheeters and

---

2   "Hare Krishna" is something of a misnomer. Technically speaking, the specific spiritual system popularly called Hare Krishna would more accurately be described as "Krishna Consciousness." The official institutional promoter of Krishna Consciousness is the International Society for Krishna Consciousness or ISKCON, which was founded in New York City by the Indian-American emigre Srila Pradhupada, who opened the first ISKCON temple at 26 2nd Ave. in 1966, not far from the punk club CBGB at 315 Bowery, where Youth of Today would often headline the venue's famous hardcore matinees.

3   The term "cult" is controversial within the academic study of what I will refer to in this paper as New Religious Movements (Urban 8).

others have noted, his post-Youth of Today work with his next band Shelter took this preachiness to garish, nearly parodic levels that nevertheless and perhaps ironically found a much larger audience than Youth of Today.

Shelter started rehearsing in 1990, just as Youth of Today was ending. Within a year they would release the *No Compromise* 7" and the *Perfection of Desire* LP. Cappo started a new label Equal Vision, a subsidiary of Revelation, dedicated solely to Krishna-related material, including cassettes that featured devotional chanting in the Krishna style.[4] Once the band started touring, Cappo and his bandmates, including John Porcelly, who had played guitar in Youth of Today, were fully-dedicated Krishna monks. Perhaps because of their devotional flavor, these tours, incredibly, inspired a small subgenre of hardcore punk that is sometimes called "Krishnacore," though this name was probably never promoted by the actual bands who played the music. This small coterie of bands, which released most of their music on Equal Vision, achieved some success in the mid-1990s, releasing hardcore music that is still revered by fans and allows some of the musicians to keep performing on the hardcore revival circuit—Ressurection (whose name for some reason was intentionally misspelled), 108, and Inside Out, to name a few of the most popular. Among these bands, Inside Out, which actually recorded the least material, is perhaps most notable because it featured lead singer Zach de la Rocha, who would go on to found Rage Against the Machine, one of the most critically and commercially successful rock bands of the 1990s.[5]

Krishnacore was a short-lived musical trend even within the endless cycle of microgenres that tend to populate the hardcore underground, but it was a particularly interesting one because of its spiritual overtones and its controversial proximity to a New Religious Movement that many outsiders still accuse of being a cult.[6] As scholars of New Religious Movements generally argue, this sort of sensationalistic dismissal of groups like Hare Krishna is

---

4   As discussed by Dines and others in Bryant and Ekstrand, the chanting of mantras (kirtan) is an important spiritual practice in ISKCON and other Hindu sects.

5   Inside Out also performed at an infamous Shelter gig in June 1990 that was picketed by other hardcore bands. See Alva; and McPheeters, 142. The band's song "Burning Fight" provides the name for an oral history of the nineties hardcore scene edited by Brian Peterson and published under the Revelation Records imprint (2009).

6   As Stewart and Peterson mention, other forms of spiritual commitment, including Christianity and Islam, eventually flourished within the hardcore scene. Krishnacore was unique for its association with a New Religious Movement, not one of the Abrahamic religions.

both narrowminded and discriminatory. Frances Stewart has pointed out, in her survey of religiosity among punk fans and performers, that most of them adopt the anarchist-derived attitude towards organized religion summed up in the slogan, "No Gods, No Masters" (12). The particular society that Ray Cappo railed against at the end of "No More" and re-confronted during his spiritual crisis in 1989 has been described by scholars like Talal Asad and Peter Berger as "post-secular" (qtd. in Stewart 81). Though rates of religious participation fluctuate, what used to be construed as the progressive ideal of secularization has never come to fruition. Indeed, religion, as a sphere or system of social participation (in the sense suggested by functionalist sociologist Niklas Luhmann) is ineluctable.[7] The music of Shelter and others in the Krishnacore tradition, including precursors like Bad Brains and Cro-Mags, stage the conflict between the sacred and the secular or profane, between a worldview that is thoroughly imbued with religious meaning and one that is impatiently doing away with old myths. Just how eccentric would it be to feel so conflicted at a moment when the masters of the universe are celebrating the fact that history is about to end? What problems did the appeal to religion solve for Cappo and his fans?

"P.M.A." or "Filler?" Thinking About Religion in Early Hardcore

The dialectic between dogma and individual expression that engenders Krishnacore's emergence in Ray Cappo's music is already heard in hardcore's earliest recordings, especially in the work of Minor Threat, who inspired the Straight Edge movement, and Bad Brains, who, in turn, inspired Minor Threat. Ian MacKaye, lead singer of Minor Threat, and a towering presence in the hardcore scene, has described his music as "sacred" (qtd. in Lahickey 30). In 1981, his band released their eponymous first EP. The first side of the lightning-fast album (eight songs in under ten minutes) closes with the track "Straight Edge," a song that many listeners heard as a rallying cry. In less than a minute, MacKaye outlines an anti-drug message that expresses his personal convictions and reflects the difficulty of supporting a do-it-yourself

---

7   See Luhmann, *A Systems Theory of Religion*, whose theory of secularization, or rather secularization's "disappearance," undergirds this essay's approach (223). The conceptualization of the post-secular deployed in this essay is also influenced by Asad and Berger, whom Stewart also cites. Luhmann cites Berger (217, n. 43).

all-ages scene in the context of a nightlife industry predicated on liquor sales. On later tracks, like "Out of Step," from the band's second EP *In My Eyes* (1983), MacKaye would match this anti-drug message with a commitment to sexual abstinence outside of committed relationships (though MacKaye would consistently stress throughout his career that both messages were misconstrued). As is well known, over the next several years, MacKaye's message would congeal into what became known as Straight Edge hardcore, named after his song. In the hands of later bands, the messages of MacKaye's songs, which he intended only as a personal expression of his commitment to sobriety, congealed into a dogma. The leaders of these groups preached the Straight Edge message like a gospel.[8]

Ironically, given the pseudo-fascistic militancy that emerged in some corners of the Straight Edge scene, MacKaye's lyrics and Minor Threat's extraordinarily aggressive music, in terms of tempo and volume, were at their core expressions of non-conformity. The first track on the eponymous EP, and hence the band's recorded introduction to their audience, is the song "Filler." The extreme volume and rapid presentation of "Filler" is mechanistic to the point of almost sounding robotic. The lyrics are an expression of stinging rage. In a recent analysis by musicologist Evan Rapport he mentions that the tempo of the track can be counted at a speed of 370 bpm, incredibly fast, even for a hardcore song (212). In the lyrics MacKaye lashes out at a friend who has discovered what the friend calls "romance" and "religion." MacKaye thinks the friend is "full of shit." In what sounds like a semi-improvised coda to the song MacKaye accuses the friend of being a "sheep looking for a shepherd," a fairly bitter dismissal of Christian iconography. Hence, a rejection of religious values was an important if somewhat underappreciated aspect of MacKaye's original Straight Edge message.

There was an almost immediate resistance to this anti-religious attitude from *within* the hardcore scene that was expressed, in fact, by the hardcore band that MacKaye specifically named as his inspiration for starting Minor Threat—Bad Brains. In stark contrast to the atheistic, anti-religious sentiments expressed by MacKaye, the members of Bad Brains adhered to the

---

8   Stewart discusses Straight Edge itself as what she describes as a "surrogate" form of religion. See also Dines who has written on the way in which Krishna punk performance practices are congruent with yogic beliefs about sacred sound ("The Sacralization of Straightedge Punk").

tenets of Rastafarianism, a syncretic New Religious Movement within Christianity that emerged in Jamaica in the 1930s. In addition to adopting Rastafarian clothing, hairstyles, and slang, the members of Bad Brains adhered to a strict vegetarian diet (similar to the Krishnas); consumed marijuana as a sacrament; and integrated soulful, devotional reggae pieces into their otherwise blistering hardcore sets and recordings.[9] Indeed, given the laid-back vibe associated with mainstream reggae music, the band members even viewed the more aggressive, energetic aspects of their presentation to be a part of their spiritual practice, including violent moshing in the audience and acrobatics, like backflips, on the part of lead singer HR. They self-consciously understood punk's lack of boundaries between performer and audience as a means for establishing a spiritual link that was fed and fostered by their exquisite musicianship and unrivaled energy.

Making the overall blend of perspectives and ideologies in the hardcore punk scene much more confusing, but also compelling, Bad Brains further combined this visionary spiritual message with the humdrum self-help philosophy promoted by author Napoleon Hill in his 1937 book *Think and Grow Rich*. The title of one of Bad Brains's most popular tunes "P.M.A.," which is often incorporated into hardcore tattoos and graphic design, is an abbreviation for one of Hill's terms, "positive mental attitude," a state of mind that Bad Brains embraced and promoted among their followers. For instance, Cro-Mags' singer John Joseph frequently cites this principle in his performances and autobiography, *The Evolution of a Cro-Magnon*. If a listener only heard Minor Threat and the other more militant straight edge bands that emerged in their wake, one might get the sense that there was no room for spirituality in hardcore. Nevertheless, for the band that all of these other bands emulated, Bad Brains, spirituality was, in a sense, the *hardcore of the hardcore*. Bad Brains' spiritual commitment arguably inspired a countertradition within hardcore of spiritually-informed performance that, as part of a New Religious Movement, was also not traditional in terms of its posture towards organized religion. For these musicians, spiritual expression was what gave the hardcore genre its strength and distinguished it, ideologically and stylistically, from the nihilistic punk that had preceded it. Like the Straight Edge punks, the

---

9   Examples of Bad Brains' oscillating styles appear on all of their records—for instance, their 1982 debut self-titled cassette contains three lengthy reggae numbers, "Jah Calling," "Leaving Babylon," and "I Luv I Jah," in a dub-style. The rest of the album is packed with their signature hardcore rants.

hardcore punks invested in spirituality, like Bad Brains, Cro-Mags, and later Shelter, understood the stance they were taking as a dialectical reversal of the spiritual nihilism that earlier punk bands had embraced.

This dialectic between spirituality and non-conformity repeats itself throughout the history of hardcore. In general, hardcore lyricists evince a no nonsense, no bullshit attitude towards politics and everyday life, whether those politics are couched within a specific scene or wider social concerns. The genre is also populist in the sense that almost all bands involved in it are respectful of the genre's traditions. As the genre's name suggests hardcore punks sought to represent the vital center of the wider punk genre, a genre that at the end of the 1970s had begun to display some of the same rock star excess punks had originally rejected. Even though the Bad Brains were extraordinary musicians, they were committed to promoting, at least initially, a scene in which everyone could play. The barrier to entry in hardcore punk, at least in terms of technical musical skill, was low. In fact, audiences were suspicious of technical proficiency outside of the ability to play quickly, like Bad Brains. To this day, hardcore shows sonically resemble staging grounds for the communal aspects of the genre—slam dancing, gang vocals, the elimination of barriers or borders between audience and performer. Hardcore shows often have the air of ritual and the music is compared to traditional folk music forms in the sense that it is easy to play; immediate; and organically expressive of social concerns shared by a subcultural community. A paradigmatic expression of this view is offered by Brendan Mullen, owner of the L.A. punk club the Masque in the 1981 documentary film *Decline of Western Civilization*,

> Some of the better of the punk bands developed into sort of like folk music. I don't mean folk music that's a traditional folk music, but the allegory can be drawn to the sixties when protestors used acoustic guitars. Now instead of acoustic guitars you know they have high speed 300 beats-a-minute speed rock and are yelling about the same things, about how the air is poisoned out there. The air in utopia is poisoned—the final joke.

The music is self-consciously anti-commercial. Band members and fans often indulge in acts of violent self-sabotage (including suicide) that delimit hardcore scenes as magic circles, liberated from the necessarily commercial orientation of traditional rock or pop music, as well as the humdrum concerns of social reproduction in bourgeois society. As MacKaye might put it, hardcore shows are a sacred space.

In spite of this tendency towards certain notions of the sacred, mystical, or ritualistic in punk performance, at the time when hardcore kids got interested in Hare Krishna, the religion was perceived by the public as a cult full of eccentric scam artists with shaved heads, dressed in saffron covered robes. They mindlessly chanted a well-known mantra, popularized by George Harrison in his song "My Sweet Lord"—"Hare Krishna Hare Krishna / Krishna Krishna Hare Hare / Hare Rama Hare Rama / Rama Rama Hare Hare"—while asking for donations and peddling religious literature and trinkets. Suspicion of the movement was of a piece with a wider social concern about cults, New Religious Movements, and the social hysteria around "brainwashing" (Urban 201-19).[10] The rejection of Krishnacore by some in the hardcore scene was reflective of this wider antipathy towards the movement in society-at-large. However, Krishna Consciousness actually had deep roots in the New York scene, not least of all because its founding as a religious movement occurred in the late 1960s almost immediately before the emergence of the punk scene in the same Lower East Side neighborhood that would eventually house the important club CBGB, which started featuring punk bands like Suicide, Television, the Ramones, and Patti Smith in 1973. Only a few blocks away, in Tompkins Square Park, ISKCON's founder Srila Prabhupada began his mission (Bryant and Ekstrand 2-3).[11] As punks like John Joseph and his compatriot in Cro-Mags Harley Flanagan point out, joining the Krishnas for free lunches was a rite of passage on the Lower East Side, even though most of the punks who joined the Krishnas for lunch didn't become converts.

---

10   Urban's book also discusses the 1980s controversies around "Satanic Panic" and considers Rastafarianism as a New Religious Movement.

11   As discussed in Bryant and Ekstrand, ISKCON is a missionary movement within the Hindu religious philosophy of Gaudiya Vaishnavism, that is, the branch of Hinduism that venerates Vishnu as the supreme godhead. Perhaps confusingly to non-adherents, followers of Hare Krishna hold that Krishna, whom the Hindu scriptures stipulate preceded Vishnu temporally, was the godhead's supreme, dominating form. In other words, he was not an avatar of Vishnu but his dominating essence. In this way, the specific Vaishnavism practiced in the Hare Krishna religion is different from the Hinduism most widely practiced globally. Technically-speaking, it is monotheistic and therefore controversial within a traditionally religious Hindu theological frame, but it is not blasphemous or philistinic as some of its critics in the West have claimed.

Cro-Magnon Consciousness: Hardcore Goes Krishna

In 1986 New York hardcore band Cro-Mags released their debut album *Age of Quarrel*, a milestone in the genre that continues to be admired and emulated. Lead vocalist John Joseph and bassist Harley Flanagan drew on their experiences as New York street kids who, in Joseph's case, had survived horrific child abuse, imprisonment, and drug addiction, before ending up on the Lower East Side, a member of the Cro-Mags and a devotee of Krishna.[12] Flanagan, for his part, was also dedicated to Krishna Consciousness, though he had not lived as a devotee. His home life as a child was somewhat more stable than Joseph's. He lived with his mother and at age nine actually published a book of stories with a preface by the Beat poet Allen Ginsberg, who was coincidentally one of the earliest supporters of ISKCON in the U.S. and is reported to have given Prabhupada funds to build his first temple. Flanagan's mother ran in the same circles as Ginsberg and apparently this association encouraged her to foster her son's talents as a storyteller, however limited. On one hand, Flanagan's book was a gimmicky byproduct of the hippie subculture in which Harley's mom raised him; yet it also indicates that he grew up at a greater distance from the harsh New York City street life of the 1970s and 80s, but also a greater proximity to the 1960s counterculture, than Joseph.

By age twelve, Flanagan was drumming in the New York punk band Stimulators. Recordings by the Stimulators are scarce, but they were infamous in large part because of Flanagan's youth, look, and antics. He was one of the first members of the early U.S. punk scene to specifically incorporate the working-class skinhead style he discovered during Stimulators' trips to England (before the movement became associated with the neo-fascist National Front). Over time, Flanagan's skinhead style would evolve into the heavily tatted, shirtless, working-class style of the Cro-Mags, not dissimilar from the look of some pro-wrestlers.

---

12   From the beginning, the Cro-Mags band history was notable for the intense rivalry between Flanagan, Joseph, and guitarist Paris Mayhew, whom Joseph frequently smears in his autobiography as a spoiled poser. Among fans, the band's work after *The Age of Quarrel* is controversial, as they increasingly embraced a more generic speed metal sound. For his part, Joseph didn't even appear on the band's second album *Best Wishes* (1989), and ended his working relationship with Flanagan on 1993's critically-panned *Near Death Experience*. Since 2018, Flanagan, Joseph, and drummer Mackie Jayson have been involved in litigation regarding the band name, and there are currently two versions of the band, Cro-Mags and Cro-Mags JM.

The intensity of Joseph's upbringing on the streets of New York City is echoed in the band's music and reflected in the lyrics and iconography they used to deliver their message. *Age of Quarrel*'s cover features an image of a mushroom cloud generated by the Castle Romeo thermonuclear test explosion. On one hand, the image is a remnant of a Cold War visual archive that so many in the U.S. and elsewhere have sought to disavow or forget, either out of paranoia or resentment. On the other, it is a brutal reminder that the threat of nuclear annihilation is still as omnipresent today as it was in 1986 (or 1953). In a sense, the image represents a return of the Cold War repressed at a new moment of paranoid rage on the part of the band members. In one of the album's most paranoiac lines, tinged with conspiratorial thinking, Joseph sings, "If AIDS don't get you than the warheads will." A line like this reflects the album's overall orientation towards both the streets and apocalyptic themes, terms that pop up throughout the album not just in specific lyrics, but in emblematic song titles like "Hard Times," "Signs of the Times," "Street Justice," and "Survival of the Streets."

Perhaps surprisingly, this apocalyptic orientation in the Cro-Mags' lyrics was not just a byproduct of their origin in the rough and tumble, crime-ridden streets of New York City in the late 1970s and 1980s. It was also a result of Joseph's devotion to Krishna Consciousness. As he explains in his autobiography, Joseph chose the title *Age of Quarrel* for the album in reference to the Hindu conception of the *kali yuga*, the fourth and current stage in the development of humanity in which it hurtles to a chiliastic point of strife ("quarrel") before regenerating itself in a new golden age in harmony with the Hindu pantheon (320). This harmony will involve a wholesale reordering of reality—the death and rebirth of the entire universe as we know it.

Once understood, this reference in the album's title suggests a greater depth to the concerns in the album's lyrics, which on the surface may seem like working-class, punk anthems, reminiscent of contemporary bands in the anti-racist skinhead, Oi!, and street punk scenes overseas. Joseph sings from a point of view that is paranoiac and dramatic, accentuated by his manic singing style, but grounded in material concerns about food, shelter, survival, and belonging. The lyrics are concrete and borrow stock phrases from politics, advertising, scripture, and the media—"Do Unto Others," "Don't Tread on Me," and the other titles mentioned above. On the track "Survival of the Streets," Joseph describes life in a squat, "a burned out building," where police, "the beast," are liable to "pull the trigger" and end his life. These urban narratives are as gritty as any crime drama, but their social realism serves a higher spiritual purpose. As the band puts it on another track, they are "Seekers of the Truth," locating a deeper reality beneath the surface or "street" level of appearances.

Seeking Shelter: The Krishnacore Revival

In the early nineties, the spiritual blueprint created by the Cro-Mags was embraced and expanded by Krishnacore bands. As 108 guitarist Vic Dicara put it,

> Nobody would have cared for [Krishna Consciousness] if it wasn't for musicians making it a part of their art. If it wasn't for Bad Brains and their amazing mixture of Rastafarianism, metal, and punk none of this would have happened. The Cro-Mags would have never been the band they were ... And if it weren't for the Cro-Mags and the mind-boggling, concrete-tough expressions of Krishna conscious strength and power that they delivered in ... *Age of Quarrel* then Ray Cappo would never have become interested in Krishna and Shelter would never have formed. (qtd. in Peterson 134)

Based on this immanently reasonable description by Dicara, it is slightly surprising that fellow New York hardcore performers like McPheeters, his bandmates in Born Against, and others in the ABC No Rio scene they helped start would have been so harsh towards Krishnacore's emergence.[13] After all, as Luhmann emphasized in *A Systems Theory of Religion*, the cultlike theological excesses of contemporary religion are limited or contained within the modernist conception of culture: "Here we are only interested in what it means for religion once it is observed in society as a partial domain of culture" (225). In other words, once religion becomes the domain of culture, it loses its sacred value, or at least it should from the perspective of non-adherents, but it did

---

13   ABC No Rio is a non-profit art space and concert venue on New York's Lower East Side that began as a squat in 1980. In the early nineties, it became home to an anarchist hardcore scene that was notable both as an alternative to the violence that had basically ruined the CBGB hardcore scene and also for what many have characterized as its politically-correct, some might say censorious booking policies. Like its West Coast cousin 924 Gilman Street, directly associated with Tim Yohannan and *Maximum Rocknroll* (*MRR*), ABC No Rio had a strict policy of not booking artists with racist, sexist, or homophobic lyrics and would require performers to submit lyrics before appearing (see Rettman, *NYHC* 335-40).

not appear this way to the denizens of the hardcore scene who resented Krishnacore, perhaps because their scene was already functioning as a pseudo-re-
ligion. As McPheeters mentions in his memoir *Mutations*, the Cro-Mags were
his favorite band (16). Still, he recounts a famous early Shelter show that he
and others from ABC NO Rio drove to Connecticut to picket (142). Elsewhere,
in the pages of the most prominent punk fanzine of the time *Maximum Rocknroll*, editor Tim Yohannan, a famously cantankerous New Left holdout took
Cappo to task for what he called his "insane" new beliefs in an interview that
ran alongside a long exposé of ISKCON that engaged in highly inflammatory
and arguably prejudicial criticisms of the movement.

In order to understand Cappo's appeal to Krishna Consciousness, one
must consider both the immediate social context of the New York hardcore
scene that Cappo had helped revive, as well as the more global context to which
many in the hardcore scene thought they were responding. A telling observation comes from Anthony "Civ" Civarelli of fellow Straight Edge hardcore
band Gorilla Biscuits, who were inheritors of the specific "Youth Crew" style
of hardcore that Cappo had pioneered.[14] At an intriguing moment in Beth
Lahickey's oral history of the Straight Edge punk scene, *All Ages*, she quotes
Civ, who recalls touring Europe with his band in 1989, "when the wall was
falling down" (43). Civ mentions that a gig in former Yugoslavia was cancelled
because of the revolution there during the tour. Back in the U.S.A. Reagan
was out of office and his policies, under successor George H.W. Bush, had not
brought about the nuclear cataclysm predicted by millenarian punks like the
Cro-Mags on *Age of Quarrel*. But certainly, there were problems. The U.S. was
back in recession and regressive social policies like the War on Drugs, mass
incarceration, welfare reform, and the offshoring of jobs would all wear on the
U.S.'s social fabric. By January 1991, the country would be in a hot war, invad-
ing Iraq. Despite the fact that most in the hardcore scene were not affected by
these social problems directly, in political-economic terms, they nevertheless

---

14   Youth Crew is a subgenre of Straight Edge hardcore. It was inspired by the Reno, NV
hardcore band 7 Seconds and emphasized positivity and male bonding, along with
the other anti-drug and anti-sex trappings of the Straight Edge philosophy. Its proponents like Cappo and Civ adopted a subcultural fashion style that favored clean cut
sportswear like varsity jackets, Swatch watches, and cargo shorts, instead of the ripped
jeans, piercings, and other "cut-up" fashion styles of earlier punks. Haenfler provides
an overview of the Youth Crew style in a section of his book focused on "straight edge
trends" (12–14). Youth Crew bands are also discussed in Lahickey and Peterson.

sought to address them in their music, which broadly speaking documented a felt sense of social decay in the early post-Cold War period.

The "In Defense of Reality/The News" single was Shelter's first release after all of the members had committed themselves full-time as Hare Krishna monks. On the record's cover, they are pictured wearing devotional hairstyles, shaved heads with small tufts of hair tied at the back, but they have traded the movement's traditional saffron robes for baggy early-nineties streetwear not dissimilar from the contemporary hip-hop and earlier Youth Crew clothing styles of that time. The music on the record is a significant step away from Cappo's work with Youth of Today. That band was notable for their commitment to a stripped-down style of hardcore that was in essence revivalist, resisting the trend towards hardcore/metal crossover that was common in East Coast U.S. hardcore at that time.[15] While the Shelter record is not a punk/metal crossover, it is significantly looser than Cappo's work with Youth of Today. The first track "In Defense of Reality" starts with a dreamy intro section that features chiming guitars and a busy, upbeat bassline. When the verse kicks in, the band reverts to a fairly traditional hardcore beat, but Cappo has shifted his singing style from the alternately gruff and yelping style heard on Youth of Today records, to a chantlike style that immediately summons a mystical atmosphere without seeming overly indulgent. On this record and others by Shelter, like their most popular, *Mantra*, there is a charm to Cappo's voice when listeners realize they are hearing a regional U.S. accent, rooted somewhere between Stamford, CT and the Bronx, articulating esoteric spiritual messages with the utmost sincerity. The lyrics reference Krishna Consciousness as an alternative to what the singer calls the "religion" of "modern science," invoked precisely with the image of the "big bang," disparaged as a "creation without a creator." Released at the cusp of the commercial explosion of "alternative rock," it is not hard to imagine how this music that is aggressive and uplifting might have appealed to a wider audience than Cappo's work with his previous band, but it is still a left turn from what Cappo had been doing previously.

Shifting thematic focus from the cosmic to the worldly, the B-side of the single indexes some of the social milieu that surrounded the record's creation in a more explicit way than the A-side or Shelter's more esoteric later material. Cappo was a longtime punk fan who cited bands like the Business,

---

15   The popularity of the crossover style is discussed in Waksman, especially Ch. 6, "Metal/Punk Reformation" (210-55).

Sham 69, and X-Ray Spex as his earliest influences (qtd. in Lahickey x).[16] In other words, for all his ethical dogmatism, Cappo was a student of punk with diverse tastes. The B-side "The News" begins with a generic punk element that is nevertheless unique on a Shelter record—a sampled clip of a U.S. television news report on the recently completed invasion of Iraq by the first Bush president, which took place in January and February of 1991, the year in which the single was released. The invocation of a wider social context, filtered through the mass media, resonates with later Shelter songs like "Surrender to Your T.V." and "Civilized Man" on *Mantra*, while simultaneously contrasting dialectically with the clips of Krishna devotional music (*kirtan*) that begin certain songs on *Mantra* and other Shelter albums. The tune is barely a hardcore song in the traditional style, sounding a bit more like the kind of grunge metal that was about to become popular on U.S. radio by a band like, say, Alice In Chains. In contrast with the sample that begins the song, the lyrics are ambivalent about the singer's relationship towards what he calls "the news" (really, the news media). As he repeats in the chorus, "Before I want to hear your news / I want the news on me." This is exactly the kind of rejection of political context that would have annoyed other scene denizens—like *MRR* editor Yohannan or the ABC No Rio protestors. Cappo draws a contrast between his spirituality and the prevailing political ideology common in hardcore at that time, which was specifically concerned with the tyranny of social institutions like the media over the individual. He does not reject this ideology outright but insists it must be supplemented by spiritual awareness.

Despite the esoteric message on the record, which could not have been more out of step with the prevailing social atmosphere of the early 1990s, Shelter were nevertheless very popular and arguably became the most visible U.S. hardcore band when they released their album *Mantra* in 1995. Though this later album clearly incorporated what by that time were mainstream alternative rock influences, it still included authentic hardcore blast beats and riffing on tracks like "Appreciation" and "Chance." After signing with Roadrunner, a more widely distributed independent label than Cappo's own Reve-

---

16   X-Ray Spex vocalist Poly Styrene (Marianne Joan Elliott-Said) was also a Krishna devotee after her time in the band. Cappo writes, "I was reared on punk rock, ska, and Oi! from Sham 69 to X Ray Spex to the Business" (qtd. in Lahickey x). Elsewhere, Cappo mentions early punk and hardcore bands as diverse as the Damned, Siouxsie Sioux, the Residents, the Police, Patti Smith, the Ramones, UK Subs, Minor Threat, Void, Agnostic Front, SS Decontrol, and 7 Seconds as his formative influences (ix-xi).

lation or Equal Vision, they toured with the then incredibly popular ska-punk band No Doubt, which was a launching pad for pop megastar Gwen Stefani. Shelter had evolved significantly by that time, most notably on the album *Beyond Planet Earth*, to something approaching the "mall punk" style of groups like Stefani's and others like Green Day or blink-182. Cappo, while still presenting himself as a Krishna devotee, would nevertheless duet with Stefani at shared live performances. To some extent, Cappo and Shelter's pursuit of mainstream success at this stage in their career might have seemed to contradict both Hare Krishna and hardcore music's anti-materialistic ideological stance and aesthetics. On the other hand, if we understand Shelter's embrace of Krishna Consciousness as a sincere act of religious devotion and not an ironic misappropriation of Hindu religious philosophy, reaching out to mainstream audiences can be understood as an extension of ISKCON's evangelical zeal.

In one sense, the lyrics of "The News" are a repudiation of the social and political context invoked by the sample that begins the song. As spiritual seekers, the band members are rejecting the material trappings of the social and political world. In another sense, however, the band is also uncovering and addressing the deeper spiritual and philosophical issues raised by the U.S. invasion of Iraq during the Gulf War and the wider sense of ideological confusion at the end of the Cold War. The phrase "your news," as opposed to *the* news, captures the singer's alienation from the U.S. imperial project even as the embrace of esoteric religious tradition imported from India signals a more global perspective.

Coda: Repeating the *Mantra*

Although Krishnacore bands like Shelter, the Cro-Mags, and 108 still occasionally reunite for on-off shows, none of them have released new music in many years. Some bands' members like Cappo, Porcelly, and DiCara are still devotees, while others, like John Joseph, cite the spiritual texts and wisdom he discovered in the Krishna consciousness movement as part of a larger, syncretic life philosophy. The latter, for instance, maintains a strong online presence and as of early 2022 has written three books.[17] He regularly appears on

---

17   Regrettably, Joseph is also notable on Twitter for promoting COVID-19 conspiracy theories.

podcasts, including Joe Rogan's podcast, which is the top-rated podcast in the world ("#1152 - John Joseph").[18] Ironically, Joseph has probably received more exposure from that one appearance than he did during his entire musical career. On Joseph's Twitter feed and Instagram and in his books, he promotes a life philosophy that is equal parts Eastern spirituality, street smarts, and the self-help approach of Napoleon Hill that was introduced to him by the Bad Brains. In Joseph's telling of his conversion to Krishna Consciousness, it was conspicuously linked to his alienation from Bad Brains, for whom he worked as a roadie. Joseph mentions that the members of the Bad Brains were beginning to sympathize with the specific form of black nationalism promoted by the Nation of Islam leader Louis Farrakhan. As Joseph explains, he chafed at Farrakhan's insinuation that all whites were the devil and he specifically resented the hangers-on that exposed Bad Brains to this sort of philosophy (261-62). Joseph avers that as an anti-racist he could not stomach this resentment on the part of the Bad Brains—his musical and spiritual heroes.

That figures like Cappo and Joseph have been able to maintain a profile apart from the hardcore subculture that nurtured them is, in a sense, predictable, because despite Shelter's limited success, none of the music they made in their careers ever made much sense as a commercial proposition. In other words, the specific kind of religiosity Cappo and Joseph were promoting works better as a lifestyle brand than a musical style. Brendan Mullen's reference to hardcore as a kind of "traditional folk music" has never been more a propos. Hardcore is not now nor ever was mainstream music. Aesthetically, the genre has continued to grow and mature in ways that almost seem to contradict the way in which it was originally intended to simplify punk rock music and return it to its working-class roots. Through the process of diversification, hardcore has also become a kind of people's music or folk music, to which Cappo and Joseph indelibly contributed, and with which its listeners strongly identify in a way that Ian MacKaye, despite his anti-religious sentiments, described as "sacred."

As Niklas Luhmann and other sociologists have argued, secularization is no longer a useful rubric for understanding the relationship between religion and society (223). Yet this is just the approach that McPheeters, Yohannan, and others seem to have taken when they protested Ray Cappo's conversion to Hare Krishna in the most bitterly critical way possible—the idea that the

---

18   Rogan has also interviewed Cappo, whom he met through a shared interest in combat sports ("#1430").

rationalization of religion will lead to its disappearance. While rates of religious participation continue to decline, society as a whole, especially within particular geographic regions and populations, remains devoted. In the U.S., evangelical Christians are perhaps more powerful now than they ever have been, especially in Southern states and the rural Midwest, and religious extremism appears to be on the rise. Musicians like Cappo and Joseph were creating art, passionately and effectively. This art is both a contribution to and comment on the civic culture of hardcore that fostered it. Religious devotion, for these artists, replaced Straight Edge militancy. *Age of Quarrel* still garners fans and it will be listened to and appreciated for many years to come. Records like "The News" or Shelter's most popular album *Mantra* may not fare as well. Yet in order to understand hardcore as an ongoing and incomplete political and aesthetic project, they should not be forgotten—or misheard.

References

Alva, Freddy. "The Anti-Krishna Flyers Incident of 1990." *No Echo.* July 22, 2020, noecho.net/features/anti-krishna-flyers-incident-of-1990. Accessed 31 May 2022.

Annabella, "The Truth, the Whole Truth, and Nothing but the Truth, So Help Me Krishna?" *Maximum Rocknroll.* December 1989.

Asad, Talal. *Formations of the Secular: Christianity, Islam, Modernity.* Stanford UP, 2003.

Bad Brains. *Bad Brains.* ROIR, 1982.

Berger, Peter. "Secularism in Retreat." *The National Interest* 46, Winter 1996/1997, pp. 3–12.

Bryant, Edwin, and Maria Ekstrand. *The Hare Krishna Movement: The Postcharismatic Fate of a Religious Transplant.* Columbia University Press, 2004.

Cro-Mags. *Age of Quarrel.* Profile, 1986.

Cro-Mags. *Best Wishes.* Profile, 1989.

Cro-Mags. *Near Death Experience.* Century Media, 1993.

The Decline of Western Civilization. Penelope Spheeris, dir. Nu-Image Film, 1981.

Dines, Mike. "The Sacralization of Straightedge Punk: Bhakti-Yoga, Nada Brahma and the Divine Received: Embodiment of Krishnacore". *Musicological Annual* 50.2, April 2015, pp. 147–56.

Fukuyama, Francis. *The End of History and the Last Man.* Free Press, 1992.

Haenfler, Ross. *Straight Edge: Clean-Living Youth, Hardcore Punk, and Social Change*. Rutgers University Press, 2006.

Harrison, George. "My Sweet Lord." *All Things Must Pass*. Apple, 1970.

Hill, Napoleon. *Think and Grow Rich*. The Ralston Society, 1937.

Joseph, John. *The Evolution of a Cro-Magnon*. Punkhouse, 2007.

"Krishna Bakhti in Hardcore - Part 1 of 3." *YouTube*, uploaded by kencredible, November 15, 2019, youtu.be/l7Pwr7veQ7E.

Lahickey, Beth. *All Ages: Reflections on Straight Edge*. Revelation Books, 1997.

Luhmann, Niklas. *A Systems Theory of Religion*. David A. Brenner and Adrian Hermann, trans. Stanford University Press, 2013.

McPheeters, Sam. *Mutations: The Many Strange Faces of Hardcore Punk*. Rare Bird, 2020.

Minor Threat. *In My Eyes*. Dischord, 1981.

Minor Threat. *Minor Threat*. Dischord, 1981.

Peterson, Brian. *Burning Fight: The Nineties Hardcore Revolution in Ethics, Politics, Spirit, and Sound*. Revelation Records Publishing, 2009.

Rapport, Evan. *Damaged: Musicality and Race in Early American Punk*. University of Mississippi Press, 2020.

Rettman, Tony. *NYHC: New York Hardcore, 1980-1990*. Bazillion Points, 2014.

Rettman, Tony. *Straight Edge: A Clear-Headed Hardcore Punk History*. Bazillion Points, 2017.

Rogan, Joe. "#1152 - John Joseph." *The Joe Rogan Experience. Spotify*, 2 August 2018, https://open.spotify.com/episode/77D01nImfM59exlzjgApIK?si=3Q FGbmVNRdqZid1V5ooGKQ.

Rogan, Joe. "#1430 - Raghunath Cappo." *The Joe Rogan Experience. Spotify*, 21 February 2020, https://open.spotify.com/episode/4MAMTrx7K6qKQFUa PLjCvm?si=Sv-zYyoYS6uPQ4ZME3QlVQ.

Shelter. *Beyond Planet Earth*. Roadrunner, 1997.

Shelter. "In Defense of Reality b/w The News." Equal Vision, 1991.

Shelter. *Mantra*. Roadrunner, 1995.

Shelter. *Perfection of Desire*. Revelation. 1995.

Stewart, Francis. *Punk Rock Is My Religion: Straight Edge Punk and "Religious" Identity*. Taylor & Francis, 2017.

Urban, Hugh. *New Age, Pagan, and New Religious Movements: Alternative Spirituality in Contemporary America*. University of California Press, 2015.

Waksman, Steve. *This Ain't the Summer of Love: Conflict and Crossover in Heavy Metal and Punk*. University of California Press, 2009.

Wood, Robert. *Straightedge Youth: Complexity and Contradictions of a Subculture*. Syracuse University Press, 2006.

Yohannan, Tim. "Ray of Yesterday Meets Ray of Tomorrow: It's Enough to Make Me Start Drinking!" *Maximum Rocknroll* 79, December 1989.

Youth of Today. "No More." *We're Not in This Alone*. Caroline, 1988.

Something Better Change: Hardcore and the Promise of a Liberating Punk Education

David Ensminger

For well over a decade now, the notion of punkademia has taken shape, creating a subculture within the academia via dissertations, peer-reviewed articles, especially those found within the journal *Punk & Post-Punk*, seminars, symposiums, hashtags, and common parlance. Other developments include the Punk Scholar Network,[1] which held an online Global Punk Conference in Dec. 2020. Older antecedents include Punk Kongress, sponsored by the Federal Cultural Foundation in Germany, which in 2004 convened four days and nights of activities, including panel discussions, live acts, lectures, films, and an exhibition. Such efforts prove that hardcore punk has migrated from being a shunned outlier, an anti-intellectual hodgepodge, to an integral part of the scholarly and education theory ecosystem.

In 2006, the *Chronicle of Higher Education* ran an article about straight-edge academics covering their own musical terrain in an article titled "Studying Rock's Clean, Mean Movement," while in 2011, the *Boston Globe* ran an article penned by Leon Neyfakh in which the byline declares "How do you study a movement that doesn't want to be studied?" That piece included the input of myself and others that attempted to explain how we combine scholarly rigor with the fervent countercultural ethos of the hardcore punk and Do-It-Yourself underground, which Estrella Torrez summarizes as providing fertile ground for a pedagogy that may manifest qualities ranging from equity and a sense of community to various forms of emotional interplay and meaningful collaboration: all of this occurs in the name of re-imagining teacher-learner dynamics (136).

In essence, I believe we attempt to practice what we preach—to carve a hardcore punk praxis that helps students empower themselves and even be-

---

1   Cf. the article by Bestley, Dines, and Stewart in this book [the editors].

come liberated from existing power structures. This has become more necessary during the shift to on-line education during the Covid pandemic as students become more reliant on big business platforms, from Zoom to Blackboard, which often lack privacy while also aggregating data, too.

For me, this has been nearly a 25-year exercise in persistence, resilience, and flexibility. People have variously described me as a hardcore punk historian, even a sociologist, when in fact my university training is grounded within the folklore program at the University of Oregon and the creative writing program at City College of the City University of New York. I study the lore and material culture of hardcore punk; hence, my punkademics is an actual hybrid practice born of emic ("insider") insight and pro-creative urges. I am a child of hardcore punk, raised in its tumultuous bosom since I was 9-10 years old, when my brother began to swarm me with albums (from Pere Ubu and Butthole Surfers to Cockney Rejects and Public Image Limited), vinyl 45s (Joy Division and Sisters of Mercy), and homemade cassettes containing bands ranging from Crass and Articles of Faith to Die Kreuzen. He also gifted me fanzines like *Maximum Rocknroll* and *Last Rites* that smelled mysterious and contained page after page of revolting renegades, Jello Biafra and the like, many of whom were intent on overturning hegemony, existing norms, or systems.

Yet, too often hardcore punk pedagogy has been imagined as a discursive undertaking linked to aspects of complex and nuanced theory instead of practice. That is, one might assume that if hardcore punk professors inject and inculcate "radical" intellectual constructs and perspectives into their curriculum—advanced Marxism, performance studies, contemporary feminism, critical race and queer theory, post-colonialism, and post-structuralism—then such rhetorical positioning will catalyze students' profound education assault on powers-that-be. While I firmly believe that adding doses of Foucault, Baudrillard, Eagleton, Freire, Lippard and countless others may add weight and heft to a reading list, plus sharpen students' critical thinking repertoire, reading alone does not produce skills, social capital, and meaningful activities. It can also become intellectually passive, a means of retreating into the tomes/tombs of language and philosophy, in which paradigms and hypotheses matter more than concrete or direct action.

In effect, mastering the specialized language of the academy, itself a kind of hegemony, serves as the process of weeding out: it acts as a gatekeeper for an elite meritocracy often loathed by hardcore punks. When I attended high school, that was the tattooed teenager with a Social Distortion graphic on his arms who threw aluminum soda cans at me in the hallways, while in the age of the Internet it is those who simmer with vitriol against experts, technocrats, "deep state" government career professionals, and teachers/professors who seem to police language and behavior. The latter constitute the deplored "libs," according to the argot of the right-wing.

Despite being used by those adhering to so-called progressive values, such elite discourse (incentivized and buttressed by colleges and universities) often raises the bars of participation, creating fewer and fewer opportunities for those who question, shun, or cannot participate in the intellectual rigor of the discourse. It is not a tool of democracy and participatory culture or a means of active learning and engagement. As Craig O'Hara, author of the groundbreaking work *The Philosophy of Punk: More Than Noise!* and co-founder and editor at PM Press, noted to me: "I completely agree with the practice over theory idea. But how can teachers use this? I don't know. [Perhaps] throw away the Marxist books and make everything interactive, inclusive, and hands-on." That is, hardcore punk pedagogy should likely spend less time on the dialectic literary theory of Fredric Jameson and more time creating 21st century opportunities to explore John Dewey's notions of community-minded, learner-centered problem solving that can be linked to a holistic experience. Yet, in the extensive age of the Internet, not everyone is guaranteed such access or net-working, so "aligning appropriate technology" in the development of projects and curriculum becomes essential (Williams 94).

"Punk Rock, much like anarchism, is more of a practice than a theory," continues O'Hara:

> Once upon a time, Marxism and other post-modern pursuits involved both a revolutionary critique of the existing social order and practice against it. Presently, Left-wing theoretical critiques of society are little more than insulated fields of study by the academic classes. Anarchism can be a field of study as well: it has a rich history dotted with fascinating people from all over the globe. But without practicing anarchy—exposing, naming, and working against unjustifiable conditions for a more equitable future—there is little value in the study alone.

"Surely, there are some rough theoretical boundaries for punk rock: loud, aggressive, angry music and cultural works that protests the dull, unquestioning lives of mainstream sheep as well as the greedy existence of ruling elites," he argues. "It's got to be rebellious with an egalitarian bent. Without some punk rock theory you'll end up with talented musicians, artists, and creators who join capitalism and sell their DIY skills to the highest bidder. A little bit of theory goes a long way, but without the practice you'll have nothing at all." So, a punk pedagogy, in essence, should be equally rebellious, trying to upend the status quo and dismantle norms, plus it should be pro-democratic and participatory; as a result, that means it will be messy and novel, fractured and incomplete, too. Such praxis is a doing rather than a reading and knowing. It is not hard-line but hardcore: it is flexible and adaptive.

In addition, in terms of educators handling issues rippling through culture, like the quest for racial justice, as Prof. Benjamin Fong recently pointed out in *The New York Times*, creating a diverse reading list is mere stagecraft, not an impetus for a revolution. The desire to "de-prejudice" minds is not itself a significant enough act of social transformation, since it is done often in a newly "approved manner," for the "future of American society does not hang on our collective syllabuses being carefully weighted for race and gender." Adjusting a reading list may present a notion of equity, at least in terms of diversifying the representation of intellectual and cultural history, but real change is a series of actions—organizing, strategizing, problem-solving, coalition building, and deploying social strategies that happen in the streets and halls of power. In fact, Fong suggests too often academics are simply displaying "self-flattery" and "cynically deployed 'cultural intelligence,'" as well as "tokenism" that do little to create structural, concrete change. Teaching students to overcome their hidden biases and "exclusionary attitudes" is to be commended, but it often "inflates" a university's sense of importance. In the end, "if we free ourselves of the notion that education is social change," Fong asserts, "then we can begin to think of education about social change."

In addition, as studies of corporate implicit bias training seem to indicate, well-intended top-down programs often result in both short-term gain only and even some unexpected negative or undesirable consequences: "short term educational interventions do not change people," whether related to at-work safety behavior like wearing gear appropriately or curbing racist attitudes; "anti-bias" initiatives can actually "activate stereotypes," since the attempt by someone to "suppress" a stereotype may actually make those thoughts "cognitively accessible"; "training inspires unrealistic consequence in anti-discrimination programs," which can cause people to become even more complacent, and training makes the majoritarian/white populace (or hetero, Cis-gendered, etc.) "feel excluded"; and generally speaking, "people react negatively to efforts to control them" (Dobbin and Kalev 49-50). This has become crucially evident during the Covid-19 era regarding social distancing and mask mandates, which has hardened the "freedom first" libertarian philosophies of citizens. Other routes and methods that make more sense are increasing diverse social face time (creating classrooms that are actually diverse in terms of enrollment), molding everyday multicultural dynamics that are not exclusionary to whites, and making the overall efforts feel voluntary and a mere portion of larger, multi-effort systemic change.

Hence, in my own way, as a teacher, rather than focus on the enduring problems of systemic racism and intolerance, I propose solutions that acknowledge limits and offer alternatives to the above practices. We work through issues of mandatory military service, like Israel and South Korea, weighing issues and drawbacks, and discuss national service efforts, both historic, like the Civilian Conservation Corps and Works Progress Administration, to modern efforts like Teach for America and beyond. The students also debate the attributes of eliminating grades in favor of a pass/fail system and debt-free tuition proposed by some politicians. These reforms or changes could mold different environments for the academia or citizen spaces, which might embody fuller integration, contact, inclusion, and bridge-building between people and communities. Project-based learning becomes part of those efforts.

Hence, as I would argue, hardcore punk professors should spend more time deploying their soft skills learned through the hardcore punk subculture and less time on self-satisfying deconstructions, disassembling, and critiques. "DIY punk remains at the axis of an interesting tension," noted Prof. Daniel Makagon, who teaches at Depaul University and penned the lauded book *Underground: The Subterranean Culture of DIY Punk Shows* in our correspondence:

> On one hand, punk is very much about trying to challenge cultural norms, to do something different. On the other hand, in order to put on a show, for example, people have to be organized, they have to communicate clearly with partners on projects, they have to have a plan for promoting the show and what to do the day of the show. A good punk show doesn't just happen; the show emerges because the promoter has developed some organizational, problem-solving, and communication skills.

And those traits are not relegated to the punk subculture itself. That is obviously true amid the uproar and uprising of Black Lives Matter, a lengthy contested 2020 presidential election in America, and a raging worldwide health pandemic and crisis fueled by virulent misinformation campaigns creating a wide swath of people who believe it is a fraudulent and a hoax. This is, a section of citizenry believe doctors inflate numbers or conflate the virus with other diseases and morbidities, etc. The rallying cries of such distinct sub-cultures, like anti-vaxxers and others, which at times correlate to neo-Nazi propaganda, seem very akin to the notion of "Don't Believe What You Read," the punchy opus from 1978 by the Boomtown Rats ("I look at the papers to see what they say / I know most what I read will be a lot of lies"). Hence, the uber-right has infused their own media networks with a Do-It-Yourself media, which gains a varnish of legitimacy: NewsMax seems authentic due to their rabid critiques, while Fox News has become just another sideshow of the corporate press. In addition, on the Left, people have eschewed the semiotics of the society of the spectacle in favor of forming human chains and wielding leaf blowers to dissipate tear gas (suburban moms and dads in the Portland riots), burning sections of neighborhoods or creating short-lived autonomous zones of self-rule (Minneapolis and Seattle), or taking to the streets in festive defiance, joy, and relief as Joe Biden won the race for the presidency, even as Republicans declared it a sham.

Hence, now is the time of change underfoot. I contend that a shift towards applied knowledge, immersive learning, and kinetic education praxis needs to occur. To become more fully self-empowered and liberated, students across the cognitive, physical (diff-abilities), as well as socio, ethnic, class, and cultural spectrum need soft skills that often directly relate to the DIY hardcore punk context: time management, personal communication, social intelligence and interaction, problem solving, and ongoing curiosity and day-to-day critical thinking, etc. All of these can be understood as multi-modal, democratic, inclusive, and hands-on. Doing so will lower the barriers of participation and foster a multi-modal approach from the classrooms smelling of still-wet Clorox to the invisible airwaves of the Internet. Doing so will serve to diminish the importance of industrial scale, one-size-fits-all education modes that have failed to create equity, power-sharing, and common ground.

In addition, such teaching relates directly to underground hardcore punk community activities: the production of music and related goods (T-shirts, cassettes, albums, skateboards), the construction and maintenance of environments (from basements, galleries, and skate parks to all-ages venues), independent 'micro-influencer' media (fanzines, flyers, blogs and other web forums), time-sensitive gigs, protests, and bookings (music and political events), and personal identikits (the ongoing subculture of youth style). By gaining such skills "learned through doing," as progressive philosopher and educator John Dewey proposed in the 1930s, students can cement their ability to analyze, deconstruct, resist, and subvert the present day education system and fulfill hardcore punk's promise to re-make an unfair world.

But whether this will lead to liberation is debatable. "DIY has been an important historical feature of punk culture," Makagon pointed out to me in an email:

> but often what is less clear in the arguments about DIY is how punks learn to do DIY. That is, one can quickly pick up that a variety of features of punk culture are created by punks for other punks: flyers for shows, records, cassettes, fanzines. But it takes some time to figure out that each DIY artifact is an invitation for other people to participate. Moving from implicit invitation to explicit forms of communication that invite further participation also requires some desire to mentor. Punks need to be able to read an audience, to understand how different kinds of mentoring are needed in different contexts.

Hence, teachers cannot simply telegraph their intentions: teaching, mentoring, and modeling are the essential tasks at hand for any professors that subscribe to, or identify with, hardcore punk identity and culture.

First, Manage this Meme and Gig, Then You Can Manage the Revolt

Intuitively, most people understand the real politics of time itself. It is finite, relentless, and can easily break a person's habits and spirit. Managing time is a vital asset that embodies the manifold practice of subtly shifting skills and mindsets: the ability to prioritize and follow through with tasks, to delegate and consult as needed, to seek effective means of organization that act as precursors and facilitate certain preferred outcomes. In the ever-quickening world of online life, with its surging velocity of information, time management now occurs within seconds, as media theorist Sherry Turkle posits in her 2011 book *Alone Together*: for instance, recent noteworthy actions include thousands of citizens brainstorming nearly instantaneous hashtags and seemingly effortless satirical memes about Rudy Giuliani's media fiasco calling for a Biden-Trump ballot recount while awkwardly stationed in front of a landscape store that shared the name of a luxury hotel and porn shop in a neighborhood more known for dildo reviews than presidential politics. Those media savvy undertakings and self-made media, full of computational and even crude graphics, embody guerilla tactics and have an in-built sense of obsolescence: the news cycle only lasts for days, even hours.

When K-Pop fans deluged Twitter with images of pancakes to hijack President Trump's "Million MAGA March" hashtag, they understood that a day later would have been dead on arrival. Immediacy is a pre-eminent mode of the viral ecosystem. However, due to the interpenetration of politics and pop culture, some content relating to similar occurrences, albeit with a slight change from context to context (hence a sense of continuity), will have a second life. The potency, though, like a dissipating half-life, will decline until it becomes merely ironic and nostalgia-inducing and not an alarming metaphor for a debauched administration suffering from its own decline. Now, exceptions do occur, such as Green Day hijacking, appropriating, and re-imagining/re-invigorating the lyrics of Millions of Dead Cops, which morphed from "No War/No KKK/No Racist USA" to "No Trump/No KKK/No Racist USA" under the nasally bellowing of Billie Joe Armstrong at the 2016 American Music Awards. The lyrics have since become a fixture of marchers decrying the current state of affairs in a country struggling with the heightened presence of white militias, police violence, and terrorists groups.

Black, African-American, and Social Justice media subcultures also offer pointed lessons about the variance, usability, and potency of memes. Hardcore punk history is steeped in graphics and logos repeated ad infinitum—the Circle Jerks skanker drawn by female artist Shawn Kerri, the cocktail toting skeleton of Social Distortion, the "icons of authority": the cross common in Christianity, the Union Jack, the swastika, and the two-headed Ouroboro (snake and/or dragon) amalgamated by Crass, and an illustrated pistol pointed at viewers used by DOA, and many more. Meanwhile, memes and murals depicting victims of police brutality, such as Breonna Taylor, have become highly politicized and rampant, an inherent part of the visual vernacular of communities of color attempting not only to pay tribute but to instigate change. Outlets including *Washington Post*, *Vox*, *NBC News*, *National Public Radio*, *Huffington Post*, and *The New York Times* have committed time and space to the issue of their effectiveness; as writer Jenna Wortham insists, in the case of Taylor, her image lingers like a ghost, a wormhole into other times and places (or a collapsed sense of time and space) in which the atrocities and indignities suffered by such communities feel continuous and ever-present. Time then is time now. The pain is simply a continuum. And though each meme is in fast elastic and may mutate and morph beyond control (or spawn other "feral attempts" that seemingly lack the depth and authenticity),

Wortham notes it all amounts to hyper-visibility that hopefully does not drown out the resourceful actions of people working on behalf of the issues.

In the meantime, hardcore punk seems to have lost its focus and bite, its ability to replicate that sense of urgency and mass appeal. Gone are the days when Sham 69 bemoaned the jailing of George Davis (wrongly convicted armed robber), the Pogues sang adamantly about the Birmingham Six (men falsely accused of a pub bombing), DOA agitated on the behalf of the anarchist Vancouver/Squamish 5 (imprisoned urban guerrillas), or Anti-Flag penned a song for imprisoned journalist Mumia Abu-Jamal and Leonard Peltier (Native American activist). No Rock Against Trump cohered like Rock Against Reagan did in the 1980s or Rock Against Bush in 2004. The age of the internet, in some ways, has left hardcore punk in a stagnant self-satisfied wake. While K-Pop and hip-hop cultures have aggregated their activism and gone viral, hardcore punk has been described as the fuel for Antifa by outlets like the Guardian, which published the article "'No Fascist USA!': how hardcore punk fuels the Antifa movement." Though, the loose-knit members are as likely to listen to rap as they are to listen to Hard Left, Appalachian Terror Unit, or even Strike Anywhere. In fact, in the same article, Jello Biafra of the Dead Kennedys denounces Antifa's escalating embrace of violence, which he believes "plays into the hands" of the Trump supporting, fascist-leaning cohorts. Instead, he advocates for "raised middle fingers" that lets the right-wing understand that a critical mass is ready to reject them (qtd. in Thomson).

To be fair, hardcore punk bands have participated in the cause and zeitgeist of Black Lives Matter, each with their own modus operandi, including a band from Pico Rivera, Vandalize, who rode through the streets of Los Angeles belting out their music from the back of a pick-up truck in the summer of 2020 after the death of George Floyd. As members of the Latin community, they understood too-well the menace of policing, so this opportunity to unveil their riffage during taut and tense times of tumult meant a way to shed light on the multi-generational, multi-ethnic anger simmering in the wake of unjustifiable killings (Brown). Though they may not have the cultural clout, currency, or heft of hip-hop bands with large-scale followings, Vandalize's commitment and conscience indicate hardcore punk's continuum and continuity.

But perhaps a hardcore punk pedagogy should be concerned less about that state of ire and revolt and more about providing tools and skills that allow students to self-define and navigate their own pressing concerns and issues. That is, students should exercise some "ownership" of their issues and projects.

The online sense of incessant speed, the internet's millisecond rhythms, has a hardcore punk counterpart: memes act as the visual and textual equivalents of D-beats pounding like machine-gun fire in a vociferous thrash punk tune. They replicate endlessly, almost effortlessly. And students need to understand their potency, less they become less engaged and less involved in the elastic cultural conversation (the wide rippling tide of the "attention economy") under way. They experience political crisis in real-time through transmedia navigation—jumping from platform to platform, fluidly. Hence, my students use a range of possibilities to share and network their research and create communities of discourse: among them, students have authored and shaped Facebook feeds, Reddit accounts, PowerPoints and Prezi presentations, YouTube videos, Pinterest boards, and the walls of the college to pin up their research with tape and scissors, causing a great debate amid faculty about the contested space within the staid architecture. Students felt these mediums were more pregnant with possibilities and timeliness than a word processor's typical bland and routine process: such contemporary mediums convey a vital ability to share and disseminate, percolate and network, infuse and inject, all quickly and in real-time.

In all likelihood, many of my students, reared in the attention economy, in which capitalism becomes an ever-flowing ecosystem of information often masquerading as connectivity and bonding, are likely far savvier than myself in regards to that universe. They continuously deal with trolls: I mostly do not. They adore Anime: I avoid it. They argue about the merits of K-Pop: I am mystified. Some of them, without my knowledge, might be not just pop fans but members of stan culture, a more fervid version of the subculture embraced by stars like Lady Gaga, whose URLs include www.ladygagoreostanclub.com, where visitors can provide their names, email address, and even birth dates to receive "the latest breaking news surrounding the Chromotica-inspired collaboration including drop dates for the cookie and Lady Gaga OREOgrams as well as chances to win in the Sing It With OREO promotion." The cross-promotion is unabashed.

Diehards understand, unlike casual fans known as "locals" (side note: in hardcore punk and surf culture, coveted beaches were branded as "Locals Only" by youth who sometimes were associated with racist behavior), how the systems operate: they learn the governing metrics of Billboard and streaming platforms, which can boost artists' success; they offer endless tips to other users and members of the ARMY, like avoiding bulk purchases, choosing to build playlists rather than rely on loops; avoiding the use of mute; and much more than celebrating birthdays, making donations on a band's behalf, buying an album ten times, or posing for an infinite variety of selfies with band-related ephemera. All of this amounts, according to one Gaga super-fan, as free labor, all deftly done on a phone. They are not mere evangelicals, they are virtual soldiers on TikTok and Twitter—creative, committed, agile, and un-dettered—funneled into a centralized, commodified interface. Gone are the Usenet chat rooms, mailing lists and bulletin boards of the 1990s (Coscarelli).

Hence, assigning the same-samey routines of essay composition, literally pulling a student from the nuances of a 21st century environment to a rudimentary means of intellectual production, like composing paragraphs with strict guidelines championed in the 19th century, needs a re-imagining. To those connected, the "Internet … is this bazaar of obsessive worlds," which perhaps first gestated in its contemporary form via the rise of FarmVille, notes Ian Bogost, a game designer that teaches at Georgia Tech: that Facebook embedded game acted as a precursor to an everyday reality of "gamefied attention" that "encourage[s] interaction loops in a way that is now being imitated by everything from Instagram to QAnon" (qtd. in Victor). Similarly, music subcultures are now gamefied too: competitive environments propel fan behavior, like stans. Hence, while hardcore punk fans may compete for alternative prestige by posting flyers on-line from 1982 or use straight-edge memes to mock people, stans are gaming the system, finding ways to boost their artists and causes by any means necessary. Hardcore punk pedagogies should take note.

To meet that challenge, all of my "Composition I" students explore, research and attempt to synthesize key segments of new media literacies proposed by Henry Jenkins and his Project New Media Literacies, which began at MIT and has re-surfaced at the Annenberg School at the University of Southern California. As a longtime writer, public intellectual, and teacher, he has proposed a series of such literacies as building blocks and precursors of successfully empowering oneself as a citizen, worker, and student in the 21st century. That means keeping a pace of change and innovation that occurs as convergence culture continues to unfold. That is, the world shrinks from computer systems that once occupied entire rooms to no more than the palm of a hand, and technology grows smaller and more intuitive, powerful, and artificial-intelligence enabled. Jenkins sketches and defines an array of traits that define and underscore such efforts, from play (play as a form of learning), performance (developing an on-line identity), and visualization (graphic inter-faces of information) to distributed cognition (flowing one's thoughts through a machine tool), transmedia navigation (switching platforms and modes), and collective intelligence (the pooling of knowledge, like Wikipedia).

In essence, my students "back into" theory, since they are likely already participating in such ventures, in some form, on a daily basis. So, their projects sharpen their understanding of how technology is impacting their learning and living. They address topics ranging from Fortnite to Google Glass, One Laptop Per Child to Kiva micro-loans (on-line lending platforms meant to change people's lives and support causes like female-run agri-cultural businesses in the "Third World"), driverless cars to warehouse and medical robots. At first, many students have some degree of trouble grasping the salient details, but as we "unpack" the concepts and bridge the gap between theory and lived experience by showing how much they have already mastered, they "connect the dots," become better informed of their agency. They can better predict consequences, like losing a sense of direction due to the over-use of Google Maps, or losing long-hand math skills or even spelling capabilities due to both calculators and spell-check software.

These skills/abilities may not seem hardcore punk in the musical sense, but they are hardcore punk in the sense of conscience and consciousness. They involve a sense of community-mindedness, choosing action over inac-tion (studying what is happening rather than what happened), and are tied to contemporary shifts in subject matter decided relevant by the student learner and not arcane philosophy and theory. Their choices reflect the "throbbing nerve-pocket of the now," to quote writer Sam Anderson. Or, as summarized by writer Mike Dines, "punk pedagogy seeks to remain far-reaching, *up-to-date* and exploratory" (31).

Such undertakings are also hardcore punk in theme: punk has always ad-dressed contemporary times like a newssheet—DOA howling about general strikes, Dead Kennedys' agonizing over chemical warfare, Against Me! nar-rating tales of transsexuals coping with life's crushing unfairness and bigotry, War Against Women and Petrol Girls challenging and attempting to dismantle patriarchal traits and structures, MDC opposing Nazi tendencies from John Wayne and Ronald Reagan to Donald Trump. Though the students may not choose to explore environmental degradation and systemic racism heads-on, bluntly, by decrying police policies, they instead unveil how Black Lives Mat-ter use tools of media literacy to network, organize, and challenge and change such policies. Rather than being merely descriptive and reactive, they attempt to be solution-oriented, to claim not a riot of their own but a new future, one that may better resemble a punk rock rooted in the notion, as Joe Strummer once said (and now is the headline on his foundation web page), "exemplary manners to your fellow human beings."

For instance, the ability to create, manage, and manipulate information flow within a still merging information system, to make research meaningful, of-the-moment, and intuitive, plus memorable and penetrating, is like creating punk tunes off the cuff, derived from news of the day, whether 1977 Britain or the dirty neon vitriol of Los Angeles during hardcore's zenith hour. For decades, hardcore punks have managed their own education, their own didactics and auto-learning, by understanding the time sensitive nature of the output, whether a benefit gig in a rented hall whose money cannot be recouped if cancelled for a cause that needed funds immediately, to fanzine articles about bands that are on the road as the Xerox machine started whirring. The albums by bands like Dead Kennedys, in which they eviscerated Ronald Reagan in their lyrics and gig commentary, are optimal, in terms of their impact, only when carried out stealthily within the volatile era. Change occurs not due to accidental factors played out at random with little link to time and space. Effective change occurs because participants understand both leadership and efficiency, the crunch of time, and how to manage the moving parts of a gig (lighting and PA, flyers and posters, message board postings, "likes," and concentrated use of algorithms), protests (optimal sites and signage, surge capacity and alternative routes), and albums (home demos, studio recording, mixing, mastering, production, and distribution). Hardcore punks learn this empowerment paradigm hands-on in an immersive, hands-on series of environments in which "time is everything."

Compared to Foucault arguing about contested truths and the Panopticon and Baudrillard pontificating about simulacra, these are activities that prepare hardcore punk teachers for the difficult, contested space of pedagogy. Teachers must create easily adaptable content, flexible calendars and schedules, and meaningful learning outcome measurements and assessments that propel students to become contemporary and effective agents of their own change. And sometimes the templates may be borrowed from other music subcultures as well, hence insuring that hardcore punk and its pedagogy will always remain an unstable but vivid hybrid.

References

Anderson, Sam. "Watch This Snowball Fight From 1897 for a Jolt of Pure Joy." *nytimes.com.* 25 Dec. 2020, nytimes.com/2020/11/05/magazine/snowball-video-fight.html. Accessed 26 Dec. 2020.

Brown, August. "Meet the punk band that provided the soundtrack for DTLA protestors from a moving pickup truck." *latimes.com.* 1 June 2020, https://www.latimes.com/entertainment-arts/music/story/2020-06-01/black-lives-matter-protests-downtown-hardcore-band-truck. Accessed 28 Dec. 2020.

Coscarelli, Joe. "How Pop Music Fandom Became Sports, Politics, Religion, and All-Out War." *nytimes.com.* 25 Dec. 2020, https://www.nytimes.com/2020/12/25/arts/music/pop-music-superfans-stans.html. Accessed 25 Dec. 2020.

Dines, Mike. "Learning through Resistance: Contextualisation, Creation and Incorporation of a 'Punk Pedagogy.'" *Journal of Pedagogic Development* 5.3, 2015, https://uobrep.openrepository.com/bitstream/handle/10547/584233/226-584SM.pdf;jsessionid=050AFC86BDB32736FB1F4EB425FE4B06?sequence=1. Accessed 29 Dec. 2020.

Dobbin, Frank, and Alexandra Kalev. "Why Doesn't Diversity Training Work? The Challenge for Academia." *Anthropology Now* 10.2, Sept. 2018, tandfonline.com/doi/full/10.1080/19428200.2018.1493182. Accessed 31 Dec. 2020.

Fong, Benjamin. "Teaching Racial Justice Isn't Racial Justice." *The New York Times.* 18 Nov. 2020, nytimes.com/2020/11/18/opinion/college-antiracism-teaching.html. Accessed 19 Nov. 2020.

Makagon, Daniel. Email to the author. 14 Dec. 2020.

O'Hara, Craig. Email to the author. 23 Dec. 2020.

Project New Media Literacies. newmedialiteracies.org. Accessed 1 Jan. 2021.

Thomson, Jamie. "'No Fascist USA!': how hardcore punk fuels the Antifa movement." *theguardian.com.* 9 Sept. 2017, https://www.theguardian.com/music/2017/sep/09/no-fascist-usa-how-hardcore-punk-fuels-the-antifa-movement. Accessed 26 Dec. 2020.

Torrez, Estrella. "Punk Pedagogy: Education for Liberation and Love." *Punkademics*, edited by Zach Furness, Minor Compositions, 2012, pp. 131–42.

Turkle, Sherry. *Alone Together: Why We Expect More from Technology and Less from Each Other.* Basic Books, 2011.

Victor, Daniel. "FarmVille Once Took Over Facebook. Now Everything is FarmVille." *nytimes.com*. 31 Dec. 2020, nytimes.com/2020/12/31/technology/farmville-zynga-facebook.html. Accessed 1 Jan. 2020.

Williams, Morgan K. "John Dewey in the 21st Century." *Journal of Inquiry and Action in Education* 9.1, 2017, files.eric.ed.gov/fulltext/EJ1158258.pdf. Accessed 23 Dec. 2020.

Wortham, Jenna. "The Lives They Lived: Breonna Taylor." *nytimes.com*. 26 Dec. 2020, nytimes.com/interactive/2020/12/23/magazine/people-who-died.html. Accessed 26 Dec. 2020.

"There is no hope for the USA": Bad Brains and The Sounds of Race in DC Hardcore

Shayna Maskell

Popular music has long been understood as a force for socialization and of marginalization, acting often as a link between the self and the collective. Of course, such positioning within society means that music can also be used to enact and sustain hegemony, dominant ideologies that privilege some and sideline others. This ideological power of popular music comes from both its origins in and representation of human agency (intentionality) and in its function as art (symbolic meaning). From Plato, who believed music could be a way of harmonizing the soul but also warned that breaking conventional aesthetic modes of music was dangerous to the social and political fabric, to Immanuel Kant, who in his *Critique of Aesthetic Judgment* (1790) claimed that we must understand art as purposefully produced, deliberately allowing for interpretation, to theories of popular music insisting on the social meaning constructed by music, as well as the sociopolitical implications of such meanings: Music acts as a purposeful expression of individual thought. That expression is then interpreted, read, so to speak, by consent and mutual understanding of cultural and social norms, thereby conferring publicly accepted and (nearly) universally recognized meaning. Such meaning is nearly always political, reinforcing cultural norms such as definitions of gender, race, class, and age, or, alternatively, emphasizing dissent and defiance, using noise—that is, the subversion of what proper aesthetics are in music—to upset the conventional social order. This chapter situates itself firmly amidst that fertile sociopolitical framework, building on these theoretical tenets of music's intentionality, expressive symbolism, and subsequent political potential.

Bad Brains, the founding fathers of DC hardcore, are still known today as pioneers of hardcore punk, not only for their technical virtuosity and musical innovation, but also as one of the only all-black hardcore bands.[1] The band and their eponymous album, even with the unusual composition of four black males, was, in many ways, in line with the cultural and musical milieu of the time: punk rock names (HR, Dr. Know, Darryl Cyanide), do-it-yourself fashion sensibilities that combined militancy with shocking design (including half-shaved heads, peroxide-bleached hair, and Johnny Rotten jackets), the sociopolitical inflected lyrics of songs, and the near-abounding energy and rawness of punk sound. Yet, the narrative of Bad Brains, as both social beings within the DC and larger punk rock scene and the music itself, which they generated and played, cannot and should not be disassociated with the production and reinforcement of, and resistance to, how race is constructed. The elements of sound in their album serve as a performance of racial identity in one contested site of struggle—music. From the complicated aesthetics of racialized sound through the reinterpretation of rock 'n' roll to the lyrical parallels to folk music, to the inclusion of reggae on a hardcore album, *Bad Brains* performs multiple, often contradictory, racial identities.

The Racialized Sound of (Punk) Rock

As much of popular culture would have us believe, Elvis Presley was not just the King, but also the progenitor and near-deity of rock 'n' roll. But as any passing fan of rock also knows, the origins of this genre are firmly implanted in the marginalized, threatening, and subversive (at least to white audiences in the 1950s) sounds of rhythm and blues. Most of the first rock styles were variations on black musical forms that had taken shape before white audiences took note and, consequently, almost all of rock's most influential and formative innovators were black (with some exceptions, of course, including Bill Haley and the Comets). Singers like Chuck Berry and Little Richard, black artists who sang a hard-driving version of R&B that would bridge the gap between rhythm and blues and rock 'n' roll, were musicians with whom young people—both black and white—could identify. These musicians were younger and wilder than the traditional R&B artists, and despite the difference in skin color, they expressed a freedom and a lack of inhibition for which (white) adolescents yearned.

---

1   Of course, credit must be given to the handful of black punk predecessors of Bad Brains, including Poly Styrene of X-Ray Spex, Death, Pure Hell, and punk producer Don Letts.

While rock, including the glamour and spectacle of it, was critical to bridging the sociocultural relationship between blacks and whites, it also conjured up arguments about leisure, work, and freedom, as whites have been entertained by blacks since the time of slavery (cf. Bloomquist; Lott; Sharpe; Taylor and Austen). Moreover, the history of 1950s rock is littered with the appropriation of black music by white musicians. For record labels, such musical commandeering became the preferred way for white wealth to exploit black talent; in doing so, countless black R&B and rock musicians lost money and credit to lesser remakes of their most successful songs. The complicated racial history of rock resumed with the onslaught of the British Invasion of the mid-1960s. Black-based R&B reemerged in the country's consciousness when British bands—the Animals, the Rolling Stones, the Beatles, the Kinks (to name but a few)—charted with both blues and R&B covers and with their newly-formed, blues-inspired rock. Unlike its 50s precursors, these bands weren't trying to assume wealth from current hits; instead, they tended to cover older material in order to pay it homage. In this way, R&B represented cultural capital, with these British bands valorizing "blackness" as the personification of difference from or opposition to the mainstream. Ironically, the white, British versions of black, American sounds came to symbolize the pinnacle of rock 'n' roll.

Unsurprisingly, the musical influences of Bad Brains themselves fulfill this portrait of rock's muddied racial past, including their entrance to and enchantment with punk music. Growing up in Southeast DC, Bad Brains bassist Darryl Jenifer was consuming a steady musical diet of not only traditionally black music—jazz, soulsters like Aretha Franklin and Stevie Wonder, and funk in the form of Sly and the Family Stone, and George Clinton and the Funkadelics—but also early heavy metal, by British and American acts like Led Zeppelin, Kiss and Black Sabbath (Andersen and Jenkins 27). Jenifer credits his cousin's playing of The Doors' "Light My Fire" as "the day I fell in love with music and instruments" (209). The Hudson brothers, Bad Brains drummer Earl and lead singer HR, part of a military family who travelled extensively (including a childhood in Liverpool) before settling in Maryland, grew up singing Beatles songs with their parents, cementing their decision to play music. Much like the history of rock itself, the members of Bad Brains connected to the music of singers and bands who performed a complex and often multi-layered representation of race.

More interestingly, perhaps, is their foray into and subsequent adoption of, punk rock. Sid McCray, Jenifer's neighbor and friend, is credited with introducing punk to the band members after seeing a 1977 TV report on British punk. Immediately, Bad Brains were drawn to the music of the Sex Pistols, the Ramones, the Dickies, and the Damned. The volume, speed, urgency, and anger of punk reflected their own sociopolitical and cultural racialized selves. In a city marred only years earlier by race riots, where African Americans were hurting from drug problems, economic decline, poverty, and crime, as well as the active threat of gentrification and neighborhood destabilization, Washington, DC continued to suffer from flagrant racism and less overt forms of marginalization during the 1970s. Punk offered a reprieve from these social realities. It gave expression to the indignation and frustration borne from the death of prominent black leaders like Martin Luther King Jr. and Malcolm X, and its "uninhibited sounds ... seemed to be the perfect deflection from everyday DC existence" (Jenifer 210). Promoting the rejection of establishment-generated truth, punk urged listeners to think for themselves, a message not lost on Bad Brains, who struggled with employment, drugs, and even a life trajectory. With the ideology of violence dominating the landscape of Washington DC—that of the State against other countries, and the State against minorities, both figuratively and literally—the violence of punk's sound acted as a sort of reclamation of violence as representation for Bad Brains. Rather than violence on behalf of authority, punk was violence in reaction to authority, violence *instead* and *as* their own authority.

Bad Brain's hardcore encapsulated both this violence and this authority through the force and energy, the power and the skill, of the band's first album, *Bad Brains*. Hudson's drums are militaristic, clashing, and clattering with the ferocity of the hi-hat, and as forceful as a pummeling of fists. His tempo is astonishing, beating out the menacing tracks' rhythm with determination and vehemence, inducing a seizure-like pace of toe-tapping, and a head-shaking pulse that could cause whiplash. The guitar of Dr. Know is equally spectacular. In a genre where technical expertise is eschewed, his playing is not only skillful but also compellingly intoxicating. He rips into guitar solos with exhilarating force and impossible speed; his riffs have a heavy, penetrating distortion that, in combination with his thrashing tempo, are at once aggressive and enthralling. Jenifer's bass adds considerable heft and antagonism to the sonic assault; his riffs and use of stop-time redefined what bass could be in a punk band, recalling the bebop era of jazz. Pounding and throbbing, the stamina and thrust of Jenifer's bass rounds highlight the sense of menacing possibility in the fury of these tracks. Then there's HR's vocals: his yelps and gasps convey the desire, wrath, and urgency of the music. This debut 1982 eponymous album not only defined and inspired what DC hardcore was and would be, but also who Bad Brains—black men in a white scene in a black city—were.

Lyrical Protest: The Tradition of Multiracial Protest Music from Civil Rights to Punk

Borne from centuries of immigrants and submerged in the democratic ideal, folk has stood as a symbol of not only "authenticity" but also of the American mythos of individuality, freedom of speech, and challenge to political authoritarianism. This music arose from the fields of slavery, where the blues acted as a unifying force, lyrically by sharing mutual tales of woe and hardship and musically by creating simple refrains that could be memorized and repeated. Continuing the multiethnic strand of music, the agrarian populist movement of the 1880s focused its music on the sociopolitical themes of shared experience; yet, the most influential era of politically-themed music stems from the International Workers of the World (the Wobblies) and the radical tradition of folk in the 1930s. Known as the "singing movement," the Wobblies created songbooks as political text, contending that "a pamphlet, no matter how good, is never read but once, but a song is learned by heart and repeated over and over" (Regon 54).

As one of the most famous political songwriters, Woody Guthrie (as well as his contemporaries Pete Seeger and Aunt Molly Jackson) merged the style of the talking blues—brought to the American musical tradition by African Americans—with the overt politics of the Wobblies, a predominantly white movement, to propagate the popular folk song. This laid the groundwork for the music of the civil rights movement. "We Shall Overcome," "Oh Freedom," and "We Shall Not be Moved," with their recurring choruses, rhyming verses and emotionally charged lyrics, act to concurrently solidify a shared political identity and to give literal voice to the utopian political and social goals of the movement. This music and oppositional consciousness continued into the 1960s, with Bob Dylan, Joan Baez, Phil Ochs, Tom Paxton and others exemplifying musical rebellion against the hegemonic forces that determined social mores. Yet, the best-known artists in this genre were white. It wasn't until the mid-1960s that the social consciousness of folk music was linked once again to the music of African Americans in the form of a gospel and R&B fusion with singers like Curtis Mayfield and Sam Cooke. Bad Brains, nearly twenty years later, reinterpret the sociopolitical lyrics, and, in some ways adhere to and contradict, the structure and sound of the folk music tradition. Incorporating both locally and nationally germane cultural and political issues of the day, *Bad Brains* echoes the still-relevant themes of folk's 60's heyday—alienation, antiauthoritarianism, class struggle, and the fight for marginalized voices to be heard.

"The Regulator," the fourth song of *Bad Brains*, parrots the sentiments of such classic protest songs as Dylan's "Subterranean Homesick Blues" (1965) and the Who's "My Generation" (1965), with their near-universal theme of anti-authoritarianism. Just as Dylan envisioned a government that tapped your phones and arrested you regardless of any wrongdoing and the Who lamented mainstream society's inability to understand the cultural choices of the youth, Bad Brains bemoans the intersection of government and cultural control: "You tell me what to say and when to say it/You tell me what to do and how to do it/And if I ask you why, you'll arrest me/And if I call you a liar, you'll detest me." Yet, the song's political remonstration is more than simply a youth-specific attitude of rebellion; instead, it is an explicit reaction to the particular sociopolitical environment of Washington DC in the late 1970s.

The city's political infrastructure was, until the 1970s, completely dependent on the federal government. Despite President Nixon's endorsement and Congress' eventual approval of home rule for the city, there were still burdensome and near-paralyzing restrictions on local authority, which produced a massive disconnect between the appearance and execution of power, the veneer of control and the performance of command (Gillette 190–91). This dichotomy of power masked an even more nefarious imbalance—that of race. The overarching hand of the white majority in Congress superseded the black-based local government: "it wasn't a question of right and wrong, it was a question of race and power—white lawmakers ... telling black people in the city how to run their lives" (Jaffe and Sherwood 24). This patronizing relationship tended to exemplify the still-overt racism in the city, as well as the divergence between white "idealism" and black "reality." Bad Brains speak to this situation with clarity and conviction, singing "You control what I'll be/You control who I see/And if I let you/You control me." In the very literal sense, the "you" was the nearly-all white Congress, who controlled the city's court system, budget, and veto power over any DC-approved legislation it didn't agree with. But the "you"—the regulator—was also a stand-in for the historically consistent inequitable racial relationship between traditional society and blacks.

Implicit in this lopsided power balance was the inability to self-represent, not only in the traditionally political sense (in having a voice in Congress, and over one's district) but in the broader notion of voice and representation. Indeed, protest music of the previous decades was created, in part, as a way to give literal and metaphorical voice to social issues that were hidden, that were silent—civil rights, worker's rights, human dignity and anti-war sentiments. Even music's ability and responsibility to act as an enunciation of marginalized issues was fodder for protest songs. Buffalo Springfield's 1966 "For What It's Worth" ("Young people speakin' their minds/Getting so much resistance from behind/It's time we stop/Hey, what's that sound?/Everybody look – what's going down?") and Simon and Garfunkel's 1964 "Sound of Silence" ("People talking without speaking/People hearing without listening/People writing songs that voices never share/And no one dare/Disturb the sound of silence") both warn of the dangers of muteness and extol the power of sound. In this way, protest music serves as an emblem of free speech, linking the capacity to be heard, to give voice, with the American ideal of democracy.

Conversely, Bad Brains' "Pay to Cum" articulates what they see as the redefinition of "free" speech, identifying the ways in which money has come to replace the concept of egalitarianism—free is not free anymore. As HR sings, "I came to know with now dismay/That in this world we all must pay/Pay to write, pay to play/Play to cum, pay to fight." In one way, these lyrics suggest a literal understanding of paying for speech, reflecting the dominant corporate culture of the time, particularly in the music industry; with the music market concentrated in the hands of very few in the 1970s, the diversity of sound was muted, and cultural production tended towards homogeneity (Peterson and Berger). The market for punk music, particularly with its anti-authoritarian attitudes that had fallen out of vogue, was dwindling, if not outright nonexistent, and "Pay to Cum" addresses, seemingly *ad absurdum*, the ways in which freedom to speak, protest, even enjoy leisure activities (including sex) had become commodified. What once was seen as the purview of freedom, an absolute right of Americans, had become a privilege of those who were able to pay. In another way, "Pay to Cum" is addressing the recurring folk song theme of speech as representation, conflating the ability to play music, to literally be listened to, with social protest. When HR howls, "the end is near/hearts filled with fear/don't want to listen to what they hear/and so it's now we choose to fight/to stick up for our bloody right/the right to sing, the right to dance/the right is ours," he is alluding to the way in which noise, music, and the concurrent message contained within those sounds, is controlled, ignored and imbued with authority. Socially, the delineation of sound "effectively define[s] which type of people are acceptable … and which are not" (Loughran 152); that is, the intolerance for and rejection of hardcore by mainstream society acts as intolerance for and rejection of their specific social positions and political opinions. Bad Brains' protest speech about protest speech, then, is excluded by the social barriers constructed around their particular kind of sound, or form of speech.

More than just on the cultural level, "Pay to Cum" addresses the silencing that is occurring on the legal level as well. With the federal establishment of the Noise Pollution and Abatement Act in 1972, the government legislated the concept of sound, arguing that citizens consider street noise "disturbing, harmful or dangerous" (U.S. Department of Housing and Urban Development). In particular, DC's Noise Control Act of 1977 bans "any sound which is loud and raucous or loud and unseemly and unreasonably disturbs the peace and quiet of a reasonable person of ordinary sensibilities" (D.C. Law 2-53),[2] leaving space for the stifling of Bad Brains' brand of protest song. In doing so, the federal and city laws embody the song's claim that society doesn't want to listen to what they don't want to hear—figuratively and literally. At least tacitly, the irrationality and obscenity of the song's title "Pay to Cum" is equated with the incongruity and offensiveness of regulating and commodifying speech.

The intersection of class, race, and representation is explored more overtly and even more concisely, in Bad Brain's less-than-ten-line song "Fearless Vampire Killers" ("FVK"). "The racial and class divisions loom larger and become more stark on the national stage," and DC, which, in 1960, became the first city with a black majority, still suffered from massive income and socioeconomic disparities in the late 60s and early 70s (Jaffe and Sherwood 15). These economic inequalities were exacerbated by the race riots of 1968. Sparked by the assassination of Martin Luther King Jr. and culminating in looting, violence, the destruction of many black neighborhoods, and the use of federal troops to quell the uprising, the city suffered a near-decade long economic and social recovery. With over 800 fires, twelve deaths and over a thousand more injured, a number of consequences, beyond the fiscal, surfaced, including the rapid protraction of self-selected segregation and the flight of middle-class blacks from the once-flourishing U Street and Cordoza neighborhood (Kersten Wills). As a consequence of the rapidly shifting city demographics,

---

2   The Noise Control Act of 1972, 42 USC 4901 was passed on October 27, 1972.

the fissure between races and classes became both conflated and more pronounced: "[...] with residents who have sought refuge from wards across the world, in a city with a huge gap between rich and poor, the connection between the local and the global becomes crystal clear when you're 16 blocks away from the White House where social welfare cuts are proposed [...]" (Modan 38). "FVK" casts the band into the role of heroes (vampire killers) and assigns the villain's character to the (implicitly) white rich living dead who are taking over their city. HR warns, "The bourgeoisie had better watch out for me...we don't want your filthy money/we don't need your innocent bloodshed."

Beyond the lyrical parallels that Bad Brains' punk music had to the protest songs of the 1960s and 1970s, its use of sound and structure simultaneously mimic and contradict folk music. Much of folk music (not to mention the similar 12 bar blues structure) has simple repetitive verses and sticks to the strophic structure, wherein the song has a uniform melody but different lyrics for each stanza. Songs like Bob Dylan's "Don't Think Twice Its Alright" (1963), "Blowin' in the Wind" (1963), "The Times They Are A'Changin'" (1964), and the Byrd's "My Back Pages" (1967) are all strophic in their macrostructure. This uncomplicated structure is most often used in short, straightforward songs, delivering a unity of sound that allows a focus more on lyrics and narrative. In addition, such consistency permits audience anticipation of melody, fostering participation in singing and lending itself towards the idea of collective performance. Integral to this is the appearance of a unified front such singing granted—rather than signifying the political expression of just one musician (e.g. Dylan, Pete Seeger or Woody Guthrie), the collective performance announced the communal acceptance and expression of the music's sociopolitical content. This strophic structure, and its accompanying musical and social solidarity, is evident throughout the songs on Bad Brains. From "Big Takeover," to "Pay to Cum" to "Don't Need It," nearly every song employs the short, repetitive lines and structure that mirrors the construction of 60s folk songs. And, similar to folk music, these brief, recurring lines can motivate uncomplicated understanding and unproblematic memorization, ultimately offering the same sort of sociopolitical community of music that folk did. In this way, it wasn't just four black punks singing—it was all of Washington, DC. The effects of these songs, these voices and this emotional and musical community was a collective protest.

Despite the structural parallels of hardcore and folk, the two genres diverged in an obvious and important way: sound. While "the quiet sounds of folk music perhaps encouraged a focus on a text as prime source of meaning [...]" (Eyerman and Jamison 122), Bad Brains did the opposite, with screeching guitar, thumping bass, ferocious drums, and lyrics that weren't so much sung as shrieked or squealed. Yet, the seemingly contradictory sounds of folk and hardcore actually function in a similar fashion: as a performance of authenticity. For the protest singer, the music was often subordinated to the message, and the vocal style of the singer was influenced almost exclusively by the emotional undertones of the words. The central musical instrument for folk singers was the voice. In folk, this emotion was characterized as intimacy, empathy, compassion, sorrow, or heartbreak. These evocations were, to an extent, an expression of privilege. The whiteness of folk assumed *a priori* attention paid; that is, the communication of white emotion already implied importance. Bad Brains' hardcore emotion, on the other hand, embodied blackness—marginalization, outrage, anger, and desperation. The obfuscation of Bad Brains' sung/shouted lyrics should be understood as a counterpart to the voice itself; in this case, the visceral emotion of HR's voice—hoarse, urgent, loud, and angry—underline the anger of the lyrics. Similarly, the vocals of Dylan, steeped in eagerness and weariness, plaintiveness, and hopefulness, correlate to the content of his folk songs. Bad Brains' sound represents blackness and folk whiteness, but they both serve the same purpose—sincerity and truth in sound.

Race and/in DC Hardcore

The history of the punk scene is, by and large, a history of whiteness. While punk's predecessor, proto-punk, has sonic and political ties to the black community, and British punk boasts the reggae-inspired Clash, "punk has been largely, and largely correctly, defined as a White subculture" (Duncombe and Tremblay 207). Proto-punkers like the Patti Smith Group, Iggy Pop, MC5, Richard Hell, and the Velvet Underground, along with the first wave of British and American punk bands like the Ramones, Sex Pistols, the Cramps, the Damned, X, the Dickies, and the Misfits, are all white. Even the arrival of hardcore, which was spurred by punk's creeping commercialism and sought to play louder, faster and harder, in the form of Los Angeles' Black Flag and San Francisco's Dead Kennedys, did nothing to change the racial complexion of the scene. As Greg Tate (1957-2021), music writer for the *Village Voice* (and black himself) notes, "hardcore is white ... no matter how much Hendrix and

Berry they ripped, it still ain't nothing but some whiteboy *sounding* shit now" (216).

The DC scene was no different. Not only were the early punk bands uniformly white, including the Slickee Boys, Overkill, the Razz, the Urban Verbs, and the aptly named White Boy, but also the accompanying audience was primarily white. In fact, two of the most comprehensive photographic histories of the DC punk scene, Susie Horgan's *Punk Love* and Cynthia Connolly, Leslie Clague and Sharon Cheslow's *Banned in DC* exhibit this dearth of black participation. A mere twelve of 450 black and white photographs in *Banned in DC* and only five of 100 black-and-whites in *Punk Love* reveal any black punk fans.[3] Covering six years, and countless concerts around the DC area, less than one-third of the photographs have just one black face amongst the sea of white punk rockers. Yet, Washington DC itself was a black majority city, making the white DC hardcore scene more of an incongruity. Since 1957, DC was a majority-minority city, embracing the funk moniker "Chocolate City" after it finally obtained home rule in 1973. The 1980 Census shows that 70.3% of the city's inhabitants were black, only slightly down from 1970's 71.1%. And the city was home to not only black activists, including the re-located Stokely Carmichael, Marion Barry, and Sterling Tucker, but also a parallel coalition of black political power. Bad Brains, then, was both an anomaly and normality, straddling the line between whiteness and blackness, marginalization and power.

The innovation of Bad Brains and hardcore, then, should be understood as a re-creation of racially appropriated folk and rock, and, to a certain extent, of punk itself. Bad Brains was constantly formulating and performing multiple identities, one of which was a complex musical negotiation between blackness and whiteness. The use and transmogrification of black constructed rock into hardcore seems to afford these men a mode of condemnation of mainstream white culture, while seizing upon the musical language for "airing feelings of marginality and contestation" (Lipsitz 55).

---

3   This count excludes any black punk musicians, including a significant number of photographs of Bad Brains, as well as two each of Toni Young and David Byers of Peer Pressure, and Skeeter Thompson of Scream, a DC punk band of the mid-1980s.

Hardcore Meets Reggae: Black Essentialism in Sound

Bad Brains' hardcore, however, was even more complicated than the musical melee of folk, rock, and punk. Given their positioning both within the DC hardcore scene (as majority white) and within DC proper (as majority black) there was an internal racial tension that ultimately was expressed sonically through a form of so-called "authentic blackness." On the one hand, Bad Brains rejects the essentialization of blackness, particularly through the mode of consumption, singing "We don't need Ivory Liquid/Don't want no Afro-Sheen…" in "Don't Need It." They likewise rebuff the societally constructed concept of blackness in "The Regulator:" "You control what I'll be/You control who I see/And if I let you/You control me." These lyrics attempt to buck both the more general concept of social controls and, more specifically, the constructed physicality of blackness through consumer products and assimilation into a white bodily ideology. Even more blatantly, "Big Takeover" warns "all throughout this so-called nation prepare yourself for the final quest/your world is doomed with our own integration/Just another Nazi test." Regarding race relations as a mere experiment, the band imagines a future contemplated by the Nazis—one of ostensible racial purity, which eliminates minorities and obliterates resistance. And Bad Brains makes clear, this country would fail such a test; "So understand me when I say/There's no hope for the USA." Yet these songs do more than simply assert an alternative black identity lyrically; even more importantly, they do so musically, within the context of (white) hardcore. That is, the space Bad Brains creates for a marginal black identity in these songs is created inside an already-white dominated identity; their construction of blackness in hardcore is a reaction to and should be understood within the context of an already-established white terrain, rather than a racially mixed "outside" world.

On the other hand, outside the (white) structure of hardcore, and perhaps in reaction to such a white-washed identity, Bad Brains engage in palpable and deliberate essentialization of blackness with their reliance on so-called "black authenticity," most clearly with their utilization of reggae in their 1982 album, and their concurrent conversion to the Rasta lifestyle. While the notion of authenticity is clearly a difficult, if not completely artificial, construct,[4] the

---

4   The previous use of quotes and the inclusion of adjectives like "so-called" and "ostensible" around and in front of the word authenticity have been my attempt to acknowledge the highly constructed nature of the concept. For the reminder of the chapter I

stakes of such a definition—who generates these delineations and who is able to claim membership within the authentic group—are quite real and tangible. As Johnson argues,

> Many times these arbiters of authentic blackness have the economic and/or social clout to secure particular attributes of blackness—for example, dreadlocks, vernacular speech, living in a particular part of town, etc.—as the components of the template from which blackness originates. Often, it is during times of crisis (social, cultural, or political) when the authenticity of older versions of blackness is called into question. These crises set the stage for "acting out" identity politics, occasions when those excluded from the parameters of blackness invent their own. (2)

Bad Brains, then, existing within the paradoxical crisis of racial identity, are "acting out" their identity politics by participating in this performance of black authenticity, an authenticity produced by a specific set of sociopolitical circumstances and accepted by the band as an entrée into a legitimate black identity outside of white hardcore. Central to this adoption of an authentic black identity was the assumption of a distinctively black musical and religious identity—Rasta and reggae.

Reggae, as a continuation and new growth of and from historically raced black musical identities, arrived sonically also as a derivation of those black musical genres, and ultimately, as a symbol of authentic blackness. Emerging from Jamaica, reggae, much like American rock 'n' roll before it, borrowed and reconstructed R&B and the blues, reinterpreting the sounds with an idiosyncratic local flavor (Bennett 75). It is this amalgamation of sound, and its sonic birthplace of Africa, that helped lionize reggae as an authentic black music. Representing the literal and musical African diaspora, reggae harkened back to a nostalgic, if not overly idealized, symbol of blackness. In a country that consistently and continuously tried to marginalize, if not assimilate, blacks, reggae stood as "a precious inner sanctum, uncontaminated by alien influences, a black heart beating back to Africa" (Hebdige 38).

Connected nearly inextricably to reggae is Rastafarianism, the Jamaica-based religion founded, like reggae, on the combination of African and European influences, in this case the white Bible and black Africa. Espousing a revolutionary theology that spurns capitalism (epitomized by the concept of

---

will refrain from using such qualifications, while still recognizing the artificially created definition of authenticity.

Babylon, which refers to the entire raced, classed system of capitalist oppression), Rastafarianism demands race and class equality, which will ultimately result from the destruction of Babylon (Ruggles 107–8). Such a dogma had already been explicitly expressed in the reggae of Jimmy Cliff, Bob Marley and the Wailers, and other artists, making the relationship between the music and the theology explicit. This potent combination of black musical expression and the religious tenets of racial egalitarianism (with its tacit promise of the downfall of white hegemony) became an appealing, if not idyllic, interpretation of black identity, "draw[ing] strength from the ideal of a black community working in harmony" (Tate 216). Much like the performance and consumption of jazz and blues (before its transformation and appropriation into white mainstream society), reggae and the accompanying Rasta lifestyle acted as a deliberate sign of Otherness, as a contemporary mark of musical black authenticity. It delineated African from black or Other from assimilated and compliant American. In other words, it symbolized authentic blackness.

In 1978, the members of Bad Brains (who then still called themselves Mind Power) went to see Stanley Clarke and Chick Corea, the jazz fusion masters, and happened upon Bob Marley, who was also playing that evening. The band, and, more precisely HR's, identification with reggae and the Rasta started that summer night. Their affinity for the Jamaican-based music and the lifestyle had elements of both the aesthetic and the spiritual; describing reggae as "so incredible, so beautiful" (Andersen and Jenkins 58), HR's vision of the music fit the idealized principles of Rastafarianism and offered a spirituality that he claims helped him kick his heroin habit. Even more importantly, the music and theology offered a choice in how the band and its members represented their selves, specifically their black selves. As bassist Jenifer explains, "Rasta was a way of life we chose to recognize. I was raised Catholic but that was a white man's religion and that's not my heritage" (67). The decision to embrace and embody reggae and Rasta was a conscious effort to, at once, resist the collective white identity of hardcore and assert their authentic blackness to a community which did not accept hardcore as a genuine black musical identity.

In addition to the alternative black identity Bad Brains establishes in their hardcore songs, they also include three unadulterated reggae songs on 1982's *Bad Brains*, thereby performing authentic blackness for both the hardcore and black community. "Jah Calling," which references the Rasta term for God, is the sixth song and the first reggae tune on the album. An all-instrumental song, "Jah Calling" is an abrupt and somewhat shocking fissure in a hardcore album, given its massive slowdown in tempo and juxtaposition against the previous five lightning-fast, raging songs that opened the album. Following the traditional reggae musical structure—with an emphasis on the off-beat, simple harmony, and temperate tempo—the song acts as a disruptor to the assumption of a specific (white hardcore) identity. This acts, in part, as a deconstruction of the hegemony of sound parallel to the deconstruction of the hegemony of whiteness in punk. As philosopher Jacques Attali argues, "[s]ubversive noise ... betokens demands for cultural autonomy, support for differences or marginality" (7). Indeed, reggae has had a historically subversive status since "the preservation of African traditions ... has in the past been construed by the authorities (the Church, the colonial and even some 'post-colonial' governments) as being intrinsically subversive, posing a symbolic threat to law and order ... hint[ing] at that darkest rebellions: a celebration of Negritude" (Hebdige 31). The inclusion and contrast of reggae in a hardcore punk album forces the listener to decelerate—both in the music itself and in the construction of Bad Brains' musical identity;[5] the song's brazen performance of difference (sonically and, through it, racially) demands a more complicated understanding of the band's race and concurrent character.

Two songs later is "Leaving Babylon," whose reggae sound is overlaid with lyrics straight out of Rastafarian principles of class and racial equality, as well as its emphasis on the evils of a Babylon typified by America. The placement and content of "Leaving Babylon" acts to reiterate the band's identity of black authenticity, while still allowing for a connection with its white audience. As the eighth song on the album, only one hardcore song stands between the bookends of reggae—"Jah Calling" is followed by "Supertouch/Shitfit," which is immediately followed by "Leaving Babylon." In doing so, the band reaffirms that the first interruption of the sound and attending consciousness (in "Jah Calling") was neither fluke nor caprice; it was an intentional and expressive proclamation of sound and meaning. The lyrics themselves, while sung in a conventionally reggae style (which could be off-putting to the ears of punks more accustomed to the shrieking singing of hardcore), offered a

---

5   It should be noted, however, that part of the Rasta ideals embraced by the members of Bad Brains was homophobia. When asked about a trip to San Francisco to play a show, HR responded, "Well, it's okay, but too many faggots . . . most of them act so crazy even out in public, it disturbs me, makes me want to go and shoot one of them" (*Flipside* #31). In addition, when Bad Brains stayed with fellow punk bands Big Boys and Dicks (both having gay members) in Texas, the band stiffed the Dicks money they owed them for marijuana, leaving a note that said, "Burn in hell, bloodclot faggot" (ibid.).

relatable theme of disillusion and alienation, albeit in the language of Rasta rather than punk. But it was successful in its merging of the white hardcore and black reggae/Rasta ethos of anti-capitalism and disaffection for the hegemonic structures sustaining the system. The final song of the album is also the third and last reggae track, "I Luv I Jah." Despite the same reggae musical styles as the previous two songs, these lyrics are a pointed effort to demonstrate their authentic blackness and challenge those who would deny them that mantle. Describing how "two young men call me not their brother/they try to make I feel ashamed" and "my lovely sister, judge me by my clothes, yeah/only to learn her mistake, not everyone's alike," Bad Brains continue to affirm their faith, both in Jah, and in themselves and their authentic (if not conventional) black selves. While the other reggae songs seem to be a declaration of blackness to the white audience of hardcore punk, "I Love I Jah" seems to offer a defense of that blackness to their racial peers.

Building an authentic black identity within the chiefly white punk scene necessitated an overlap of the two racialized musical identities. As HR says, "Reggae music is punk and punk music is American ... [and] here I am in this predicament, here I am African in a European environment, so I find myself with two likenesses [...]" (*Flipside* #31). But there was a kindred spirit in both hardcore and reggae—a rebellious, revolutionary attitude. Like its musical predecessors of R&B and rock, reggae's music explored the tension between African roots and European hegemony. Retaining influences from its history as a former British colony and sounds from its musical position in Jamaica, reggae acted as a representation of the African diaspora. As with hardcore, reggae acts as both a cultural representation of marginalized identity and rebellion to the dominant white hegemony. While the band's performance of "authentic blackness" does, as Johnson states, "delimit the possibilities of what blackness can be" (19), the physical realities and sociopolitical conditions of the late 70s and early 80s help to clarify why such performances were necessary to the individual construction of Bad Brains' identity.

Conclusion

Music making, as well as music consumption, is a site for the creation of collective cultural identity. Discrete and overlapping cultures of music provide and have provided crucial sites within which marginalized people, whether they are black, lower-class, women or disaffected youth, can negotiate their own representations in varying degrees of opposition to, or collaboration with, hegemonic narratives. Every history that is created and disseminated within US rock music culture, from jazz and blues to Motown to folk to heavy metal, has been formed within this very particular struggle for social and cultural agency. Through these narratives, and the construction of sociopolitical and historical-specific identities, music "comes to stand for the specificity of social experience in identifiable communities ... captur[ing] the attention, engagement, and even allegiance of people" (Lipsitz 127). Music, then, provides space for people to negotiate their historical, social, and emotional relations to the world; the way fans define and understand themselves—what they believe and value—is intertwined with the varying codes and desires claimed by a taste culture associated with a specific genre of music. Using performance and sound as a political form to interrogate issues of gender, sexuality, race, and class, music has created a praxis based on the transformation of the private into the public, consumption into production, and in doing so, has not only reflected popular culture through the years, but has had a hand in changing how we understand and how we define what popular culture is. And while it is clear that music contains no inherent racial identity, no essence that brands it black, white, Asian or Indian, it is equally obvious that sound contains racial and social meaning. This meaning is, of course, socially constructed and historically contingent, and it carries with it the norms, values, and cultural constructions of its people. The music of Bad Brains' 1982 album, *Bad Brains*, also forty years after its release, allows for an intricate, involved, and frequently ambiguous, understanding of how race is performed through sound, and, more specifically, through the band's particular version of hardcore.

References

Andersen, Mark, and Mark Jenkins. *Dance of days: Two Decades of Punk in the Nation's Capital*. Akashic Books, 2009.

Attali, Jacques. *Noise: The Political Economy of Music*. University of Minnesota Press, 1985.

Bad Brains. *Bad Brains*. ROIR, 1982.

Bennett, Andy. *Cultures of Popular Music*. Open University Press, 2001.

Bloomquist, Jennifer. "The Minstrel Legacy: African American English and the Historical Construction of 'Black' Identities in Entertainment." *Journal of African American Studies* 19.4, 2015, pp. 410–25.

Connolly, Cynthia, and Leslie Clague. *Banned in DC*. Sun Dog Propaganda, 1988.

D.C. Law 2-53. D.C. Noise Control Act of 1977. 30 December 1977.

Duncombe, Stephen, and Maxwell Tremblay, editors. *White Riot: Punk Rock and the Politics of Race*. Verso, 2011.

Eyerman, Ron, and Andrew Jamison. *Music and Social Movements: Mobilizing Traditions in the Twentieth Century*. Cambridge University Press, 1998.

Flipside #31, April 1982.

Gillette, Jr., Howard. *Between Justice and Beauty: Race, Planning, and the Failure of Urban Policy in Washington D.C.* The Johns Hopkins University Press, 1995.

Hebdige, Dick. *Subculture: The Meaning of Style*. Routledge, 1979.

Horgan, Susie J. *Punk Love*. Universe, 2007.

Jaffe, Harry S., and Tom Sherwood. *Dream City: Race, Power and the Decline of Washington, D.C.* Simon and Schuster, 1994.

Jenifer, Darryl A. "Play Like a White Boy: Hard Dancing in the City of Chocolate." *White Riot: Punk Rock and the Politics of Race*, edited by Stephen Duncombe and Maxwell Trembley, Verso, 2011, pp. 207–12.

Johnson, E. Patrick. *Appropriating Blackness: Performance and the Politics of Authenticity*. Duke University Press, 2003.

Kersten Wills, Denise. "'People Were Out of Control': Remembering the 1968 Riots." *Washingtonian Magazine*. 1 April 2008, https://washingtonian.com /2008/04/01/people-were-out-of-control-remembering-the-1968-riots/. Accessed 14 June 2020.

Lipsitz, George. *Dangerous Crossroads: Popular Music, Postmodernism and the Focus of Place*. Verso, 1997.

Lott, Eric. *Love & Theft: Blackface Minstrelsy and the American Working Class*. Oxford University Press, 2013.

Loughran, Maureen E. *Community Powered Resistance: Radio, Music Scenes and Musical Activism in Washington, D.C.* Dissertation. Brown University, 2008.

Modan, Gabriella Gahlia. *Turf Wars: Discourse, Diversity, and the Politics of Place*. Blackwell Publishing, 2007.

Peterson, Richard A., and David G. Berger, "Cycles in Symbol Production: The Case of Popular Music." *American Sociological Review* 40.2, 1975, pp. 158–73.

Regon, Bernice Johnson. *Songs of the Civil Rights Movement 1955-1965: A Study in Culture History*. Dissertation. Howard University, 1975.

Ruggles, Brock. *Not So Quiet on the Western Front: Punk Politics During the Conservative Ascendancy in the United States, 1980-2000*. Dissertation. Arizona State University, 2008.

Sharpe, Christina. "Blackness, sexuality, and entertainment." *American Literary History* 24.4, 2012, pp. 827–41.

Tate, Greg. "Hardcore of Darkness: Bad Brains." *White Riot: Punk Rock and the Politics of Race*, edited by Stephen Duncombe and Maxwell Trembley, Verso, 2011, pp. 212–16.

Taylor, Yuval, and Jake Austen. *Darkest America: Black Minstrelsy from Slavery to Hip-Hop*. WW Norton & Company, 2012.

U.S. Department of Housing and Urban Development. As reported by Kenneth Eldred. *Noise at the Year 2000*. Fifth International Congress On Noise As An International Problem. 1988.

Ms. Bob Davis and *Hardcore California*: A Conversation About a Forty-Year-Old Document of Hardcore Research

Ms. Bob Davis in Conversation with Konstantin Butz and Robert A. Winkler

Peter Belsito and Ms. Bob Davis's book *Hardcore California – A History of Punk and New Wave* is one of the first-ever books to use the term "hardcore" in its title as a reference to subcultural music scenes. It provides a comprehensive overview of early punk, new wave, and hardcore movements in Los Angeles and San Francisco by presenting a whole variety of band photographs, cover artworks, posters, and insightful texts that introduce the main protagonists of these scenes and document the importance of the two cities as musical hubs for punks, hardcore kids, and musicians from very diverse backgrounds. *Hardcore California* was first published in 1983 so that the publication of our anthology *Hardcore Research* happens to coincide with its 40th anniversary.[1] However, this celebratory occasion was not the only reason for us to reach out to the editors. We consider Peter Belsito and Ms. Bob Davis as very early—if not the first—quintessential "hardcore researchers" and are very happy that Ms. Bob found the time to sit down with us and share her memories about conceiving, writing, editing, and publishing *Hardcore California*.

Ms. Bob combines an academic background with a unique career as a musician and transgender activist that struck us as extraordinary. Her experiences show to what extent research on subcultural phenomena such as punk and hardcore, almost naturally, relies on extensive collaborations, unforeseen coincidences, and—first and foremost—dedicated individual work that will still always leave some recipients and participants of the respective scenes unsatisfied. It was inspiring to see that already 40 years ago, basically right around the very emergence of what became known as hardcore, there

---

1   Cf. the introduction to this anthology.

were people out there that not only shaped but also dedicatedly documented subcultural scenes and created historical archives with a rigor that was hardcore in itself. The interview with Ms. Bob offers insights into the genealogy of the book and the editors' involvement in early punk and art scenes around the famous DIY venue Valencia Tool & Die in San Francisco.

Konstantin: Let's start by considering how you got involved in the work on the book Hardcore California and the events that led to its publication. At the time you got involved, you were already teaching at college, right?

Ms. Bob: Yes, I joined the faculty of City College of San Francisco (CCSF) in '76. It was the American bicentennial. They had planned a class in American folk music. The person who was going to teach the class was unavailable, but he knew that I knew the subject and asked me to teach it. I was still in grad school and got an emergency hire. I taught that class in the summers for several years and eventually began teaching more and more there.

Konstantin: How did you meet Peter Belsito, and how did you get involved in this terrific project that eventually became Hardcore California?

Ms. Bob: Here is how it happened: Even before I left graduate school, I got involved with a group called Ubu Incorporated. It was named after the Alfred Jarry play about the anarchist King Ubu (Ubu Roi). In that group we were doing what is called free music, a sub-set of new music, which basically was improvised music, structured improvisations of various kinds. Things were cheap enough in San Francisco and we had our own storefront performance space where we could rehearse and present concerts. After we lost our space, we had a meeting where we tried to figure out how to get a new space. Peter attended together with a guy named Joegh Bulloch. That was the first time I saw Peter. Joegh had just finished art school at San Francisco Art Institute and Peter had moved here after finishing art classes at the University of Massachusetts. Peter didn't really vibe with the group and Joegh went on to do his own thing. He's now the administrative director of Burning Man. Anyway, Peter was living in a storefront near my home with his girlfriend, painter Lisa Fredenthal. They wanted to create a gallery on the first floor with a space for bands to play in the basement. One day, as they were cleaning out the basement, they found a sign saying: "Valencia Tool & Die." This place had obviously been a machine shop many years before and that's how the space got its name: from the sign found in the basement. As there were concerns about the noise from the bands that would play there, they tore up the floorboards in the first floor and filled the space under the floor with sand because sand absorbs sound. Then they closed it all up and you couldn't tell that the sand was there. It worked. You could stand upstairs; you would feel the vibrations in the floor, but you could talk at a regular volume with someone and not have to shout. But as soon as you'd open the door and go down those stairs—it was a low ceiling, concrete floor, stone walls, nothing to absorb the sound—it was loud. I got involved with Peter with the idea that I'd come and help when there were bands, if I could produce performance art events, new music, and free music in the first-floor gallery. So that's how we started working together. Peter was the art director for a punk magazine called *Damage*, so he had a lot of insight into local bands. I think there were a total of ten issues of *Damage*. It was through this connection that we got bands to play at Tool & Die. It was often people who had appeared in *Damage*. There were a lot of bands looking for places to play. The quality of the bands was very uneven. We never had the money to pay anyone up front. It was always a split of the door.

Robert: When was it? Are we talking end of the 1970s?

Ms. Bob: I think it was in 1980, it might have started in '78. When the Western Front festival was happening in San Francisco [cf. Lefebvre], Susan Pedrick, a local punk scenester, had the idea to have an exhibit of punk posters at Tool & Die for the festival. The gallery on the first-floor room had posters covering all four walls. The first night, we were going to have a gallery opening for the posters; we may not even have had a band that night, but it was still really well attended. A lot of people were there. I had a vague connection to Ron Turner, who owned Last Gasp of San Francisco, an underground comic book publishing company. It's still around. I phoned Ron and told him that I had something I wanted him to see, "This could be a book." And he came over before the event started, looked around, and said we should get in touch with him. We were very lucky as Ron had already made the decision to move into entertainment books and here we were with a book about punk posters, something very, very current. That is how our book *Street Art: The Punk Poster in San Francisco 1977-1981* got published. Peter did the layout, a woman named Marian Kester, who wrote for *Damage*, wrote the text, and I dealt with all the artists and the bands. Then Peter had the idea to do *Hardcore California*.

Konstantin: How did you come up with the idea to use the term "hardcore" for the title of the book?

Ms. Bob: Peter wanted to do a San Francisco and L.A. book and from the very beginning the notion of using the term "hardcore" in the title was discussed a great deal because we knew we weren't only going to be covering hardcore bands. The original title was *Street Music*, trying to capitalize on the success of *Street Art*. Now, this is my interpretation of why we called it "hardcore," Peter would probably say something else, but I think it was just the most current term. To just call the book *Punk California*, wasn't as exciting as *Hardcore California*. When people asked me about it, I said it had to do – and I still believe this – with the dedication to the music. The people who were doing this kind of music, even if it didn't have all the trappings of hardcore, had an intense dedication that was hardcore – in their hearts. It is something they're doing because they have to, right?

Konstantin: That's also in the preface of the book. There is this one very strong paragraph where it kind of summarizes what you just said. It ends with the sentence: "Not everyone in this book has continued in the hardcore, but they all know what it means" [cf. Belsito and Davis 7]. That struck us as crucial: Even if not everyone in the book subscribes to the label hardcore, they all know what it means.

Ms. Bob: They know what it means, and they have that kind of commitment. That's what it is about.

Konstantin: What was your personal take on this? Did you also consider yourself or your work as "hardcore"?

Ms. Bob: It was not the kind of music I would listen to at home. I was still involved in the new music scene, and I was not playing in any bands. I was composing for a theater company, and I performed one or two gigs with a band named Novak. But I didn't fit their image. I was at least ten years older than anybody else in the band. And, also, I insisted on performing in drag. Musically, I sounded fine, but Novak, the leader, asked me to leave the group because my presence gave the band an inconsistent image on stage. It was amicable. No hard feelings. For me, I enjoyed the excitement. I enjoyed being part of Tool & Die, a venue I could go to that was so cutting edge. And I enjoyed being able to wear high-heels and a big wig and talk to people while I worked the door. But most of the people didn't know that I played an instrument. So,

I wasn't involved musically. I was there because I wanted to produce performance art events.

Robert: Would you say that back then the scene was more open, more open-
minded? There is a tendency to say that at some point hardcore turned into
this more masculine and tough subculture that is not so tolerant when it
comes to gender issues. Was that different at the beginning of the 1980s?
Was it more of an open space? I mean, you were showing-up in drag...

Ms. Bob: It was, especially at Tool & Die, because remember, it was founded by art
students who knew other art students. And we were doing gallery shows
and performance art events. It was an arty scene. That kind of testosterone-
driven music went on at other places in town. There were other places who
did that better than we did. We drew what I think was a clientele that was
mostly made-up of college students, especially art and music students.

Konstantin: Let's get back to the book again. Can you tell us a little bit about the
writers you enlisted for *Hardcore California*? Besides Peter Belsito and you
there are three other authors involved: Craig Lee, who wrote the part on Los
Angeles and played in the bands The Bags, Catholic Discipline, The Bone-
heads, and Funhouse, a young writer with the name Shreader, who added to
Lee's text, and Jonathan Formula who wrote the introduction. How did you
find them?

Ms. Bob: Craig Lee wrote for *LA Weekly* and the magazines *Damage* and *Flipside*.
He's the only one in the book who was a professional writer. He brought
along a guy called Shreader. Craig said: "Well, the real recent stuff, the music
of the past 18 months, I haven't been dealing with, but Shreader can take care
of that for you." Shreader was still in high school. He sent us a manuscript
that was, pardon the expression, terrible. I spent hours and hours rewriting
that thing. Turning fragments into sentences, you know. He had no objection
to my edits, so I think I was true to his intention. But what he had submitted
wasn't printable. I think the second-best section in the book is by Peter. At
this point, he was in a "Bohemian" period. He was spending a lot of time in
cafés, writing in notebooks. I don't know how Peter knew Jonathan Formula.
I don't know how he got involved. I don't think he was a musician. He was a
sound engineer. I know he toured with The Residents. Those were the writers. I wish Craig Lee hadn't dumped Shreader on us, because I think it's the
worst writing in the book, even with my editing.

Konstantin: In the book it says that you were working with about 7.000 photographs. That sounds like a lot of work.

Ms. Bob: The sorting process for both the posters and for the photos was infinite. We established a system of Yes – No – Maybe. Those were the three piles, and then we had to keep track of that and return the photos back. The hardcore scene has a lot of photographers involved and it was my job to keep it straight as to whose photos are whose and get them back to them. So, Peter and I went to Ron Turner, the publisher at Last Gasp, and pitched the book idea. Ron liked the idea and told us this: "I'll do the book on one condition. I want to do the book square, 12 inches by 12 inches, and I want you to get permissions to reproduce album covers from at least some of the punk bands in the book." If we could get the bands or record labels to agree to let us use the album covers, we would get the contract. In those days, when you got a publishing contract, you got money out front, not like it is today. And it was quite a bit of money, too. We may have gotten as much as $5,000 each. In 1981, that was a lot of money. So, we talked to all the record labels that were producing punk bands. We took a trip to L.A. to talk to record labels. I can't remember all the names. I think one was Slash, or was Slash a magazine?

Konstantin: It is also a label. They released the Germs (GI) record for example. And you probably also talked to SST, right?

Ms. Bob: SST, yes. Those guys were a lot of fun. They were the guys out by the beach. After the end of our interview, they went surfing. They wanted us to go surfing with them, but I'd never been surfing in my life. However, I could not get in touch with anyone from the Dead Kennedys. I just didn't know how. All the contact information on the records was out of date. I kept sending them letters and getting them back. Finally, we did get permission to use one of their records. I don't know exactly how we did it. I think we went to the distributor. The way it worked was that the printers had the films of the record jackets. The record labels did not have them, the printers did and they would not do anything with it, like make a copy, unless they had an authorization. I think we got an authorization from the distributor and that was good enough for the printer. Then, after the book comes out, I hear from the Dead Kennedys. And they were nasty. They're angry: "We're gonna do this and that, and we're gonna sue" and all that. So, I sent them all the letters I had sent out. I photocopied the envelopes with the cancelled stamps from the post office and said: "Look, hey, I tried to get to you." But they said, we did this on purpose, that we purposely used old addresses to reach them. But that was all I could find, man. I went to the record stores; I copied the addresses down. It's all I could find. That was one of the things that happened afterwards. Anyway, we got the contract and Ron dealt with the Dead Kennedys.

Konstantin: All of this actually sounds like a whole lot of research that you were doing, which relates to the title of this anthology. Would you consider your work on *Hardcore California* as a research project? Has it been a mere documentary or have you been doing hardcore research?

Ms. Bob: This is interesting, because you asked me whether it was a research project or a documentary. I'm not sure I know the difference, you know. Pardon me for getting academic on you: We were researching lived experience – while it was going on. So, we were asking people about last week, last month, last year. I don't even think we used the local punk magazines for facts. Peter interviewed people. And after the book came out one of the things that I heard a lot of people object to was the coverage of a performer named Mary Monday. Mary was from Canada and Peter presented her as the woman who brought punk to San Francisco. That's basically what she said in an interview and Peter ran with it. That did not please a lot of people who said: "We were punk before Mary Monday ever got to town!" That was one of the more contentious things in the book.The only other point of contention I know: We made a decision, perhaps one that should have been thought about more, but we decided to limit the part on San Francisco pretty much to bands actually from The City. I don't think we covered any of the East Bay bands at all and a number of people were angry about that – the East Bay bands, for sure. What they pointed out to us was: "You didn't apply such limitations in L.A. In L.A. you're covering bands from Redondo Beach, and you're covering bands from the city, too. Why didn't you do that in San Francisco? Why were you inconsistent?" That was something I, frankly, did not have an answer for. We made this decision, and I'm not sure it was a good one. But it was the decision that we made.

Konstantin: Do you remember any explicit objections from the "hardcore" hardcore scene? That is, from bands that did not relate to the "new wave" side of punk at all?

Ms. Bob: Generally, people liked it. I don't say this with no modesty: It was impressive when it first came out. However, I had a voicemail machine and I got one phone call from some guy who wouldn't identify himself and he was like: "You're gonna be blackballed from every club in town, pal!" He was really angry. For me this was odd, because few people in the punk scene actually knew me. Peter was much better known. I also happened to be walking by a bar once and stopped to talk to a woman I knew. She was dating a guy who was in one of the East Bay bands. As soon as he heard I was Bob Davis, he walked away. She explained that he was so upset because his band wasn't in the book. But in general, it was well received. I happened to have drinks with some people among whom was the manager of City Lights Bookstore, which is the bookstore founded by poet Lawrence Ferlinghetti. City Lights also published *Howl* by Allen Ginsberg and all those beat poets. So, someone said that I edited *Hardcore California* and he told me it was one of their bestsellers at Christmas the first year. That made me feel great!

Konstantin: Would you regard *Hardcore California* as a historical document? Is it more from within the scene or about the scene? Where would you locate it?

Ms. Bob: It was done by people who were either in the scene or people who were in the periphery of the scene as in my case. See, my job was to be the publication professional. I had worked with Ron before; I knew more about how the process worked. I had taken a number of workshops from Bay Area Lawyers for the Arts in contracts, in taxes, and in copywriting. I'm not a lawyer, but I had this background. And Peter had so much to do with the art and the writing; I was an administrative editor. So, I was more outside of the scene. But Peter was in the scene. I think we worked kind of both sides of that equation. I do definitely consider *Hardcore California* a kind of snapshot of what was happening at that time. An imperfect telling, but one that does not do violence to what was going on. I think we presented what was going on, accurately. Yes, there are omissions. But what can you do about that? There always are.

Konstantin: To our knowledge *Hardcore California* is the first-ever book that is using "hardcore" in its title. The term "hardcore" was probably used in other contexts before but this is the first publication we could find that uses it within the contexts of punk, music, and subcultures. In that way, it presents a kind of pioneering work and it is logical that it cannot cover the associated scenes in their entirety. It's a first — if not the first step — and we would say it's a very big step in covering the early California hardcore and punk scenes. Particularly, as there are really many bands in the book.

Ms. Bob: And the great thing is that you get to see the bands. I love the way Peter organized the book. I love the visuals. I love the way he decided to put that column down on the side of the page, so that we could have more photos in there. And, frankly, if it had been a book that only covered the strictly hardcore bands, I don't think that we would have found the same publisher, who was willing to invest the money to print all those photos. Printing a photo costs money, and printing a colored photo, or an album cover, costs even more money. So, I'm not sure, just from a marketing point-of-view, that a book about just "hardcore" would look like or sell as well as *Hardcore California*.

Konstantin: When we first contacted you, you said that you hadn't been working on or thinking about punk or hardcore lately as you had been concentrating on other projects for a long time. You founded the great Louise Lawrence Transgender Archive, became an expert in that field, and also were the first transgender person to become a member of the tenured faculty at City College of San Francisco. To us, that sounded truly amazing and actually kind of hardcore, both in terms of an academic career and a life's journey. Did these experiences and your experiences in the transgender community overlap with the time you spent close to the early hardcore and punk scenes?

Ms. Bob: Slightly. I would always dress in drag to collect money at the door. There was a magazine in town called *Punk Globe*. Ginger Coyote was the name of the editor/publisher. She is a transsexual – there's a photo of her in *Hardcore California*, too [cf. Belsito and Davis 93]. So, I got to know her, and talked to her. There is overlap there. And I was expressing myself as a transgender person a lot. I did an hour-long performance art piece that used video and slides of me in drag. It was called "Madame of Many Faces." A lot of my friends had art names at the time, for example Fast Forward, Phil Harmonic or Laszlo Bean-Dip. They started calling me Madame. It was part of what I was doing, but I didn't do punk drag too often. It was more glamory drag, which I did poorly. I make a lousy drag queen if you want to know the truth. But what started then with collecting drag magazines ultimately became the Louise Lawrence Transgender Archive forty years later. It was a long evolutionary process. To my surprise, I don't perform music anymore. I don't even play very much. I write a lot on transgender history. And I really enjoy running the archive. I was able to get some grants and I was able to buy some things: old books, a lot of photos. It's really what I do now. But as for the relation to punk and hardcore: They existed together, but I don't think they mixed very much.

Konstantin: If you disconnect the term "hardcore" from the whole punk-thing and consider what you said about it before: that it stands for people who just express themselves with a strong dedication they have in their heart, then it seems as if it could be quite accurate to call what you are doing hardcore.

Ms. Bob: Yes. It involves doing things that you love and not only doing it for the money.

Konstantin: Exactly. Maybe we can finish at this point. Thank you so much for taking the time.

Robert: Yeah, thank you very much!

Ms. Bob: I'm very happy to have helped. I know what it's like to do research.

References

Belsito, Peter and Bob Davis. *Hardcore California – A History of Punk and New Wave* [8th printing]. The Last Gasp of San Francisco, 2004.

Belsito, Peter, Davis, Bob and Marian Kester. *Street Art: The Punk Poster in San Francisco 1977-1981*. Last Gasp of San Francisco, 1981.

Lefebvre, Sam. "Bay of Punks: Remembering when Punk Rock Invaded San Francisco." *The Guardian* 23 Feb. 2017, theguardian.com/music/2017/feb/23/punk-rock-san-francisco-jim-jocoy-order-of-appearance. Accessed 19 May 2022.

Writing *from* Hardcore: Interwoven Lines of Becoming

Alain Müller and Marion Schulze

Hardcore is resolutely constructed. It is built piece by piece, word by word. It is the result—a fragile, provisional result—of a collective activity involving multiple "networks of cooperation" between a large variety of actors and operators that span well beyond the hardcore world (Becker, *Art Worlds*). It literally takes the entire world to construct hardcore as *a* world. This observation, however, is in strong tension with a narrative that not only traverses the world of hardcore but also holds it together, namely its remoteness from and its rejection of *the* world. Such a narrative has been well captured by the hardcore band Hatebreed: "In a world full of enemies, I'm an enemy of the world" ("Burial for the Living"). This means that, among the plurality of activities that underlie the making and the stabilizing of hardcore's fragile existence as a world, one set of activities, a crucial one, consists in cutting hardcore's existence from the rest of the world, i.e. in actively and continuously tracing its boundaries.

These are the main conclusions of our ethnographic research *on* hardcore, in which we described, constructed, and analyzed hardcore as a rhizomic network and thereof attempted to develop a socio-anthropology *of* hardcore (cf. Schulze; Müller, *Construire*; Müller and Schulze). To conduct our research successfully, it was fundamental for us—both having been involved in hardcore for about a decade before starting our research—to distance ourselves from hardcore as a "set of perspectives and understandings about what the world is like and how to deal with it, and a set of routine activities based on those perspectives," as Howard Becker put it (*Outsiders* 38). This meant rendering "exotic" the perspectives, understandings, and activities that were familiar to us in order to reframe hardcore as a radical alterity and construct it as an ethnographic object. In other words, it implied a great deal of decentering (*décentrement*) or bracketing (see e.g. Stewart and Mickunas). This does not mean decentering in the sense of physical distance—proximity is part and parcel of ethnographic methods. In fact, we were still *living* hardcore. It does, however, merely refer to an epistemological operation that allowed us to uncover, unfold, and untangle the many lines that weave the existence of hardcore. We could then engage in noticing, following, and tracking all of the actors and operators at play in the stabilization of hardcore as a world—both *within* and *beyond* hardcore.

Lines of Becoming

By referring to the conceptual apparatus of Gilles Deleuze and Félix Guattari, on which we rely extensively in this chapter, one could say that the main conclusion of the socio-anthropology *of* hardcore that we have developed is that hardcore is constantly *becoming* a more or less stable *assemblage*. Indeed, as Jean Hillier summarizes, the concept of *becoming* "is concerned with how something emerges and with what it can do, rather than what it is" (337). In hindsight, however, and with this definition in mind, it seems to us that our previous analysis involved insisting, almost obsessively, on the processes of the emergence of hardcore, leaving the question of what hardcore *can do* aside. In other words, after having shown that hardcore is *constructed* through ongoing, fragile and entangled achievements, a symmetric question remains: To what extent, and how exactly, is hardcore *constructing*?

This question may be too vast to elucidate in this chapter—and perhaps *at all*. We thus propose to explore an interposed question that offers heuristic potentialities to capture hardcore as a constructive force, i.e. what hardcore can do. We are *unblackboxing* a dimension that was a blind spot in our research (as product), namely the intimate relationship between hardcore and our research itself (as process), i.e. to explore how hardcore has been a constructing force in and of our academic work. Echoing music sociologist Antoine Hennion, who notes that "[he] actually feels that he has less done a sociology *of* music than written a sociology *from* music," (41, our emphasis), we examine to what extent, and through which lines of forces, hardcore has been shaping the way we frame our questions and design, conduct, and write our research. In other words, we wish to explore the possibility that we have always written *from* hardcore, rather than *on* hardcore. As our heavy use of italicized prepositions indicates, this analysis thus indirectly raises the question of the importance of prepositions. We will return to this idea.

Questioning to what extent we have written from hardcore also raises a more fundamental set of questions: What was and is the "nature" of our own attachment to hardcore? How has hardcore affected us? How has it been a line of force in our *life lines*? What has it been doing to us and made us *become*? As the wording of these questions suggests, we will address them by drawing further upon Deleuze and Guattari's conceptual framework. In their view, the world is made of lines. Lines, in this perspective, and as summarized by Ronald Bogue, are:

> Always in motion, never static [...]. [T]hey are vectors, trajectories, courses of movement and becoming, some so predictable in their journeys that they may be charted, demarcated by intersecting regular trajectories, graphed by grids of coordinated vectors, but others as erratic as the line of flight, a vital, nonorganic zigzag passing between things. (157)

Every "being" in this perspective is seen as a point, "an inflection of lines" (Deleuze 161), a fragile and impermanent point of inflection, a "becoming of forces that encounter each other and manifest themselves together," as Hillier puts it (339). Building on this ontological principle implies leaving the "obsolete figures of object and subject, the made and maker, the acted upon and the actor" behind, as proposed by Bruno Latour ("Factures/Fractures" 22). In this sense, we will not tackle the question of what hardcore has been doing to us as *subjects*. Rather, we will follow Latour's advice to adopt a "middle voice" that suspends the importance of nouns—subjects as well as objects—and focuses on webs of relationships (see also Serres and Latour 101). In this perspective, we, as "subjects," are only passage points between hardcore and academic work. Our role as subject was to ensure that the passage could happen, that is, to stay in a "pre-position," prone to taking part in a web of "relations that precede any position" (Serres and Latour 105).

In what follows and building on the above, we will hypothesize that the in-between, the *passage* between hardcore and academic work takes place on two main *planes*. First, it takes place on the plane of percepts and affects. Second, it takes place on the material and technical plane. As we will discuss, both of these planes involve materialities; all of what has been deeply *made durable* through the assemblage of bodies[1] as well as material and technical distributions and mediations (cf. Latour "Technology is Society Made Durable").

1. Hardcore Concepts, Percepts, and Affects: Ways of Noticing

> Fuck your world and fuck you too!
> *Death Threat*
>
> Fuck you, fuck you, fuck you and your system too!
> *Madball*

These two excerpts of lyrics—chosen for their representativeness of hardcore's perspectives and understandings—are traversed by and capture multiple dimensions. First, and despite their straightforwardness and apparent simplicity, both statements entail a *conceptual* dimension. Indeed, according to Deleuze and Guattari, a concept aims at grasping heterogeneity "in an absolute form" (177). Starting from this definition, we can retain that "world" and "system" are used in these lyrics (and the myriad others in the same vein) to grasp the heterogeneous whole against which hardcore stands up in its totality. Following Deleuze and Guattari's understanding—but somewhat distancing ourselves from the two authors who considered that concepts are specific to academic philosophy—hardcore is indeed populated by conceptual beings. In turn, this also explains why hardcore (and its punk origins) has been described as a form of philosophy (see e.g. O'Hara).

But besides concepts, second, these two excerpts of lyrics also capture something of a different texture: rage and anger. In other words, a "bloc of sensations, that is to say, a compound of percepts and affects" (Deleuze and Guattari 164). This is a line of thought that we would like to follow. For the two authors, percepts and affects are—in contrast to perceptions and affections that are usually feelings of a specific subject—"independent of a state of those

---

1   Here, we draw upon Eduardo Viveiros de Castro's definition of the body: "body is not a synonym for distinctive substance or fixed shape; body is in this sense an assemblage of affects or ways of being [...]. Between the formal subjectivity of souls and the substantial materiality of organisms, there is thus an intermediate plane occupied by the body as a bundle of affects and capacities" (475).

who experience them [...]," meaning that "[t]hey go beyond the strength of those who undergo them. Sensations, percepts, and affects are beings whose validity lies in themselves and *exceeds* any lived" (164, our emphasis). Such a conceptualization might assist us in understanding which forces hardcore captures and which ones fuel them. This is a necessary step in grasping which wealth of forces might likely pass from hardcore to other forms of assemblages, and in this chapter's case, to academic work.

Deleuze and Guattari go on to explain how the aim of art (and we do understand hardcore as an art form) is "to wrest the percept from perceptions of objects and the states of a perceiving subject, to wrest the affect from affections as the transition from one state to another: to extract a bloc of sensations, a pure being of sensations" (167). They add:

> Artists [...] are presenters of affects, the inventors and creators of affects. They not only create them in their work, they give them to us and make us become with them, they draw us into the compound. (175)

This definition, it seems to us, very much resonates with hardcore lyrics, and with hardcore's artistic performances in general—including aesthetics and design, as well as bodily performances. More concretely, to return to our example, it is not only about Aaron Butkus's (Death Threat's vocalist) and Freddy Cricien's (Madball's vocalist) rage and anger. Aaron and Freddy's voices and lyrics, accompanied by the musical rhythms, thrills, vibrations, and tensions, only "make perceptible the imperceptible forces that populate the world, affect us, and make us become" (Deleuze and Guattari 182). They *capture* rage and anger as pure forces that traverse and exceed hardcore in and of itself.

Approached in this perspective, hardcore is mainly about affects. Hardcore is, in fact, pure affect(s). It captures rage and anger and the frustration, deception, hate, violence, and struggles that go along with these sensations and, yes—to a certain extent—the "constantly renewed suffering" of humans as pure force (176). Listening to hardcore's lyrics and music, resonating with them, dancing along to them, then allows for *plugging into* a very specific bloc of sensations and to be traversed by these lines of forces. Interviewees told us how, even without understanding the lyrics of the first hardcore bands they had ever heard or what had unfolded at the first show they attended, the emotions of anger and rage directly resonated and vibrated with them (cf. Schulze 111f.). And this happened beyond, before, and below the sole conceptual and linguistic planes, as "newcomers" do not necessarily understand the lyrics nor identify the conceptual themes of hardcore immediately.

We are no exception. We, too, remember, while progressively *becoming hardcore*, that affections of past anger and rage were slowly finding a groove, a rhythm to follow, a force to tap into in order to express and enact themselves. Hardcore allowed us to plug into anger and rage as affects, as a wealth of forces. This was done through dancing, for example, and in catalyzing hardcore into a force to put things into action. While reading the lyrics of the bands or feeling the amount of rage, we also sensed a strength that could materialize and become actualized by *violent dancing* (how hardcore's form of dancing was called at that time) or singing along. We were learning how to use anger as a force. In Audre Lorde's words, we made a symphony of anger as we had to learn how to "orchestrate those furies so that they do not tear us apart" and hardcore resonated with us as the frame to do so (282).

The joy and passion of being able to express and share these sensations and affects with others, with a collective—friendship, in other words—was also an affect that traversed hardcore and forged our attachment to it. We profoundly felt that we were part of a world populated by like-minded, like-emotioned, like-scarred people, by affects and percepts we could resonate with, by humans and objects we could relate to and learn from, by music we could dance to; a world with an omnipresent representation of anger, rage, and violence, where we could nevertheless (or rather, because of it) live peacefully.

To this extent, once again, we do understand anger and rage—as well as the struggles and passions that go along with them—as constructing forces, *beings*, that are constantly made present and that traverse hardcore music and lyrics and, more fundamentally, hardcore souls and bodies. In hardcore's words: these sensations are more than words. Not only do they exceed individualized bodies, they are the driving force at the root of these very bodies that hardcore produces with their enthusiasm (cf. Souriau), their tensing, and their abilities to be traversed by anger. More so, these affects constitute a, if not *the*, fundamental wealth of forces in and for hardcore's existence.

In this light, and in retrospect, the epistemological maneuver of decentering that we engaged in for conducting our research was only partial. We suspended what could easily be suspended, or bracketed, in order to decenter ourselves: the conceptual, precisely because decentering is a *conceptual* operation. Even if it required effort, it is in many ways much easier to distance oneself from a conceptual view(point), from an understanding, than it is from the body as a bundle of affects, ways of being, and capacities solidified and materialized through years of becoming hardcore.

And yet—hence our hypothesis—it is precisely because the percepts and affects of hardcore were more deeply assembled in and through us as lines of forces that they also traverse and assemble our academic work. We wish to explore this line of thought in the following.

Reading Lines

First and foremost, hardcore affected our ways of reading. As for probably anyone else, some academic texts resonate with us more than others. Beyond their conceptual content, we would like to suggest that these specific texts capture percepts and affects that share proximities with those captured by and traversing hardcore. In other words, as much as hardcore resonated with us and has weaved into our life lines, it found a resonance with particular academic texts *through* us. We therefore attuned and aligned ourselves to and with texts that not only addressed similar lines of thoughts as hardcore texts and themes but also fundamentally—and this is our main point here—captured the same percepts and affects. Unsurprisingly, these texts, first and foremost, put everyday experiences at center stage as much as hardcore prides itself on telling stories through its lyrics that are rooted in the everyday. More than that, these texts usually focus on previously "almost unknown or unrecorded things," on "small things," and show that these small things are "not small after all" and, as Virginia Woolf put it elegantly in *A Room of One's Own*, "made one wonder what need there had been to bury them" (92). Usually, these texts are, to put it differently, traversed by an attention to "study the unstudied" as Leigh Star paraphrases Anselm Strauss (379); a way of doing research that opens "a more ecological understanding of workplaces, materiality, and interaction and underpinned a social justice agenda by valorizing previously neglected people and things," as Star continues. It is precisely this research,[2] made evident in the lines by Star—that often but not always captures different declinations of anger driven by different forms of injustice, as a main affect, and are animated by a passion and force to write against it. This outlines the ways in which anger can be used as a force to at least make sense of the world and, at best, attempt to change it. In other words, a percept driven by an affect—anger that makes us attentive to see the unseen, hear the

---

2   Without pinpointing specific books (as this is not our discussion), this argument stands here abrasively for literature in the social sciences and more precisely in anthropology, qualitative sociology, and gender studies.

unheard, notice the unnoticed—and simultaneously an affect driven by a percept—anger sparked by seeing the unseen, listening to the unheard. In short, this involves making sense of the world from the everyday and bringing the so-called margins to center stage.

In sum, the bridge *between* the percepts and the affects captured by both academic and hardcore texts was the first line of flight constituting a passage between hardcore and academic research, like water making its path toward a new furrow.

Assembling Research

This passage, marked by its mediation through printed paper, also affected our work in general, specifically how we designed our research. This occurred on two main planes that continuously and recursively informed each other: the way we conducted our ethnographic research and the way we constructed our reflections with regard to existing research and literature.

This means that, initially, we had decided *as hardcore kids* to write on hardcore for our doctoral research and to define the (academic) discussion on hardcore instead of letting us and our lives be defined by (other) researchers. We did not read about our experiences or that of our friends in academic texts. This lack of translation became our main force in engaging with our research on hardcore. In fact, the few available hardcore texts made us want to set misrepresentations straight. In particular, we did not resonate with the explanation of hardcore as a form of "magic solution" for socio-structural asymmetries in an illusory and temporary way by challenging a semiotic order, as the main paradigm of so-called subcultural studies had been stating for years. Indeed, we could not subscribe to the idea that hardcore kids were solely agents captured between structures and agencies. We witnessed collectively and reflexively engaged activities (that *made* a change) embedded in the assemblage of objects, concepts, and affects. However, another argument involves the absence of women/girls (not to mention other genders) in the research on hardcore. The empirical descriptions of women that did exist depicted them as passive, subordinated, and disciplined by man-made subcultural norms and structures. We read these as unthinking albeit unjust descriptions at best, and paternalistic, androcentric, and misogynistic at worst. In this regard, we set out to write against the existing analysis on hardcore and, more generally, theoretical frameworks on subcultures to put something more livable, more encompassing in their stead (Schulze 22).

This signaled the need to keep the so-called margins at center stage in our theorizing and to develop an art of noticing and listening to the peripheries. It also implied, for instance, taking hardcore seriously in other parts of the world (and not as a mere copy of the North American original, how it was done in research at a particular moment in time). We also considered *all* people engaged in and with hardcore as equally important for its existence. In fact, this aimed to decenter and undo research from an organizational elite perspective and to turn people that were formerly described as passive into active. Those who were formerly written out of the research became visible (those at the entrance, those who watch a show, those who clean the kitchen, those who drive the vans, run record stores and labels, etc.). As much as this analytical and conceptual move involved humans, it also meant including non-humans in the analysis and, therefore, highlighting the connectedness between humans and non-humans (a sensibility that 1990s hardcore and its involvements with animal rights and ecological activism traversed). More fundamentally, our starting point refused the mere idea of a unique, dominant truth by assuming and recognizing the existence of a multiplicity of "partial truths" (Clifford). This principle resonates with the idea that "there is not one truth cast into stone," to quote Hatebreed again ("Not One Truth").

2. Hardcore Materialities and Technologies: Modes of Assembling

As outlined above, the material and technical plane constitutes another passage between hardcore and academia through the mediation of our bodies. Our hypothesis enters here. As Deleuze and Guattari notice, "technique includes many things that are individualized according to each artist and work: words and syntax in literature; not only the canvas but its preparation in painting, pigments, their mixtures, and methods of perspective; or the twelve tones of Western music, instruments, scales, and pitch" (192). Hardcore, as a lyrical, pictorial, and musical art form, and the do-it-yourself ethics and modes of production it builds onto, is very telling in this regard. Hardcore indeed enacts its own techniques, its own ways of doing and assembling words and things. Here, we would thus like to argue that hardcore's composing techniques are enacted in our academic work.

In order to discuss this dimension, we will draw upon the example of creating a fanzine, an activity that we both engaged in as part of our own involvement in hardcore.[3] Fanzine making, a complex process that we have explored in depth elsewhere (Müller "Xsans compromisX"), relies on its own set of techniques as it implies writing, printing, cutting, assembling, collaging, photocopying, and so on. In sum, the constellation of activities that mark the creation of a hardcore fanzine pertains to a *composition*, where "'composition' describes both the activity and results of composing through material assembly and writing" (Lynch 450). It also implies all the activities that precede and follow the creation and the creator themselves: before a fanzine can come into being, it requires a lot of preparatory work. For us in the late 1990s/early 2000s, this included attending shows, establishing contacts, and collecting flyers or any piece of paper that we could take home with an email address and/or telephone number and (usually) a first name written on it. This also meant writing and receiving letters from around the world filled not only with handwritten scraps of paper but also stickers, photos, and flyers of shows. It implied creating mix tapes and putting them into circulation (usually as gifts to friends) and discovering new music. It meant talking to other people involved and sensing if they would want to contribute by writing an essay, making a collage, or drawing an art piece. We got hold of a recorder for interviews that we transcribed. This also implied inviting friends to fold the hundreds of pieces of A3 paper that we just had printed to be able to assemble our fanzines and, of course, the fingertip stings due to stapling gone wrong. Making a fanzine, then, implies engaging in a composition that exceeds the simple crafting of an object.

It is precisely these technical know-hows—and more broadly these ways of being-in-the-world—that have been reenacted in our academic work. This is because writing a dissertation or any other academic text or presentation pertains to a work of composition. More fundamentally, making a fanzine trains you to be part of an ongoing assemblage, including how to learn the specific arts of noticing and the importance and agency of objects and other non-human entities in these networks (cf. Schulze; Müller and Riom). Finally, and to tie back to the plane of affects and percepts, learning what it means to assemble—and more generally to be part of an ongoing assemblage—also made theories that put forward the idea of assemblages resonate with and

---

3   We consider this practice as highly representative of "hardcore techniques." But parallel activities such as writing lyrics, designing records, flyers, and posters for hardcore shows and writing a blog on hardcore could also be taken as examples to draw similar conclusions.

through us. For us, they were not mere concepts. They were tied to affects, percepts, and their experiences. In other words, concepts, on the one hand, and percepts and affects on the other, were "pass[ing] into one another, in either direction" (Deleuze and Guattari 177). It is therefore of no surprise that Deleuzian concepts, Actor-Network Theory, and, more generally, verb- and preposition-based theories appeal(ed) to us and became key for our analysis in this chapter, as well as our overall academic work. Why not *reassembling the social*—to paraphrase Latour—after having patiently assembled fanzines, flyers, and lyrics and after having enacted and brought to life networks as a daily practice for more than half our lives?

Final Words: Hardcore Ontologies

In the above we have somewhat artificially distinguished the plane of affects and percepts and the one of materiality. The conclusion of the second part, however, broke up this artificial separation because, as we have shown, the do-it-yourself techniques of material composition capture their own affects and percepts. They become a creative and constructing force that traverses artwork, to echo Deleuze and Guattari as they state that "the plane of the material ascends irresistibly and invades the plane of composition of the sensations themselves to the point of being part of them or indiscernible from them" (166).

By merging the plane of percepts and affects, plus the one of the material, we would like to conclude that hardcore designs and assembles its own modes of relations and attachments between humans and non-humans, i.e. its own modes of partnering and engaging with things of all sorts—from concepts, percepts, and affects to microphones, t-shirts, guitars, stages, stickers, buttons, printers, and copy machines (Müller "Xsans compromisX"; Müller "Modes de déploiement"; Schulze). In other words, hardcore enacts its own *ontologies*. And it is precisely these hardcore ontologies that pass(ed) from hardcore into our academic work, because, as noted by Jensen, "the writing of ethnography entails a rearrangement of elements from many sources, which not conforming to either 'theory' or 'data' always has an experimental and performative dimension" (537).

As mentioned in our introduction, the aim of this chapter was to sketch partial, provisional, and fragmented answers to the question of what hardcore, as an assemblage, *can do*. In retrospect, and as a way of concluding, we would like to note that our text itself is an assemblage, a composition of fragmented ideas and thus mirrors fanzines in their form, in which snippets and ideas here and there are coherent because they are stapled together and have a typical black & white, bold letter, and coarse, granular design as a graphical glue. This illustrates and reflects the very demonstration that we have attempted to make in this article: We have, indeed, been writing *from* hardcore.

References

Becker, Howard S. *Art Worlds*. University of California Press, 1982.

Becker, Howard S. *Outsiders*. Free Press, 1963.

Bogue, Ronald. *Deleuze on Literature*. Routledge, 2003.

Castro, Eduardo Batalha Viveiros de. "Exchanging Perspectives: The Transformation of Objects into Subjects in Amerindian Ontologies." *Common Knowledge*, vol. 10, no. 3, 2004, pp. 463–84.

Clifford, James. "Introduction: Partial Truths." *Writing Culture: The Poetics and Politics of Ethnography*, edited by James Clifford and George E. Marcus, University of California Press, 1986, pp. 1–26.

Death Threat. "Outcast." *Peace & Security*. Triple Crown, 2000.

Deleuze, Gilles. *Negotiations 1972–1990*. Columbia University Press, 1995.

Deleuze, Gilles, and Félix Guattari. *What is Philosophy?* Columbia University Press, 1996.

Hatebreed. "Burial for the Living." *Satisfaction is the Death Of Desire*. Victory Records, 1997.

Hatebreed. "Not One Truth." *Satisfaction is the Death Of Desire*. Victory Records, 1997.

Hennion, Antoine. "Objects, Belief, and the Sociologist: The Sociology of Art as a Work-To-Be-Done." *Roads to Music Sociology. Musik und Gesellschaft*, edited by Alfred Smudits, Springer, 2019, pp. 41–60.

Hillier, Jean. "Lines of becoming." *The Routledge Handbook of Planning Theory*, edited by Michael Gunder, Ali Madanipour, Vanessa Watson, Routledge, 2019, pp. 337–50.

Jensen, Casper Bruun. "New Ontologies? Reflections on Some Recent 'Turns' in STS, Anthropology and Philosophy." *Social Anthropology*, vol. 25, no. 4, 2017, pp. 525–45.

Latour, Bruno. "Factures/Fractures: From the Concept of Network to the Concept of Attachment." *RES: Anthropology and Aesthetics*, vol. 36, 1999, pp. 20–31.

Latour, Bruno. "Technology is Society Made Durable." *The Sociological Review*, vol. 38, no. 1, 1990, pp. 103–31.

Lorde, Audre. "The Uses of Anger." *Women's Studies Quarterly* 25, Vol. 1–2, 1997, pp. 278–85.

Lynch, Michael. "Ontography: Investigating the Production of Things, Deflating Ontology." *Social Studies of Science*, vol. 43, no. 3, 2013, pp. 444–62.

Madball. "Lockdown." *Set it Off*. Roadrunner Records, 1994.

Müller, Alain. *Construire le monde du hardcore*. Seismo, 2019.

Müller, Alain. "Modes de déploiement du parler politique dans le monde du *hardcore punk*." *Études de communication*, vol. 1, no. 54, 2020, pp. 157–78.

Müller, Alain. "Xsans compromisX: autoethnographie rétrospective de la création d'un fanzine hardcore punk en Suisse romande à l'aube du 21ème siècle." *Pop. Der Soundtrack der Zeitgeschichte, traverse: Zeitschrift für Geschichte · Revue d'histoire*, no. 2, edited by Erich Keller, Jan-Friedrich Missfelder, Gianenrico Bernasconi, Christian Koller, 2019, pp. 105–17.

Müller, Alain, and Loïc Riom. "À la poursuite des objets prescripteurs: modes de circulation de la musique dans les mondes du hardcore punk et de l'indie rock." *La prescription culturelle en question, Territoires contemporains*, edited by François Ribac, no. 1, 2019, tristan.u-bourgogne.fr/CGC/publications/prescription-culturelle-question/Alain-Muller-Loic-Riom.html. Accessed 24 May 2022.

Müller, Alain, and Marion Schulze. "Le Hardcore (punk) entre distribution quasi globale et géohistoire localisée et localisante : à propos d'une tension instituante" *Circulations musicales transatlantiques au XXe siècle*, edited by Philippe Poirrier and Lucas Le Texier, EUD, 2021, pp. 263–79.

O'Hara, Craig. *The Philosophy of Punk*. AK Press, 1999.

Schulze, Marion. *Hardcore & Gender. Soziologische Einblicke in eine globale Subkultur*. transcript, 2015.

Serres, Michel, and Bruno Latour. *Conversations on Science, Culture, and Time*. University of Michigan Press, 1995.

Souriau, Etienne. *Le sens artistique des animaux*. Hachette, 1965.

Star, Susan Leigh. "The Ethnography of Infrastructure." *American Behavioral Scientist*, vol. 43, no. 3, Nov. 1999, pp. 377–91.

Stewart, David, and Algis Mickunas. *Exploring Phenomenology: Guide to Field & its Literature*. Ohio University Press, 1990.

Woolf, Virginia. *A Room of One's Own*. 1928. Penguin Classics, 2000.

White Punks in the Chocolate City: Hardcore and Local History in Washington, DC

Alan Parkes

With exasperation over blaring distorted guitars and an up-tempo drumbeat, Ian MacKaye shouts, "I'm sorry/for something that I didn't do/I lynched somebody/but I don't know who/You blame me for slavery/A hundred years before I was born/[I'm] Guilty of being white" in a song that lasts just over a minute (Minor Threat, "Guilty of Being White"). When asked what the lyrics meant and whether they might be misconstrued, MacKaye offered an unreflective response: "Not at all, I don't think. But I'll explain it. I live in Washington D.C., which is 75% black ... I've been brought up in this whole thing where the white man was shit [but] whatever happened a hundred years ago, I am not responsible for" (MacKaye, "Rap Session" 53). He penned the words to his band Minor Threat's song "Guilty of Being White" in 1981 as a response to his experiences at Woodrow Wilson High School in Northwest DC. As a white student at a majority black school with a history of racial tension, MacKaye felt like the target of bullying.[1] He understood the political nature of his declarations, but, according to him, "it didn't occur to me at the time that I wrote it that anybody outside of my twenty or thirty friends who I was singing to would ever have to actually ponder the lyrics or even consider them" (qtd. in Azerrad 141). MacKaye faced criticism from hardcore scene members outside of DC, but he seemed unphased, recognizing that his lyrics represented a reality unique to his life in the nation's capital, highlighting racial anxiety in DC and the sectoral nature of punk.

While many writers have explored the significance of DC hardcore, few have worked to grasp a local history that led to MacKaye penning "Guilty of

---

1   According to the school newspaper, by 1980, whites made up 17% of Wilson High's student body (Childers 48). MacKaye states that about 80% of the students were black.

Being White."[2] Forty years since the release of the song, racial tension continues to plague US cities, including DC. The significance of locality prompts exploring the history of cities out of which hardcore grew. In DC, hardcore provides a telling vantage point for understanding tensions surrounding race in 1981, but it also implores understanding the forty years—and perhaps much longer—before hardcore originated. No one can appreciate DC hardcore without considering Washington DC beyond the hardcore scene, and, as Harry Jaffe and Tom Sherwood argue, "[n]o one can understand Washington without appreciating the debilitating impact of federal control that has been at various times patronizing, neglectful, and racist" (7). Taking account of youth culture in late-twentieth-century DC necessitates considering not only the uprising of 1968 and its aftermath; it requires understanding systemic inequities, efforts to overcome them, and the anxieties that remained among liberal whites who lived in the city and may have shared the frustration broadcasted by MacKaye. As DC hardcore reveals, the history of hardcore stands to expose not just the significance of the subculture to its members, but the histories and deep-seated political and social realities which influenced them. Assessing hardcore in a local and historical context propels our understanding of the subculture, the contexts out of which it grew, and how, as it moves forward, it can overcome pitfalls of its past.

DC Politics and History

Washington, DC has faced seemingly perpetual contestation between local interests and the interests of those beyond its border. In accordance with the Constitution, the federal government has held sole governing authority of the city, and at times, Congress's closefisted, if not negligent, relationship revealed an indifference to the interests of its population. The relationship between the federal government and DC's local population in the middle of

---

2   Shayna Maskell's *Politics as Sound: The Washington, DC, Hardcore Scene, 1978-1983* (University of Illinois Press, 2021) offers a more comprehensive assessment of hardcore punk from the late 1970s and early 1980s than this essay. Maskell offers an overview of a larger history of DC beyond hardcore as well. This essay parts from Maskell in an attempt to connect DC hardcore at the start of the 1980s to inveterate local policy implications and a dominant conservative discourse signified by individualism that influenced hardcore.

the twentieth century signified national disquietude. Black Washingtonians began outnumbering whites at the end of the 1950s, and by the end of the 1960s, the tension between Washington as home to over 600,000 residents and its place as the seat of government came to a head (Feinberg B1). Unrest of the 1960s that culminated in the city's uprising of 1968 most starkly placed DC at odds with the interests of white conservatives who had long held sway in the capital.[3]

During the midcentury, the seeming antipathy toward DC's majority black population symbolized racial anxieties throughout the country. In 1963, *Washington Evening Star* editor Haynes Johnson opined that "what happens in the capital affects Negroes everywhere" and could not "be dismissed as of only local interest" (qtd. in Walker 6). The reason, he argued, was that "Washington is the crucible of our democratic system," and "if democracy fails in Washington, it will fail in all of our cities" (ibid.). Black collective action in response to history of black suppression, propelled collective responses to improving representation in the district. Still, in the face of prominent opponents and codified inequities, identifying the best way to promote the interests of the black community challenged black Washingtonians. Post-World War II civil rights efforts often centered on issues that could garner popular support and white alliances such as youth recreation and public accommodations, at the cost of challenging economic inequities that might stir allegations of communism. By the mid-1960s, the "March on Washington for Jobs and Freedom" had marked a high point for the promise of civil rights, but persisting challenges plagued black communities throughout the US, and DC symbolized a unique reality as a majority black city and the nation's capital. In 1967, President Lyndon Johnson appointed Walter Washington the District's first mayor. A black Howard University graduate who became chairman of the New York

---

3   This paper only offers a cursory glimpse of race and systemic racism in post-World War II Washington DC. The use of "conservative" demarcates political figures who actively attempted to limit home rule in DC, often as members of Congress, and oversaw policy in DC as members of the Senate and House of Representatives Committees on the District of Columbia. White liberals in many cases, and, as argued here, hardcore, unwittingly adopted discourses with parallels to conservatives and thus fell short of promoting improved conditions and home rule for black Washingtonians. For a more thorough analysis, see Chris Myers Asch and George Derek Musgrove's *Chocolate City: A History of Race and Democracy in the Nation's Capital*.

City Housing Authority, Washington appeared to offer experience and understanding of the needs of Washingtonians. He thought of his position as a "challenge to make [his work as mayor of DC] a showcase and model for the nation," but Congress still held most of the power in the District (Asher A16). Segregationist congressmen maintained a lasting distain for self-government in DC when it meant empowering a majority black population (Green A1). Supporters of federal government control in DC claimed that the city became "inundated with poorly educated people who are ill-prepared for electing responsible city officials" and who fail to understand "citizen's responsibilities," representing black Washingtonians as both a problem and undeserving of self-rule and purported fruits of individual responsibility that conservatives cherished ("Rep. McMillan Makes Complaint" B3). In response, black activists faced the challenge of straddling the line between "civil rights" and "black power" (Asch and Musgrove 343). Unfortunately, Mayor Washington "was not a visionary, civil rights crusader, nor a power broker," as Toni-Michelle C. Travis writes (57). While he saw himself as a champion of the District's black population, Washington understood that advocating for home rule could impel reactionaries to undercut steps already taken in that direction and threaten the city's budget. Washington successfully marked a transition to increased home rule in DC, but the city continued to suffer from engrained economic and racial strife.

The turmoil of 1968 affirmed the mayor's calm leadership and authority over DC police, but it also proved that his limited power and efforts to ensure the representation of black Washingtonians in government had not gone far enough. Before the 1968 uprising, DC police and Washington's black communities clashed often, and police as well as city officials offered little by way of responding to the concerns of Washingtonians who complained of police misconduct and brutality. In the wake of uprisings throughout the US, the local government and police forces in DC began anticipating similar events in the city. The Kerner Report on civil disorder, created by a Presidential Commission under President Johnson in 1967 revealed causes of uprisings that divulged the failures of national and local governments to address the needs of black communities:

> Pervasive discrimination and segregation in employment, education, and housing ... have resulted in the continuing exclusion of great numbers of Negroes from the benefits of economic progress [and created] black ghettos, where segregation and poverty converge on the young to destroy oppor-

tunity and enforce failure [while] a climate that tends toward approval and encouragement of violence as a form of protest has been created by white terrorism directed against nonviolent protest" ("Report of the National Advisory Commission On Civil Disorders")

DC's uprising of 1968 thus came as a not wholly surprising response to economic inequities and racial oppression, but of cities that saw uprisings in the wake of Martin Luther King Jr.'s death in 1968, including Baltimore, Chicago, and Kansas City, DC suffered the greatest costs to life. While initially reported at 10 deaths, the toll eventually rose to 13 after bodies were discovered in the wreckage of destroyed buildings. Police fire caused the death of two people. After 7,640 arrests, 1,201 recorded injuries and 15,530 troops from both the Army and National Guard being deployed to Washington, the uprising signaled a high-water mark of tension between Washingtonians and the city's police (Walker 98).

Amid recovery, Washingtonians continued pushing for home rule through collective action. While the Twenty-Third Amendment, ratified in 1961, granted Washington residents the right to vote in presidential elections, the District of Columbia Voting Rights Amendment, proposed by Congress in 1978, again thrust the question of representation for DC within the national government into state legislatures. It aimed to codify the district's full representation in Congress, but race continued clouding the question of representation in Washington, pitting black activism in the District against white liberalism and rising national conservatism. Massachusetts Senator Ted Kennedy ventured a fair guess as to why states failed to ratify the Amendment: they feared DC senators might be "too liberal, too urban, too black or too Democrat" (qtd. in Modan 43). But the issue was not only with conservatives. "The problem is the Tarzan mentality of white liberals in Washington," a black staffer for DC delegate to the US House Representative Walter Fauntroy told *The Washington Post*. "The whites are swinging on the vine through the jungle to save all the n*****s. But they don't expect a Muzorewa to stand up and say the n*****s can save themselves. They can't handle an independent black man" (Williams C7).[4] The failure to ratify an amendment that would further enfranchise black voters appeared in line with efforts to combat still looming fears of civil rights agitation.

---

4   Abel Tendekayi Muzorewa was an African nationalist leader and prime minister of Zimbabwe Rhodesia during its transition to black rule.

Largely defined by the federal government's antipathy toward DC's growing black population and the efforts of many black Washingtonians to achieve
home rule, the mid-twentieth century stands as a necessary starting point
for understanding DC youth culture in the late twentieth century. At odds
with segregationists who held sway in DC politics, many black Washingtonians championed home rule as necessary for ensuring a government that
defended their interests. Walter Washington's leadership presented a move
toward home rule, but it failed to go far enough. In 1978, however, Washingtonians elected former civil rights activist Marion Barry as the second black
mayor of Washington, DC. Barry, Asch and Musgrove write, "embraced black
power rhetoric even as [he] sought to work within the system to effect change"
(343). With activist credentials in DC, a familiarity with the local government,
as a DC Council member, as well as a willingness to work with white businessmen, Barry rallied broad support that ensured his win. Despite some misgiv-
ings about Barry's efforts to garner white votes, his win signaled the hope of
DC's black community in the midst of uncertainty, marked by civil unrest,
rising crime rates, and a middle-class exodus from the city.

Go-Go Subculture and Shared Black Values

As black politicians symbolized a hope for a new era of black representation
in the halls of power, musicians in the city likewise sought spaces to represent
cultural black interests.[5] From the 1980s onward, like hardcore, go-go music
serves to provide an understanding of the significance of culture in relation
to economic and political systems of power in DC.[6] Most significantly, go-go

---

5   While the District maintains a long history of musical innovation led by black musi-
     cians, it remains often overshadowed by other hubs of musical and cultural tastemak-
     ing. In DC music history, Duke Ellington's jazz and Marvin Gaye, who reached Motown
     stardom, stand out. More recently, New York hip-hop icon Sean Combs might deserve
     mention for his brief stint as a Howard University student. These artists, however, high-
     light a history of musical transience in DC. Writing for The New York Times, Robert
     Palmer noted that "In the 60's when Detroit, Chicago, Memphis and New Orleans were
     regional centers with their own distinctive brands of soul music, and performers from
     near and far flocked to New York and Los Angeles to take advantage of their cosmopoli-
     tan recording and club scenes, Washington was left behind" (25).

6   Roger Gastman's exhibit Pump Me Up – DC Subculture of the 1980s (23 February – 7
     April 2013 at the Corcoran Gallery of Art) along with a book of the same title is the first

scene members constructed a community in response to DC's political climate as well as a history of black suppression in the US. Kip Lornell and Charles Stephenson write, "if you don't appreciate [go-go] then you aren't black. But race is only part of it. You have to be from the city or P.G. County in order to represent for the music" (110–11). Go-go music existed largely out of sight of the white population, and even whites who might have heard go-go music or attended a go-go performance may not have been fully in-tune with the scene, as a scene that subverted white hegemony through autonomous black community formation in DC. Natalie Hopkinson reveals that through go-go's "dance and song, black actors maintained a sacred public ritual space that helped them exorcise the demons of the past, demons that cannot be separated from a troubled history of cities and race in the United States" (28). In the 1970s and 1980s, go-go, like hardcore, provided a way for young Washingtonians to navigate the world around them. Unlike hardcore, however, go-go more aptly represented DC's majority black population and the immediate political realities of the city that impelled black youths' forming communities that maintained illegibility from dominant cultural norms. Go-go centered on a black vernacular that retained cultural power. The music signified shared black values and a way to express them in spite of a history of subjugation (cf. Neal). Shared interests grew in part from a much longer history, as Hopkinson makes clear by weaving together descriptions of go-go and the cross-Atlantic interchange between West Africa and the black diaspora that takes into account centuries of exploitation.

The music inspired an organic sense of community through an impromptu polyrhythmic style best illustrated by live performances. With the beat of the bass drum pulsing as the music's heart, go-go incorporates timbales, congas, and roto-toms over driving bass and guitars. In 1985, employing words that could also describe hardcore, Richard Harrington noted in *The Washington Post*, "the music is rough and raw, pure beat incessant ... It is the live performance that defined go-go and denotes its champions" (G1). As Trouble Funk vocalists Robert Reed put it, "Go Go in its rawest form is very, very unstructured. Now we play what we call concert-style Go Go ... a non-stop continuous kind of music" (qtd. in Harrington G1). Dependence on crowd involvement helped create a performance that was never exactly the

---

attempt exploring both go-go and hardcore punk without a central focus on just one (cf. Gastman).

same. By diminishing the bounds between bands and the audiences, crowds became a part of go-go performances and reinforced community. Go-go bands often engaged in so-called roll calls, in which singers announced the names of fans over the band, and they encouraged the audience to join in with them through call-and-response. Like hardcore, go-go further inspired its own styles of dance, including the happy feet and the wop (Rogers 1). With audience participation central to go-go performances, black audiences upheld their role in ensuring that musicians remained responsive to black community interests (Neal 34). Accordingly, localization of black vernacular represented by go-go signified the contentious conditions of the capital as both the seat of government and a majority black city.

In the last half of the decade, officials' negligence and declension that marred sites of black economic and cultural significance helped mark Washington as the "Murder Capital," but go-go continued to sustain community ("Washington Remained U.S. Murder Capital" A6). The post-industrial socioeconomic conditions of 1980s DC propelled a violent drug market, revealing, as Hopkinson notes, the ruthlessness and bloodiness of the capitalist system in the US (149). At the same time, major-label efforts fell short in their attempt to commodify the DC sound to which bands such as Trouble Funk adhered. Nonetheless, go-go retained its close association with the lived black experiences of Washingtonians. As Gregory "Sugar Bear" Elliot of the go-go band Experience Unlimited put it, "a lot of groups go to Los Angeles or New York, but we're going to stay in D.C. and feed from our people their needs, desires, feelings, anxieties, because that's our lifestyle" (qtd. in Swenson 11). According to Dice, a member of the go-go scene, "[go-go is] more music of the struggle. It's more the gutter sound. In most of the neighborhoods, everybody's poor. Everybody's struggle. Go-go doesn't go mainstream. It's for the people of the D.C. area" (qtd. in Hopkinson 36). Go-go represented life in the city for many black Washingtonians and, in doing so, necessarily signified a response to decades of neglect by white leaders and power brokers in the capital.

As go-go fans gathered at venues and solidified a community centered on black music and culture, at its inception, hardcore punk offered a largely white alternative to community formation in the District. DC's past largely stood outside the prevue of many young white hardcore punks, but the subculture could not escape the capital's history. Unlike go-go, hardcore spawned scenes throughout the US, but the localized nature of the subculture resulted in distinct sound profiles and attitudes. Minor Threat's "Guilty of Being White" highlights an explicit example of the historical context that influenced subcultural formation, but DC hardcore reveals perspicuous manifestations of white conservative—as well as liberal—idealism as well. While hardcore members sought forming a community, it remained detached from the experiences of the city's black population, resulting in a seemingly nebulous position between the popularly purported leftism of punk and the white hegemony that marred DC policymaking and national political discourse. As many hardcore punks declared an apolitical stance, emphasizing personal experiences rather than political views, the subcultural sometimes assumed normative attitudes of the 1980s. The history of racial division in the city and in youth cultures underscores members' inability to escape political realities and discourses in the political capital.

HarDCore and Straight Edge in DC

Hardcore bands created their own record labels or released music on labels formed by members of the hardcore scene with less interest in marketability than fostering a DIY subculture (O'Connor). Ryan Moore argues that hardcore's emphasis on members' 'doing it themselves' "involved a quest for authenticity and independence from the culture industry, thus altogether renouncing the prevailing culture of media, image, and hypercommercialism" ("Postmodernism" 307). Similarly, Timothy Cuffman writes that hardcore's emphasis on DIY offered "the radical possibility of reconfiguring a space outside of commercial exchanges" (5). An ideal of purity, unspoiled by marketability, demarcated hardcore punk, represented by artistic control and freedom, untainted by music industry norms and embedded in the subculture's DIY ethos. MacKaye and fellow The Teen Idles' bandmate Jeff Nelson recognized the significance of documenting the hardcore scene through recording and releasing the records of local bands almost exclusively through their Dischord Records label. Dischord was "more interested in documenting the local scene than in promoting it," Mark Jenkins wrote in The Washington Post, and MacKaye and Nelson's refusal to put out music from bands outside the District exemplified that impulse (Jenkins C7). They also anticipated groups breaking up, which limited the potential for bands to reach an audience beyond the DC area. As MacKaye put it, "in D.C. right at the point when people start hearing about your band or you put out a record, the band breaks up" ("D.C./H.C."). In a scene in which bandmembers were often recycled, that "[kept] it really underground, lots of new bands" (ibid.).

While both DIY ethos and straight edge denoted independence in DC hardcore, straight edge maintained a particular potent role in signifying individualism in hardcore punk. Born the year Ronald Reagan became president in the same city, straight edge signaled a relationship between subcultural purity and individual responsibility that drew parallels to the Reagan era. Historian Kevin Mattson contends straight edge "echoed a long-standing critique of alcohol and drug abuse among predominantly leftist authors," citing Upton Sinclair, Jack London, and Aldous Huxley (33). In that way, straight edge seemed to represent a response to "the extreme ways in which massive consumerism is institutionalized in this culture. The goal of life is felt to be the satisfaction of desires by consuming something," according to San Francisco-based zine *Creep* in 1981 (qtd. in Mattson 34). However, Minor Threat quickly discounted a relationship between straight edge and leftist politics. In fact, the band sought downplaying ties to political ideology. As MacKaye put it in a 1982 edition of *Flipside*, "No D.C. bands are overtly political at all" ("Minor Threat"). The band expressed a degree of frustration with politics in hardcore: "I'm becoming immune to the 'Reagan sucks'/ 'WWIII' thing too, unfortunately," said guitarist Lyle Preslar (ibid.). The implicit politics of early straight edge thus found a connection to reactionary conservatism. A tenet of the era's rising conservatism, individualism stood at the heart of straight edge. According to MacKaye, "If people would start with themselves, to make themselves better then that's the step in the right direction" (ibid.). Straight edge furthered the creed of individualism: "I see people as people… [straight edge] was always, in my mind, celebration of an individual's right to choose his or her life" (Kirchmer and Pierschel). Nonetheless, like after writing "Guilty of Being White," MacKaye failed to foresee the influence of straight edge when he wrote the song of the same name and inadvertently sparked a movement which soon became a global underground phenomenon.

Straight edge quickly became associated with DC hardcore and aligned with an air of puritanism that outsiders attributed to the capital's scene. Minor Threat's lyrics express the sentiment. In "Out of Step," MacKaye shouts, "don't smoke/don't drink/don't fuck." MacKaye emphasized that his lyrics should not be interpreted as mandates and that he left out "I" before each line only to better fit the lyrics to the music, but the lyrics implied a directive. As Maskell notes, "the implication was that such behavior was obligatory" (166). Alternatively, in "Straight Edge," MacKaye declares, "I'm a person just like you/but I've got better things to do/than sit around and smoke dope/'cause I know I can cope." With the personal more clearly articulated lyrically,

MacKaye frames a distinction between himself and what he thought of as the outside world or outside communities while identifying with the value of individualism. Nonetheless he unwittingly created something of a movement within hardcore that became defined by abstinence as a form of purity, unadulterated by outsiders and their addictions. Maskell and Ross Haenfler show how straight edge became a social movement dependent on bounds set by the tenets established by Minor Threat. Maskell writes that in straight edge, "the 'I' became 'we,' the basis of collective identity," and it "gained a political value in [straight edge members'] ability to frustrate and provoke the expectations of most society" (177). Yet, straight edge adherents continued to embrace a discourse centered on personal over collective interests that, if not a signifier dominated by the conservative discourse of the era, hindered straight edge's collective force (Haenfler).[7]

Hardcore and Go-Go: Distinction and Connection

With an air of pride, MacKaye identified with a browbeaten and menacing, yet upstanding, form of punk that hardcore purportedly epitomized: "We're honest as shit, we never steal, we fucking go to the store, pay our money. We're poor, thank you very much ... and best of all we fucking got our heads shaved. We're like punk rockers" (qtd. in Small and Stuart).[8] The law-abiding image of punk rockers that some members of the scene hoped to establish stood at odds with perceptions of young black Washingtonians in the wake of 1968. As hardcore scene member counterparts, like other Black Washingtonians, go-go fans suffered from a history of white anxieties that propelled police persecution. Perhaps best exemplified by the murder of Cathrine Fuller in 1984, which resulted in the conviction of purported members of the Eighth and H Street

---

7   Masculinity, represented by "the traditional masculine directive of doing your own thing, being an 'inner-directed male' instead of the less manly 'other-directed' approval-seeking male," as Maskell writes, provides a basis for understanding straight edge as collective identity, one nonetheless expressed by an emphasis on individualism (163).

8   Despite ascribing a shaved head to punk style, seemingly with pride, MacKaye has stated elsewhere that his shaved head had more to do with having curly hair and, consequently, an inability to spike it. Perhaps the most well-known image associated with Minor Threat is the cover photograph of their discography album, which prominently features MacKaye's brother Alec MacKaye's shaved head (cf. Azerrad 141).

Crew, and drove the police efforts to target young go-go fans in DC. Doubt about the responsible parties persisted after the murder. According to one 19-year-old, since the murder, police "figure that now, they can nab a lot of them all at once" (Sargent 38). The case appeared to offer a basis for shaping a narrative about the violent nature of young black go-go fans: "'What the police are calling gangs is really just groups of guys who know each other and hang out together, mainly at the go-gos,'" claimed one young Washingtonian (ibid.). As increasing rates of drug use became associated with DC's black population in popular imagination, straight edge reinforced an inadvertent distinction between white and black subculture in the city. As straight edge expanded beyond DC, Mayor Barry faced attacks for allegations of drug use that were affirmed later in the decade. Moreover, as MacKaye expressed veneration for the go-go scene, he condemned property destruction and graffiti that news sources and police often associated with the black community while speaking approvingly of the DC police force ("D.C./H.C."). Tension between hardcore scene members and police flared throughout the US, but as crime signified racial anxieties, particularly in DC, declarations such as MacKaye's positioned hardcore as respectable within white society.

Still white hardcore members' semblances of working-class pride allowed them to reject their place as a part of the dominant racial majority by aligning themselves with, as Mathew Frye Jacobson states, the "downtrodden, hard-working, self-reliant, triumphant" white immigrants of previous decades (9). The association with working-class identity among hardcore fans furthered both a seemingly contradictory embrace of both community and individualism. While hardcore punks sought community, they adopted the language of, as Jacobson writes, the self-reliant. George Lipsitz describes the process of cultural internalization, in which youth cultures and subcultures "engender accommodations with prevailing power realities [...]internalizing the dominant culture's norms and values as necessary and inevitable" (16). Hardcore punks largely came from families residing in Georgetown, where the average household income was approximately triple the average of all DC ("How Household Incomes Have Changed"). The privilege of many hardcore scene members is highlighted by their involvement in the scene. For instance, photographer Cynthia Connolly began her career in DC after her mom moved the family from California to work for the Reagan administration. Aware of the punk scene in Georgetown, Connolly begged her mother to find a home there—where she took on a role as a photographer (Sonnichsen 91). Moreover, Henry Rollins recalls his DC hardcore band SOA practicing at the US Naval

Observatory, near the home of the vice president at the start of George H.W. Bush's tenure in 1981. Drummer Ivor Hanson's family lived there while his dad served as a US Navy vice admiral and Director of the Joint Staff. The choice to move to Georgetown as a consequence of a career opportunity under Ronald Reagan and chance to practice at the home of one of the nation's top military officials expose privileges that undermine explanations of hardcore as a working-class subculture (Kearney). As Maskell notes, such privileges allowed hardcore punks in DC to "explore the politics of the personal, rather than the politics of the many," despite a working-class aesthetic (89). As a subculture in which members' ostensible defiance of broader cultural norms, hardcore punk relied on the privileges and power afforded to white youths from affluent families.

Consequently, while go-go signified a communal response to centuries of subjugation, hardcore punk stood, at least in part, as a clear representation of the internalizing of white individualism that mirrored prevailing conservative discourses that existed well before the 1980s. Although the all-black Bad Brains became recognized as one of the most talented and influential early hardcore punk bands, black hardcore fans responded to hardcore punk's overwhelming whiteness by expressing dissatisfaction with a subculture that paid lip service to inclusivity while failing to create actual inclusive spaces.[9] In a scene report about hardcore in DC, one punk wrote to readers, "perhaps you have a hard time swallowing the fact that blacks can't get gigs in a town that's 75 percent black. Blacks don't own the clubs is the reason, and owners of all colors in the nice part of town ... don't want trouble, and these boys have trouble written all over them" (Jas). Bad Brains famously declared they were banned from DC, which reportedly had to do more with violence at their shows than the fact that the band members were all black and often playing in front of young white fans. MacKaye offered an explanation for why few black Washingtonians became hardcore punks: "It's not like Blacks can't be punks but they have a huge funk scene going, probably the biggest in the

---

9   The brevity with which Bad Brains is discussed in this paper is not intended to ignore their influence on DC hardcore. I recognize and appreciate that the band is more thoroughly explored in this anthology and hope to not reduce analysis of race and hardcore to the racial makeup of the scene.
     Cf. the article by Maskell in this book.

country and they have teenage bands" ("Minor Threat").[10] Young and idealistic, MacKaye challenged the problems he saw in the world that surrounded him, but "Guilty of Being White" drew on lasting anxieties extending beyond his high school. While he found reprieve in hardcore, a failure to acknowledge decades of racial inequity marked MacKaye's black peers as antagonists, and a pronounced veneration for individualism and ambiguous political ideologies lent legitimacy to systems that segregationist congressmen who held power in the district throughout much of the twentieth century aimed to uphold.

Of course, neither his peers nor MacKaye deserve blame for structural racism that opponents of home rule perpetuated. Sincere admiration for gogo proclaimed opposition to racism among hardcore members, even if they could only pose a minor threat to deep-seated inequity in DC, they should not go unrecognized. In September of 1983, Landburgh's Cultural Center in downtown Washington, DC hosted the city's first "Funk-Punk Spectacular," featuring two of the District's most influential funk and hardcore punk bands. Minor Threat offered a high energy performance complimented by the self-gibing expressionism of Ian MacKaye for the last time. The band's last song offered a reminiscent tone, pronouncing that "the core has gotten soft" (Crawford). Such a declaration seemed signified by the band's decision to cross hardcore punk bounds by opening for Trouble Funk, who by that point had achieved a level of national acclaim for songs such as "Pump Me Up" and "Drop the Bomb," which asked "Can we drop the bomb on the white boy crew?" Despite the differences between the bands and scenes they represented, MacKaye described them as both "indigenous music scenes that were really of and about Washington, DC" ("Ian MacKaye Talking"). Although unaware that the event would serve as Minor Threat's last performance, MacKaye later said that he saw it as "the perfect last gig. I felt like it was a connection with the Washington that I actually had a really deep affinity for" (ibid.). MacKaye recalls that about 1,000 to 1,500 people showed up, and while most of the audience consisted of hardcore fans, the event successfully brought together a diverse audience and blended two subcultural sounds and styles in the Chocolate City.

Ultimately, the politics and social realms with which hardcore punk engaged extended far beyond the walls of subcultural hangouts and venues,

---

10   Alternatively, Darryl Jenifer of the Bad Brains said of go-go: "'Go-go' was the music of their youth, but [we] were just straight tired of it, and found it to be not so much boring, but normal" (210).

and as DC's early hardcore scene reveals, hardcore provides a basis for understanding much more than the youth culture within a historical moment. Forty years on, racial inequities remain deep-seated, influencing youth cultures that aim to upend them, but DC hardcore maintains a legacy that has dismissed the apolitical attitudes that marked the scene in the early 1980s. Hence, hardcore should stand to impel us to do more than seek solutions to problems on an individual level. Recognizing the local histories out of which it was born, it can foster community beyond venue walls.

References

Asch, Chris Myers, and George Derek Musgrove. *Chocolate City: A History of Race and Democracy in the Nation's Capital.* University of North Carolina Press, 2017.

Asher, Robert L."Walter Washington: Back Home: Involving People." *The Washington Post,* 7 September 1967, p. A16.

Azerrad, Michael. *Our Band Could Be Your Life: Scenes from the American Indie Underground,* 1981-1991. Little Brown, 2012.

"Carl Thor Hanson Obituary." *The Washington Post,* 29 January 2008, p. B6.

Childers, Jay P. *The Evolving Citizen: American Youth and the Changing Norms of Democratic Engagement.* Penn State Press, 2012.

Crawford, Scott, director. *Salad Days: A Decade of Punk in Washington D.C., 1980-1990.* New Rose Studios, 2015.

Cuffman, Timothy. "Idle Musical Community: Dischord and Anarchic DIY Practice." *Contemporary Justice Review* 18.1, 2015, pp. 4–21.

Feinberg, Lawrence. "D.C. Population Shows First Rise Since 1963." *The Washington Post,* 20 January 1986, p. B1.

Gastman, Robert, editor. *Pump Me Up: DC Subculture of the 1980s.* R. Rock Enterprises, 2013.

Green, Stephen. "Home Rule Stall Denied by McMillan: McMillan: Home Rule Not Stalled." *The Washington Post,* 25 February 1972, p. A1.

Haenfler, Ross. *Straight Edge: Cleaning-Living Youth, Hardcore Punk, and Social Change.* Rutgers University Press, 2006.

Harrington, Richard. "D.C. Go-Go." *The Washington Post,* 19 May 1985, p. G1.

Hopkinson, Natalie. *Go-Go Live: The Life and Death of a Chocolate City.* Duke University Press, 2012.

"How Household Incomes Have Changed Since the 1980s in the D.C. Area." D.C. Policy Center. dcpolicycenter.org/publications/regional-income-trends/. Accessed 09 June 2022.

Jacobson, Matthew Frye. *Roots Too: White Ethnic Revival in Post-Civil Rights America*. Harvard University Press, 2006.

Jaffe, Harry, and Tom Sherwood. *Dream City: Race, Power, and the Decline of Washington, D.C.* Simon & Schuster, 1994.

Jas. "D.C. Scene." *Touch and Go* 5, 1979.

Jenifer, Darryl A. "Play Like a White Boy: Hard Dancing in the City of Chocolate." *White Riot: Punk Rock and the Politics of Race*, edited by Stephen Duncombe and Maxwell Tremblay, Verso, 2001, p. 207–12.

Jenkins, Mark. "Dischord: In Tune With DC's Rock." *The Washington Post*, 1 January 1987, p. C7.

Kearney, Ryan. "An Incomplete Oral History of Henry Rollins' DC Years." *WJLA*. 10 February 2011, wjla.com/news/entertainment/a-brief-oral-history-of-henry-rollins-s-brief-career-in-d-c–8387. Accessed April 3, 2020.

Kirchmer, Michael, and Marc Pierschel, directors. *Edge - Perspectives on Drug Free Culture*. Halo-8, 2009.

"LBJ Names Negro Washington 'Mayor.'" *St. Petersburg Times*, 7 September 1967, p. 1.

Lipsitz, George. *Time Passages: Collective Memory and American Popular Culture*. University of Minnesota Press, 1997.

Lornell, Kip, and Charles C. Stephenson. *The Beat!: Go-go Music from Washington*. University Press of Mississippi, 2009.

MacKaye, Ian. "D.C./H.C." *Flipside Fanzine* 29, 1981.

MacKaye, Ian. "Ian MacKaye talking about Minor Threat playing shows with Trouble Funk." *YouTube*, uploaded by PeterHutchins, 8 March 2013, youtube.com/watch?v=mZIyeRf8OPg.

MacKaye, Ian. "Rap Session." *Maximumrocknroll* 8, September 1983, pp. 50–55.

Maskell, Shayna. *Politics as Sound: The Washington, DC, Hardcore Scene, 1978-1983*. University of Illinois Press, 2021.

Mattson, Kevin. *We're Not Here to Entertain: Punk Rock, Ronald Reagan, and the Real Culture War of 1980s America*. Oxford University Press, 2020.

"Minor Threat." *Flipside Fanzine* 34, 1982.

Minor Threat. "Guilty of Being White." *In My Eyes*. Dischord Records, 1981.

Minor Threat. "Out of Step." *Out of Step*. Dischord Records, 1983.

Minor Threat. "Salad Days." *Complete Discography*. Dischord Records, 1990.

Minor Threat. "Straight Edge." *Minor Threat*. Dischord Records, 1981.

Modan, Gabriella Gahlia. *Turf Wars: Discourse, Diversity, and the Politics of Place*. Blackwell, 2007.

Moore, Ryan. "Postmodernism and Punk Subculture: Cultures of Authenticity and Deconstruction." *The Communication Review* 7.3, 2004, pp. 305–27.

Moore, Ryan. *Sells Like Teen Spirit: Music, Youth Culture, and Social Crisis*. New York University Press, 2010.

Neal, Mark Anthony. *What The Music Said: Black Popular Music and Black Public Culture*. Routledge, 2013.

O'Connor, Alan. *Punk Labels and the Struggle for Autonomy*. Lexington Books, 2008.

Palmer, Robert. "Go-Go Music Brings a Fresh Beat to Summer Dancing." *The New York Times*, 9 June 1985, p. 25.

"Rep. McMillan Makes Complaint that D.C. Press Smeared Him." *The Washington Post*, 30 August 1961, p. B3.

Report of the National Advisory Commission On Civil Disorders. United States, Kerner Commission: U.S. G.P.O., 1968.

Rogers, Charles. "Go-Go Music Seen As Next Music Crazy." *Amsterdam News*, 13 July 1985, p. 1.

Rollins, Henry. "Henry Rollins Trouble Funk 9:30 Club 30th Anniversary Birthday Washington DC May 31 2010." *YouTube*, uploaded by godieinhell2, 1 June 2010, youtube.com/watch?v=mlN4APlHas4.

Rollins, Henry. "Liner notes for Trouble Funk." *Live*. Infinite Zero Records, 1998.

Sargent, Edward. "Desolate NE Intersection Gave Name To the 'Eighth and H Street Crew.'" *The Washington Post*, 13 December 1984, p. 38.

Serviette, Nardwuar, and Henry Rollins. "Nardwuar vs. Henry Rollins (2011)." *YouTube*, uploaded by NardwuarServiette, 29 December 2011, youtube.com/watch?v=8_H4gOfourI.

Small, Adam, and Peter Stuart, directors. *Another State of Mind*. Time Bomb, 1984.

Sonnichsen, Tyler. *Capitals of Punk: DC, Paris, and Circulation in the Urban Underground*. Springer, 2019.

Swenson, John. "'Good to Go' Offers First Real Look at GoGo Music." *Afro-American (1893- 1988)*, 23 August 1986, p. 11.

Travis, Toni-Michelle C. "Walter Washington: Mayor of the Last Colony." *Democratic Destiny and the District of Columbia: Federal Politics and Public Policy*, edited by Ronald Walters and Toni-Michelle C. Travis, Lexington Books, 2010, pp. 45–61.

Trouble Funk. "Drop the Bomb." *Drop the Bomb*. Sugar Hill Records, 1982.

Walker, J. Samuel. *Most of 14th Street is gone: the Washington, DC riots of 1968*. Oxford University Press, 2018.

"Washington Remained U.S. Murder Capital in 1990." *The Washington Post*, 11 August 1991, p. A6.

Williams, Juan. "D.C. Voting Rights Stew." *The Washington Post*, 17 February 1980, p. C7.

The Musical Aesthetics of Hardcore: Straightforward, Strident, and Antagonistic

David Pearson

Hardcore is a musical style. It is many other things too: a culture, a fashion, a scene, a politics, etc. But of all the things that hardcore is, musical style has been the most neglected by academic and journalistic studies.[1] The reasons for this are basically twofold. First, musicology, the discipline that should be responsible for analyzing hardcore music, is one of the crustiest (and not in the crust-punk sense of the word) academic disciplines there is. (I have a PhD in musicology, so I can say that.) While many musicologists are now seeking to move away from a conservative emphasis on canonical Western art music repertoire, often this move is towards a canonical postmodernist theoretical repertoire that is ill-equipped to deal with musical expressions that do not fit its frameworks. In my experience, many musicologists tend to assume they know all there is to know about punk and hardcore based on a few myths about '77 punk and maybe some knowledge of indie-rock and riot grrrl bands (if I had a dollar for every time a musicologist asked me if my dissertation was about Fugazi and then gave me a funny look when I answered no...). When confronted with the existence of thriving hardcore scenes around the world for the past forty years, they tend to write it off as irrelevant (academics do this sort of thing all the time). Furthermore, musicology as a discipline has moved away from music analysis as a worthwhile endeavor in the last couple decades. (I know that sounds weird, as musicology without music just becomes -ology,

---

1   Notable exceptions are my book, *Rebel Music in the Triumphant Empire: Punk Rock in the 1990s United States*; David Easley's dissertation *"It's Not My Imagination, I've Got A Gun On My Back!": Style and Sound in Early American Hardcore Punk, 1978–1983*; and Evan Rapport's *Damaged: Musicality and Race in Early American Punk.*

but it is the truth.[2] The discipline of music theory continues to emphasize music analysis but has historically disconnected such analysis from cultural and political analysis; hopefully this is changing.)

Second, within the constellation of academics from different disciplines studying punk, there has been considerable resistance to the idea of analyzing punk music. For example, in his otherwise impressive book documenting DIY punk practices around the globe, Kevin Dunn argues that, "To define punk in musical terms is an impossible feat. Which isn't to say that people don't try. Or, more significantly, that major corporations haven't constructed a 'punk sound' that they can market" (11). The other and equally erroneous side to Dunn's rejection of the existence of a punk musical style is the idea that changes in punk musical style are made because punk bands are trying to resist co-optation. In this framework, hardcore emerged because '77 style had been commodified. Resisting co-optation might be one reason for the turn to hardcore, but only one among many. The rigid economic determinism behind the resisting-co-optation-thesis fails to account for the fact that, with a few exceptions, the mainstream music industry in the United States had largely given up on punk as a viable commercial product *before* the development of hardcore style. Moreover, the resisting-co-optation-thesis also fails to consider that many people, both in and out of bands, *enjoy* hardcore music and find in it an effective musical means to express their feelings and frustrations.

As Michelle Phillipov explained in a critique of punk scholarship:

[T]he problem is not so much one of too few close readings of individual musical texts but one of subordinating musical meanings to wider concerns about political investments. Too often music is treated as subsidiary to other institutional and ideological practices, as simply a vehicle for the expression of politics rather than something which is embedded in a variety of meanings and affects in its own right and interplays with politics in complex ways. ... The specific pleasures of snotty vocals, heavily distorted guitars, or rapid-fire, three-chord structures are simply streamlined into one-dimensional platitudes about "politics," "resistance" and "subversion." (388)

---

2   To be clear, I do not think all scholarship in musicology must have music analysis or examples using music notation, but the lack and even rejection of such methods lately is troubling, especially when they are replaced with empty jargon-heavy postmodernist "theorizing."

My point here is not to criticize punk scholars for not analyzing punk music; it is entirely up to the individual scholar what approach to take, and the more approaches the better. Rather, at issue is resistance to music analysis in punk studies. Here, it is worth asking: how differently does "punk studies" function from academia at large? Does it practice the same gatekeeping and elitism that defines academia and maintains the status quo of professorial positions and dominant ideas? Or is it (like hardcore at its best) a supportive, egalitarian community that embraces iconoclastic approaches? I would venture to say it is more the former than the latter (and, to be clear, the hardcore scene more often than not fails to live up to its ideals, but I still cherish those instances in which it succeeds).

Okay, now that I have gotten the shit talking out of the way (an important hardcore tradition, even with all the hardcore songs admonishing shit talking, such as Integrity's "No One" or No Use For A Name's "Feeding the Fire," which are, ironically, talking shit about talking shit), let me turn to the matter at hand. What is hardcore musical style? What purposes does it serve? Why does it make many of us, in the words of Martín Sorrondeguy of the hardcore band Los Crudos, "wanna fucking just start dancing and bouncing off the walls"? Why does hardcore *music* matter?

Hardcore style

The advent of hardcore in the early 1980s was an intensification of punk style in several ways. Song lengths got even shorter, often clocking in at under a minute. Vocals went from being snarled to being yelled, with considerably more timbral distortion. Guitar sounds likewise got more distorted and often emphasized the bass tones over treble (there are exceptions of course; 7 Seconds is one good example of a hardcore band whose recordings have a trebly guitar sound). Riffs got shorter, more rhythmically emphatic, and drew more frequently on minor-mode pitch material than prior punk. Whereas many late-1970s punk riffs could conceivably be thought of as short chord progressions, hardcore riffs are more decidedly and defiantly short, rhythmically accented melodic statements drenched in distortion. Late-1970s punk tempos tended to be a little under 200 beats per minute, but hardcore bands pushed the speed past what most metronomes can measure to over 300 beats per minute, sometimes pushing close to 400.

The blazing tempos of hardcore point us to the most substantial musical innovation to rock within the punk tradition. Rock beats, rooted in African American musical practices, have always been defined by a four-beat bar with heavy backbeats by the snare drum on beats two and four, with the kick drum defining beats one and three through hits on or around those beats, and a cymbal used to keep time. There are, of course, many variations on that basic pattern, including some that depart from it, but it is the basic beat we feel pulsing through our bodies when we listen to most rock songs. Hardcore does keep that basic pattern, with the kick drum on the downbeat starting an alternation with hits on the snare drum. But it speeds up the tempo so much that the kick-snare drum alternation can no longer be felt as four beats within a quadruple meter (listen to any fast hardcore song and try tapping your foot to every single "beat" in this pattern to see what I mean). Instead, the kick-snare alternation becomes a rapid blur, and the accent patterns in hardcore must be defined by other means: the arrival points of guitar riffs and the larger accent patterns on the drums, particularly cymbal crashes and kick-drum hits. For this reason, when I account for tempo in hardcore songs, I eschew "beats per minute," since the kick and snare hits are no longer beats, and instead use the measurement KSA (kick-snare alternation per minute); in transcriptions, I indicate the note value of this alternation. Though hardcore drummers often replace the kick drum with a cymbal in subsidiary metric positions within the kick-snare alternation, I like to think of it as a "felt presence" within the drum pattern. The blast beat heard in extreme hardcore genres beginning in the late 1980s takes the kick-snare blare even further by making a literal, not just felt, alternation at tempos approaching 800 KSA.

These defining musical characteristics of hardcore make it angrier, more intense, and more abrasive than earlier punk. This is in part because they condense punk musical techniques, quite literally when it comes to tempos, and thus hardcore songs get to their point in the most emphatic way possible. Hardcore is a music of direct communication unencumbered by musical excess. That does not mean it is necessarily simple, and one of the most obnoxious commonplace descriptions of punk music is that it is all just simple, three chords, no nuance. As we shall see below, it is nuances of musical expression and the creative deployment of conventions that make for a powerful hardcore song.

One way to encapsulate the aesthetic difference between hardcore and earlier punk is with the formulation *stridency over sneer*. Late 1970s punk often came dripping in bitter sarcasm and sneered at its detractors as being pathetically attached to the conventions of bourgeois society, including when it came to rock music. Hardcore, by contrast, seems to have moved beyond its detractors (quite literally by becoming a more underground cultural phenomenon), so the sneer can be de-emphasized and replaced with a strident delivery of its messages that its committed audience takes as a re-affirmation of their rejection of ... whatever it is they consider themselves to be rejecting.

When hardcore bands did use the sneer, they often appropriated musical techniques from late 1970s punk and fit them within a hardcore musical framework. A telling example is the band Charles Bronson.[3] Their vocals evoke the snarls of late 1970s punk and their riffs are often constructed with the (major-mode) pitch structures of that era, while their blazing tempos and use of blast beats put them squarely on the more extreme end of hardcore punk. A good explanation for Charles Bronson's combination of hardcore stridency and punk sneer is the fact that many of their songs are poking fun—sneering—at the hardcore scene itself.

Hardcore musical rhetoric

Let us now turn to how the musical techniques of hardcore outlined above are creatively deployed through a brief analysis of two hardcore songs and develop a beginning understanding of the musical rhetoric that articulates the messages of hardcore songs. Minor Threat's "Guilty of Being White" is one salient example of early 1980s hardcore. With a KSA of 372 and clocking in at over a minute, it exemplifies the speed and brevity of hardcore. As shown in example 1, its short verse riff moves rapidly from one power chord to the next, building in intensity by two ascending leaps of a fifth in a row, with the high point, F, given extra tension by virtue of its syncopated, anticipatory arrival.[4] Before the band begins playing, Ian MacKaye starts the song with a held-out yell on "I'm." After the full band enters, MacKaye offers short bursts

---

3   Charles Bronson was a hardcore/power violence band from the environs of Chicago, Illinois who took their name from the actor.

4   In the transcriptions in this article, I only provide the root motion of riffs. This root motion is played by bass and guitar, but the guitar plays power chords based on this root motion. Power chords consist of a root, fifth, and octave. In heavily distorted hardcore, power chords play the role of distorted timbre and thickening the texture rather than providing an underlying harmony.

of rapidly delivered syllables over the guitar riff, getting the angry words out in a seething state of exasperation.

Example 1: *Riffs from Minor Threat's "Guilty of Being White"*

The chorus of "Guilty of Being White" is a musical punktuation of the verse that precedes it, boiling down the racist lyrics into a single, six-sylla-ble refrain. At the onset of this refrain, there is a dramatic change in musical texture, with the drums departing from a constant hardcore beat and instead giving a cymbal crash followed by a rapid drum fill. Meanwhile, the vocals, guitar, and bass coalesce around the same, heavily accented rhythm to render the distillation of the song's message in a way that is most audible and em-phatic. The chorus riff starts at the high point of D, matching the exasperation of the vocals, descends down to F, and then makes a chromatic ascent that is borrowed straight from the blues tradition that laid the foundations of rock riffs,[5] landing on the functional tonic, G. The vocal line ends exactly at the arrival of the G power chord, at which point the drums return to the relent-less hardcore drum beat while the bass and guitar offer a consistent and even strumming pattern on this G, thus providing a brief moment of respite from the previous dramatic musical motion so as not to distract from gravitas of the refrain.

After another repetition of the verse and chorus, "Guilty of Being White" offers us an example of another feature of many hardcore songs: *the breakdown.* The breakdown is a section of a hardcore song in which the intensity and

---

5   I guess we can add "guilty of stealing blues licks" to the lyrics.

texture are brought down or transformed, often through a change to a slower tempo, only to be brought back to their previous levels when the breakdown ends. Breakdowns often function as a means to break the tension built up through repetitions of fast hardcore riffs and drumbeats and then build that tension back up again.

In the breakdown of "Guilty of Being White," the drums dispense with the hardcore beat and perform a drum roll that moves from snare drum to lower-pitched tom-toms, ending with crashing accents to punctuate the vocals. There is no kick-snare alternation in this breakdown, and I have notated a tempo of 180 beats per minute given the steady strumming, accents at the end of the riff, and overall rhythmic feel. The breakdown riff is in the lowest range of all the riffs on this song, reaching down to the E at the very bottom of the guitar and bass fretboards, thus dispensing, except for a brief moment at its end, with the particular tension of the verse and guitar riffs created by reaching higher up the fretboard.[6] It tonally contrasts with the verse and chorus riffs by evading the tonic, G (except for at the very end of the riff, where G's function is to lead back into the A that starts the riff), thereby creating a form of harmonic tension (as mentioned above, breakdowns do not exactly dispense with intensity, but find other means of creating tension). However, this breakdown riff diminishes the rhythmic intensity by moving from one power chord to the next far slower than the verse and chorus riffs do, and in a more straightforward rhythm that lacks any syncopated accents or arrivals. As for vocals, MacKaye delivers much sparser lyrics without the irate anger of the verses and choruses, replacing it with frustrated sarcasm. He is answered by *gang vocals*—a hardcore technique in which a group (usually of males) shouts a moment of the lyrics, usually to serve the purpose of punktuation. Gang vocals are often delivered in a very straightforward, even rhythm and heavily accented, and "Guilty of Being White" is no exception to this convention. "Guil-ty!" is shouted along with homorhythmic accents from all instruments, with the breakdown riff reaching its moment of greatest intensity here, leaping up a fifth to C and then leaping down a fourth to G for the second syllable.

Los Crudos's "That's Right, We're That Spic Band" exemplifies some of the hardcore conventions analyzed in Minor Threat's song, as well as the new musical intensities they brought to hardcore in the 1990s. For starters, the tempo of Los Crudos's song, KSA=380–392, is a bit faster than Minor Threat's song.

---

6   See Easley for an explanation of how motion up the fretboard in the hardcore riffs serves to create harmonic tension (277).

Furthermore, "That's Right..." only consists of two verses and choruses, dispensing with the need for a breakdown, and is just a bit over half a minute long. Instead of a singular yell, it starts with guitar feedback and vocalist Martín Sorrondeguy screaming the title of the song (with the insertion of "motherfucker"). The screamed vocal delivery in "That's Right..." goes beyond the yells of early 1980s hardcore in timbral distortion and dramatic intensity, and, in the verses, is delivered in relatively regular rhythmic phrasing that occupies nearly three-fourths the duration of each iteration of the verse riff. Martín's vocals in the verses are punktuated by gang vocals shouting "bullshit," interestingly in the same rhythmic place and delivery as the gang vocals in the breakdown of Minor Threat's "Guilty of Being White."

Example 2: *Riffs from Los Crudos's "That's Right, We're That Spic Band"*

The verse riff consists of four different power chords, each lasting the same duration (four KSA pulses). It offers a different kind of intensity than is heard in most early 1980s hardcore riffs by departing from diatonic modality (the use of pitches from a single diatonic scale or mode, such as the Dorian mode) by virtue of the B with which this verse riff ends. Given how accustomed we are to listening to music, including hardcore riffs, constructed from diatonic scales, Los Crudos's departures from diatonic modality create a jarring aural effect, and are one of the reasons (together with Martín's screams) their music was so consistently praised for its intensity in the pages of punk zines. (The riffs of Minor Threat's "Guilty of Being White," by contrast, are all constructed from the G Dorian mode, with the exception of the chromatic passing tone F-sharp that leads into the tonic G in the chorus riff.)

While in political meaning, the choruses of "That's Right..." and "Guilty of Being White" could not be further apart, in musical rhetoric they possess remarkable similarities. Both boil down the message given in verse lyrics to a six-syllable refrain. Both musically deliver this refrain in accented, ho-morhythmic enunciations in which vocals and instruments coalesce; in "That's Right...," Martín's voice is joined by the gang vocals heard on its verse. The cho-rus of "That's Right..." contrasts with the musical texture of its verses by virtue of the use of rapidly strummed palm-muting by the guitarist and a more em-phatic accent pattern by the band that omits accent on the beginning of the second half of the chorus riff. With just two different power chords in the chorus and with its overall brevity, "That's Right..." exemplifies the hardcore aesthetic of direct communication unencumbered by any musical excess.

I chose to analyze "Guilty of Being White" and "That's Right, We're That Spic Band" in this essay not only because they are excellent exemplars of hard-core musical style and rhetoric, but also because they deploy similar musical rhetoric and conventions to deliver antagonistically opposed political view-points. Minor Threat's song is a racist reaction by a white teenager confronted with the brutal history of white supremacy and the oppression of Black peo-ple that defines the United States and rejecting the notion that his social po-sition is a product of that long and ongoing history.[7] Los Crudos's song is a tongue-in-cheek response to the casual racism they experienced as a Latino band in the US hardcore scene; they were casually referred to as "that spic band" by white hardcore kids, whom Los Crudos in turn labeled "closet Nazis" in this song. In both songs, their messages are expressed with nothing held back, passionately and defiantly rejecting their detractors without apology. One conclusion we can draw is that while there is no inherent politics, left-ist, reactionary, or otherwise, attached to hardcore's musical rhetoric, *there is something about the way political meanings are aesthetically delivered that is universal within hardcore music.*

Take your fucking postmodernist theory and shove it up your ass

When academics write about hardcore, they make decisions about which the-ories to use to analyze it. As David Ensminger critically notes, "By 2015, punk seems like a perfect postmodern storm to many academics, for it evokes the ripe intersection of bricolage, pastiche, feminism, queer and post-colonial

---

7   In fairness to the white teenager in question, Ian MacKaye, he did change his politi-cal views over time, as is evident in the lyrics of his later band Fugazi and that band's involvement in protests against apartheid in South Africa.

theory, detournement, Situationism, and disintermediation" (x-xi).[8] Consequently, postmodernist theory is often used by academics to explain punk and hardcore. But given what has been outlined above concerning hardcore music's insistence on antagonism, it is questionable how applicable postmodernist theory is to understanding hardcore. For a central value of postmodernism is the co-existence of difference and multiple narratives (though in practice postmodernists often and ironically dismiss narratives other than their own). That is not to say there are not aspects of hardcore that could be considered "postmodern," though this term is often used so loosely as to encompass any artistic deployment of irony, juxtaposition, or appropriation no matter their aesthetic purpose and effect.

The danger is that postmodernist academics, despite all their talk of decolonizing their syllabuses, may well be, in effect, colonizing punk and hardcore with theories that conflict with punk and hardcore aesthetics in order to produce scholarship that appears innovative. The worst offenders offer up interpretations of punk and hardcore in ignorance of the actual conceptions and practices of participants in the music (which they did not bother to research), since, for the postmodernist academic, an obtuse theoretical framework is far more valuable (including literally for that tenured professor salary) than the people and cultures they are writing about. On the better end, scholars with deep connections to and/or thorough research into hardcore scenes may well be turning to the academic theory that happens to be trendy today without adequately considering how well it works to explain hardcore (and, if we are being honest, advancing one's academic career often depends on attaching oneself to whatever theoretical frameworks happen to be trendy at the moment). Oddly, for many academics, decolonizing seems to mean taking theories developed in France and elaborated in the United States and applying them to analyze social phenomena by using the most incomprehensible elitist jargon possible, rendering their analysis alien to the colonized subject both in theory and articulation. Outrageously, these days when many academics talk about decolonization, they rarely mean taking a principled stand in support of the Palestinian liberation struggle.[9]

---

8   To be clear, Ensminger has been quite critical of the ramifications of postmodernism on punk scholarship and the political commitments of academics.

9   Yes, there are important individual scholars that are, rightly or wrongly, associated with postmodernism who have taken strong stands in support of Palestinian liberation, most notably Edward Said. My point here is to call attention to how, in many

As I see it, hardcore aesthetics fly in the face (or, more accurately, stick a middle finger in the face) of the core values of postmodernist academics. For what is universal in hardcore aesthetics, no matter the particular politics of specific songs, is turning difference into irreconcilable antagonism and refusing to allow difference to co-exist. Hardcore aesthetics involve purposely seeking out sounds, words, and attitudes designed to offend those who disagree. One thing I cherish about hardcore is its honesty, for at least when hardcore bands have reactionary viewpoints, such as in the lyrics of Minor Threat's "Guilty of Being White," they are often expressed openly and can thus be sharply debated and forcefully rejected. This contrasts starkly with my experience in academia, where there is lots of talk about but much less concrete action towards diversity, equity, and inclusion, and racist and sexist attitudes are easily dressed up in politically correct language and passive-aggressive behavior.

Speaking of the postmodernist value of inclusivity, it is worth considering how the hardcore band Los Crudos went about contending with anti-immigrant racism in the United States. On patches and T-shirts, they silk-screened the words "Ilegal, y qué?" (Illegal, so what?), making clear they were not asking for acceptance by or inclusion into the American empire, but defiantly asserting themselves and appropriating and defanging the very word used to demonize immigrants. As Los Crudos and many other seminal hardcore bands demonstrate, when hardcore aesthetics were used to articulate politics of liberation, the radical nature of those politics was kept unadulterated and unconcerned with appeasing anyone who objected. Hardcore keeps it real, and that might make it tough to stomach at times, but it is that rawness that forces us to deal with its message.

To be clear, when I criticize postmodernist academic theories as ill-suited for analyzing hardcore, I am by no means suggesting that critical discussion of race, gender, and power relations more generally should not take place—just the opposite. And postmodernism is by no means the only discourse that takes up these questions—anarchism, Black nationalism, Marxism, and Pan-Africanism, for example, have all done so in their own

---

academic disciplines where postmodernism is dominant (such as musicology), there is still deafening silence when it comes to Palestine, even as (vague) talk of decolonization increases. This state of affairs likely has much to do with career concerns, as taking a stand in support of Palestinian liberation remains a political position that can tank a career in academia, as has happened to Steven Salaita and Norman Finkelstein.

ways. We should keep in mind that within hardcore and punk scenes, these questions have been addressed and people from oppressed social groups have asserted their viewpoints, often in the face of backlash, for several decades. Rather than imposing academic theories that may not fit our subject of study, we should strive to understand and learn from the way these questions have been debated within the punk and hardcore scenes, and hopefully embrace the strident attitude with which they are debated. That is not to say we should never use academic theory to analyze hardcore—I have certainly done so with the above musical analysis—but hopefully when we do, it will be in conversation with the internal discourse of the hardcore scene. For the beauty of hardcore is its stridency, which does not allow for complacency or faking it. So in that spirit, to the academics reading this: take your fucking postmodernist theory and shove it up your ass.

References

Dunn, Kevin. *Global Punk: Resistance and Rebellion in Everyday Life*. Bloomsbury Academic, 2016.

Easley, David. *"It's Not My Imagination, I've Got A Gun On My Back!": Style and Sound in Early American Hardcore Punk, 1978–1983*. PhD Diss., Florida State University, 2011.

Ensminger, David. *The Politics of Punk: Protest and Revolt from the Streets*. Bowman & Littlefield, 2016.

Pearson, David. *Rebel Music in the Triumphant Empire: Punk Rock in the 1990s United States*. Oxford University Press, 2021.

Phillipov, Michelle. "Haunted by the Spirit of '77: Punk Studies and the Persistence of Politics." *Continuum: Journal of Media and Cultural Studies*, vol. 20, no. 3, September 2006, pp. 383–93.

Rapport, Evan. *Damaged: Musicality and Race in Early American Punk*. University Press of Mississippi, 2020.

Sorrondeguy, Martín. Interview by author, San Francisco, CA, 15 July 2015.

Adventures of a DIY Oral Historian: How the Hardcore Punk Rock Scene of the 1980s Continues to Influence My Life as a Writer

Stacy Russo

> There's a certain grit to a punk rock woman.
> *Laura Beth Bachman*[1]

I went on several solo adventures around the United States in my early forties when I was in need of rebuilding my life after surviving some traumatic experiences. On one trip I flew into Bozeman, Montana, and stayed two nights at a magical wolf sanctuary. The morning I left I was given the amazing opportunity to howl along with one of the wolf packs. From there I drove through the Bighorn National Forest in Wyoming and on to South Dakota until I caught a plane in Rapid City to return to my home in Southern California. The sense of adventure during this trip and others I took around this time filled my soul and lifted my spirits. There is a connection with growing up punk rock, this experience, and many others throughout my life.

It's not that out-of-the ordinary for a woman to travel alone, but I was quickly reminded that many women would never think of doing such a thing. I was made aware of this when, shortly after my return home, I was waiting for a dental appointment and talking with the women assistants and receptionist at the office. They were shocked that I took this trip and drove around on my own in unknown and sometimes remote areas. The wolf sanctuary aspect also seemed bizarre and unimaginable to them. Hearing the conversation, the dentist appeared and called out to the women, "Do you know why Stacy did that? Because she can." It was a simple explanation, but true. I wouldn't say

---

1 Quoted in Russo, *We Were Going to Change the World* (186).

I'm a super courageous person, but I am ambitious, I want to live my life to the fullest, and I will get out there and do things even if I may not entirely know what I'm getting into. I credit much of this to my punk rock youth.

Growing Up Punk Rock

When I was a young girl, I was troubled by cruelty in the world, although I did not have the vocabulary to name what I now understand to be various forms of intersecting oppression and injustice. I was concerned about war, poverty, and violence against animals. When I looked around, I did not aspire to what many of my peers did, such as acquiring wealth in the form of homes, cars, and possessions. I also did not feel a pull toward a traditional marriage with children. I could not embrace what I believed were constricting ideas of beauty. When I saw what guys were doing and I was told I couldn't do those things, I wanted to fight against those limitations and show that I could also do what boys did. "Just you watch!" was often my attitude. All of these feelings often resulted in a sense of alienation, but I was incredibly fortunate to find other self-described "misfits" in the Southern California punk rock scene, including many who shared my social and political beliefs, and together, out of our alienation and misfit ways, we built a sense of community. Music was at the heart of this community, but we also had art, writing, and political action. When you are young and in the midst of something, you may not understand the historical context or magnitude, but looking back all these years later I feel a sense of gratitude knowing that I was immersed in an underground cultural and social movement.

Everyone who grew up punk rock has their own unique story. My story begins in the hardcore scene of the 1980s in Southern California when I was in high school. Trying to generalize punk rock or hardcore punk rock is often problematic, yet there are some elements that one could easily argue are inherent to the scene. Perhaps the strongest element is the DIY ethic that was apparent from the early stages of punk rock in the 1970s and then continued throughout the 1980s hardcore scene. One such example is the creation of fanzines (often referred to contemporarily as zines) that remained strong throughout the 1980s. Fanzines are self-published magazines, pamphlets, or booklets often created by hand using cut-and-paste techniques.

Within the hardcore scene of the 1980s, I worked on the fanzine *Anti-Establishment* with my friends, as well as various independent side projects, including creating zines of my poetry. It's astonishing in some ways to think back on my very young self as a type of independent journalist alongside my friends as we wrote show reviews, conducted band interviews, wrote activist political articles, and printed and distributed our content. I can't recall any fear in the process—only exhilaration and the belief that what we were doing was important and needed to have an audience. This boldness and level of courage and empowerment as a young girl is no small thing. I can trace this early gift from my youth directly to aspects of my life now, including my approaches to being a writer, poet, and artist. This is most definitely the case in my work with oral history and story gathering over the last decade.

Before moving into my experiences with oral history, it's important to mention a few things regarding distinctions between punk rock and its evolution into hardcore, since the latter is the scene I grew up in and where I trace much of my influence today. The music that came out of the hardcore scene carried the passion and social commentary of the earlier punk scene, but it was often faster and more aggressive. Hardcore music was also pared-down to the bones, making it minimalistic in the sense of the instruments used. The more aggressive and harder-hitting sounds led to some great tunes, but also the unfortunate aspect of increasing violence at the clubs. Some violence was stoked by police presence and harassment, but certainly not all. In today's language, I would describe the elements that led to violence at shows as "toxic masculinity." Anecdotally over the years, some women have shared with me that they did not find the scene welcoming for them when the transition to hardcore occurred. Punk gangs throughout Southern California became an unfortunate part of the later hardcore scene that wreaked much havoc at shows. The aggressive style of music could also attract white supremacist skinheads who brought violence and ruined shows for everyone who was there to have a good time. Beyond these elements, a "boys club" of jocks sometimes showed up. I did not get the impression that these jocks had much interest in the music, scene, or any form of positive political action. They likely discovered that the shows were places to go to look for fights. Considering these violent aspects and the fact that the majority of the musicians on stage and fans in the audience were male, how did I thrive and feel a sense of belonging? This is a complex question with a complex answer.

Part of the answer is problematic. I see this now as an older woman with a much more developed feminist consciousness. In elementary school, before I knew of punk rock, my favorite writer was S. E. Hinton. In her young adult novels, including *The Outsiders* and *Rumble Fish*, I identified with the adventures of the "tough" boys. Their lives were much more exciting than the girls they dated. I desired a duel role of being one of the boys while also being one of their girlfriends. This materialized in many ways for me with the punk rock scene. To be where the fun action was, I had to be "tough" enough to run with the boys and, if things like violence scared me, I would numb that fear with alcohol. Although I always identified as a girl and woman, I could not identify with the image of girlhood or womanhood society was offering, so, in many ways, I went to another extreme to get away from these restrictions. Except for a few girls who were beloved friends in the hardcore scene, I enjoyed the company of boys and longed to be accepted by them and included in their inner circle. I often felt the most empowered when I was the only girl hanging out with a bunch of boys, which happened quite often. If other girls could not keep up to or handle the danger and violence, my younger self did not have the ability to theorize this and see the complexities and inherent problems with my thinking. Part of my behavior points to an internalized misogyny that, not unlike other oppressed groups, many women unconsciously carry. So, in many ways, I thrived and felt that sense of belonging because I wanted to prove I was just as "tough" and strong as the most badass boy.

Part of the answer to my earlier question, however, is not problematic at all. In fact, I view it as something to celebrate that circles back to the positivity of the opening of this essay and certain wonderful aspects of punk rock that I lightly touched on earlier. I loved finding a space in the hardcore scene where I could completely rebel against oppressive beauty standards and find other girls and male partners who embraced and supported me. I never recall being told how I should dress, wear my hair, or anything of the sort by the punk rock boys I hung out with. This was liberating. Likewise, I was never held back or belittled, but only encouraged to write, create art, and express myself. My intellect and creativity were valued. Although I was certainly aware of sexism in the larger society, it wasn't until I was in the mainstream workforce and academic environment as a woman that I personally experienced terrible sexism and harassment. Not experiencing this as a girl is a remarkable gift. Although we were too young to articulate and fully understand our ideas of gender and equality as kids, we did have some preliminary beliefs that were quite radical. Thinking of many of the kids I knew, we certainly held feminist ideals and some of the boys I knew were genuinely concerned with women's rights. We worked collectively for human rights and animal rights by going to demonstrations and creating protest literature. We had a shared love for the music and the scene, as well as a desire for a more just world. These elements allowed me to thrive and feel a sense of community as a girl in the hardcore scene. These positive aspects of my time in the scene are what influence much of my life and still give me the courage to go out into the world and do things, even if I feel uncertain. This includes my oral history projects.

Punk Rock & Story Projects

I dream up story projects and then I go out and do them. I gather stories as a form of social justice activism in order to amplify the voices of those who are silenced or not celebrated enough. At the time of this writing, I've published two books of interviews: *We Were Going to Change the World: Interviews with Women from the 1970s and 1980s Southern California Punk Rock Scene* and *A Better World Starts Here: Activists and Their Work*, which feature interviews with diverse activists performing amazing work to eradicate different forms of injustice in our world. I recently finished interviewing older women artists who are close to age 70 or older for a forthcoming book. With this project, I wish to illustrate a positive narrative that works against age and gender discrimination. I've presented my experience with oral history and story gathering at conferences and other venues and I've heard myself described as an "oral historian," yet I'm certainly not a trained historian in the traditional, academic sense. The extent of my formal training, which changed my life as a writer, was an awesome five-day workshop for educators I attended in 2013 through the San Francisco-based social justice organization Voice of Witness titled "Amplifying Unheard Voices."[2] This inspiring workshop, coupled with my punk rock spirit, was enough for me to feel ready to embark on a large-scale project.

When I interviewed Alice Bag for *We Were Going to Change the World*, she shared that punk rock "...taught me that I don't have to wait until I'm perfect at anything to do something, whether it's creative or political or any other aspect of my life. If I see something that needs to be done, I feel empowered to do it, even if I do it in a way that's not traditional or in a way that someone else would not have done it" (qtd. in Russo, *We Were Going* 19). This gets to the

---

2   Voice of Witness provides much more than oral history training. The organization also publishes highly recommended collections of personal narratives and offers curriculum and other resources on their website. Visit voiceofwitness.org to discover more.

heart of the influence of the scene. Growing up punk rock, you learn a few important things you can hold onto throughout your life that mirror what Alice expressed: 1) You don't need to wait until you are an expert to do something; 2) You don't need to look for someone with authority to give you permission to do what inspires you—you can figure things out and do it yourself; 3) You can use what tools you have to get started; and 4) Experimentation is a good thing. These elements often go against the grain of what the academy teaches.

To be fair, I'm an academic. I have advanced degrees in English literature and library science; I'm currently pursuing my doctorate; I work as a tenured professor/librarian at a community college; and I've always loved the genres of autobiography/memoir, personal narrative, and oral history, so I've read a lot within the area that I now devote much of my time as a writer. I've been influenced a great deal by artists, activists, writers, and wonderful teachers throughout my academic journey, but the biggest influence on my life, what is at the root of my daily actions and what you could say started me down the path I'm on, is still my punk rock youth.

Imaging a Punk Rock Methodology for Documenting History

When considering oral history and personal narrative as a form of both social justice action and documenting history, it is important to imagine what a punk rock methodology or ethos might look like. I say "might look like," because my creation of a punk rock research method is still an idea-in-progress. Thinking about this and developing a framework to follow was central to my approach when I imagined and set out to complete the project that resulted in *We Were Going to Change the World*. I would like to offer several possible and interrelated ingredients for a punk rock methodology specific to documenting history or conducting oral history/story gathering projects, although much of this could be reshaped to fit other areas of inquiry as well:

A True People's History: Rejection of Idols and Celebrity Culture

Anyone who grew up punk knows that just because a person, song, book, or anything is popular doesn't necessarily mean it is good or worthy of the stage and our precious time. It's no secret to anyone reading this that the media is saturated with celebrity culture and promoting the lives of those who already have fame. The stories of the wealthy and powerful dominate across television, print, radio, and the Internet. When we see glimpses of what is dished out as "common" people under the mostly toxic umbrella of "reality" television, we often see those without wealth and power paraded around as uneducated and cruel saps who fight amongst each other. Sadly, many laugh at the reality television shows and watch with glee as people fight or face tragedies that are presented as their own making while glorifying celebrities.

Punk rock joyfully and ferociously stands against celebrity culture and the ideas of idols, leaders, or authority. Inherent in punk is a destabilization of hierarchical structures. The punk rock spirit informs us that anyone can get on the stage and once you are on the stage the audience will not give you false praise. I'm not trying to sugarcoat punk culture though, since gender and racial discrimination unfortunately appear within most contexts, including punk rock, but one cannot deny that standing up to "the man," speaking out, and knocking idols off pedestals are core elements of punk and for that matter: hardcore.

The problem we often see with historical accounts is that the powerful reign supreme. This is why accounts of history such as Howard Zinn's *A People's History of the United States* and Roxanne Dunbar-Ortiz's *An Indigenous People's History of the United States* are incredibly important, as is the oral history work of individuals like Studs Terkel[3] that elevates and respects the stories of everyday working people that are closer to the daily lives and experiences of most people in the United States and other countries around the world. The heart and soul of my book *We Were Going to Change the World* are the fans. They make up the majority of the interviews I conducted. This does not mean that I did not also include stories of those who have previously received extensive media attention, but I kept those to a minimum and thought very hard about including them. I made sure I did not lose sight of my overarching goals before I moved ahead with any interviews. I also considered the reality of our world and the truth that the stories of the fans would likely be read by more people if I included a few well-known women from the early Southern California scene.

Another reason for rejecting celebrity culture and deconstructing hierarchies is for the simple fact that cultural and political movements are composed

---

3   The 1974 book *Working: People Talk About What They Do All Day and How They Feel About What They Do* is just one of Terkel's many celebrated works. Visit the Studs Terkel Radio Archive at studsterkel.wfmt.com to listen to recordings from his long-running radio program.

of ordinary people involved in diverse ways. The hardcore scene I was part of was vibrant for its music, which was central, but surrounding that was writing, journalism, art, photography, and fashion. Often when we see historical accounts of movements the same individuals are interviewed over and over and they are usually the ones who had the most power or leadership roles. Doing historical research within a punk rock methodology does not permit a reliance on these individuals to tell the story for everyone. For a holistic and more authentic record, people performing various roles need just as much recognition. While interviewing women for *We Were Going to Change the World*, beyond the fans, I included photographers, journalists, fanzine creators, and a disc jockey. It is only when these unique voices are gathered that we can say that we are getting closer to a more complete historical record of a scene or movement.

Everyone on Stage: The Audience and the Performers are in a Shared Experience

Similar to a rejection of celebrity culture, another important understanding when conducting punk rock research is that the audience and the performers create an experience together. When I've explained this to people, I offer my experience as a poet. I can stand in my living room and read my poems out loud to myself, but standing in front of an audience to read my poems is a profoundly different experience. My poems go beyond me and become shared creations. Every fall for several years I've helped to coordinate a community poetry reading that thankfully attracts a wonderful and engaged audience. I imagine that anyone present at these events feels the energy and relationship between the poets and the audience. The poets, of course, are privileged to participate in both roles. Undoubtedly, the experience of an audience member can be just as exciting and electrifying as being on the stage. This type of understanding, namely that a shared experience happens, is definitely what I took part in at countless punk rock shows while growing up. Without the bands, there wouldn't have been a scene. Without the audience filling up the clubs, there also wouldn't have been a scene.

It is because of the relationship between the audience and the performer being a shared activity that I also wanted to include the fans (the audience) in *We Were Going to Change the World*. To ensure I maintained the goal of disrupting hierarchies while giving credit to the audience, I explained to the publisher that I did not want the women I interviewed grouped according to their roles. I surely did not want the well-known musicians grouped together. Instead, I advocated for the women to be listed alphabetically, which is how they appear in the book. It is important when conducting oral history and storytelling projects to follow ethical guidelines the whole way through from the moment of the interview until the final publication, which gets into the next important part of the process.

You Don't Own Me: People's Stories Remain Their Stories

Written into the release form each participant for my oral history projects receives and signs is my promise that they will have the opportunity to read the parts of their interview I wish to publish and make any corrections or other edits. The stories I receive are gifts that must be respected and not altered to fit into a narrative I desire. Of course, the final version of an interview is going to be different and often quite a bit shorter than the raw transcription, but I take extreme caution to preserve the original voice and only make edits when required for flow and readability. To further allow for the reader's immersion into each woman's voice, I also made the decision to remove my questions and comments in the final published interviews for *We Were Going to Change the World*, which is a practice I discovered through Voice of Witness.

Following these guidelines is relatively easy when it is just me and the interviewee going back and forth. These concerns would also be easily carried through in the realm of self-publishing a book, making a zine, or putting the interviews up on a personal website. Once a formal publishing contract is signed, that's when the importance of people's stories not being altered needs to be especially stressed. Along the way, publishers, editors, and proofreaders will be involved and these individuals may have different opinions related to how much editing should be done with first-person narratives. Thankfully, the publisher for *We Were Going to Change the World*, Santa Monica Press, valued the importance of the ethical framework I was working within and only performed minor editing for grammatical errors.

Accessibility and Elevation of a Democratic Language

A concern I didn't think much about when I was a younger academic was how inaccessible scholarly writing is to most people. When the content of such work is rooted in social justice, feminist thought, or economic justice, one has to ask, "Who is the audience?" It seems the audience is often other scholars with advanced degrees who are immersed in their academic lives. Certainly, scholarly writing done well can be thrilling and creative, but how can the world be changed and how can great written work create social action if so many people will never encounter it or understand it?

Oral history and storytelling projects are one of the most powerful ways to build community, promote social action, shine the light on injustice, and propel us forward to a more peaceful and just world. Stories provide ways for us to grow as individuals through the encounters of narratives that validate our experience and help us to feel less lonely and alienated. Stories also help us reach a common ground and aid us in understanding people who may be living profoundly different lives. This is all possible because the first-person narrative is typically accessible to a wide audience. We can consider it a democratic language. We can all tell a story and we can all listen to a story. Oral history and storytelling carries within it a punk rock ethos.

DIY: Everyone Welcome Here

Once when I was contacted via email to provide a talk on *We Were Going to Change the World* to a historical society, the person who reached out referred to me as an oral historian. When I wrote him back, I explained that I was a librarian and writer, but not technically an oral historian. I then went on to explain in a paragraph about the book and how I created it. When he wrote back to confirm my talk, his reply was something like, "I read what you wrote. You are an oral historian though." You know what? He was right. I failed in that moment to defend and validate my own DIY methods, although I would have easily been able to if I was defending a student or community activist. Perhaps I was concerned about how I was going to be described to an audience and what assumptions they would make. I've since gotten much better at standing up for DIY research regardless of the stature or formal history training of individuals around me. Within a punk rock methodology, I don't see how DIY practices would not be valued.

A DIY ethos ultimately opens up possibilities and allows one the freedom to choose the best path when it comes to building a research toolkit. For some individuals, this could be just getting out there and doing a project with little or no training. Writers, educators, and researchers with traditional university training who understand and encourage DIY methods must remain aware that a formal path is not necessary for someone to create works and contribute to the historical record. As with the earlier discussion of dismantling hierarchies, the same is true when it comes to determining who gets to document history. Embracing a DIY philosophy is a beautiful approach that values the different ways people learn and create.

Creating *We Were Going to Change the World*

Before concluding, I'd like to share about the creation of *We Were Going to Change the World*, including some nuts and bolts of the process. When I attended the weeklong oral history training with Voice of Witness, I went there with an open mind and heart without any specific projects in mind. It turned out to be the exact experience I needed at the perfect time. Voice of Witness helped me to see how I could connect my DIY approach with oral history/story gathering, writing, and social justice. While at the training, along with the other participants, I discovered different projects people conducted. One project was focused on men who all worked in a specific profession in the Bay Area. Another project involved interviewing individuals who all grew up in a certain Black neighborhood in Richmond, California. Learning about these projects was highly stimulating. I discovered how such projects could be conducted with any group with a shared history who are not celebrated enough. It was shortly after the training that I had the idea for *We Were Going to Change the World*.

Beginning my project was easy. Once it was underway, it took a great amount of dedication and endurance, but doing a project like *We Were Going to Change the World* is possible for anyone who has the desire and commitment. I like to share this with others, because I want people to know they can do it too. You do not need to travel to San Francisco or another location to complete in-person training. There is a great amount of free or inexpensive information out there. Voice of Witness, for example, provides some helpful information on their website and they also published the wonderful *Say It Forward: A Guide to Social Justice Storytelling* (Mayotte and Kiefer). You can also just dream up what you want to do and get out there and do it.

For my project, I bought two small and inexpensive digital recorders. The reason for two was to ensure that I would capture someone's story and not waste their time if one of the recorders stopped working. I then created a flyer, which was much in the spirit of the old punk days. I hung the flyer up at different locations in Southern California and posted it on social media. In a short amount of time, the flyer was shared quite a bit and I started to receive emails and phone calls from women who were interested in learning more. Roughly two-thirds of the women I interviewed contacted me directly and the remaining women I reached out to and asked them if they would be willing to participate.

Before beginning the interviews, I created a list of questions I would ask each woman, considering there may be additional questions based on each woman's response. I also crafted a document of important ethical standards I wanted to share before each interview, including the fact that the women would be given a chance to review their interviews and make any edits. I did this to hopefully make them more comfortable speaking with me. Beyond this, I made simple tracking sheets to help me keep on top of everything. This way I could ensure the version of the interview I placed in the manuscript was the one the woman agreed to since I tracked the dates of each step of the process with each interview.

Many of the women I interviewed still live in Southern California, so almost all of them I met in person. I conducted interviews in homes, outside at a park, at a restaurant, and once in a noisy cafe with an espresso machine. Something I wasn't anticipating was that I would become friends with several of the women I interviewed. I believe this is because I also grew up in the punk rock scene, so the women and I had a rich common ground. What a blessing the project turned out to be for so many reasons.

Approximately four years passed from the time I conducted my first interview and *We Were Going to Change the World* was published. At times it felt like an endurance test, but I'm glad I hung in there. One of the most exciting things about the book is that it has inspired others to do their own projects or make positive changes in their lives. I hope that reading about my adventures as a DIY oral historian and the possibilities of a punk rock research methodology will also inspire you in whatever unique and wonderful way that may be.

References

Dunbar-Ortiz, Roxanne. *An Indigenous People's History of the United States*. Beacon Press, 2014.

Hinton, S. E. *Rumble Fish*. Delacorte Press, 1975.

Hinton, S. E. *The Outsiders*. Viking Press, 1967.

Mayotte, Cliff, and Claire Kiefer, editors. *Say It Forward: A Guide to Social Justice Storytelling*. Haymarket Books, 2018.

Russo, Stacy. *A Better World Starts Here: Activists and Their Work*. Sanctuary Publishers, 2019.

Russo, Stacy. *We Were Going to Change the World: Interviews with Women from the 1970s & 1980s Southern California Punk Rock Scene*. Santa Monica Press, 2017.

Terkel, Studs. *Working: People Talk About What They Do All Day and How They Feel About What They Do*. Pantheon Books, 1974.

Zinn, Howard. *A People's History of the United States*. 1980. HarperCollins, 2015.

Whose Loud Fast Rules? – Always Already Post-Hardcore

Daniel S. Traber

Almost forty years since my first (purposely) hearing punk rock and then hard-core in 1984, I had recently tried to convince myself that I'm totally bored by eighties hardcore. But that turned out to be a lie, a self-delusion, a halting retreat from my past obsessions. This self-assessment was made all the more clear to me after I was invited to contribute to this collection and, therefore, had to allow myself to be sucked back into the music and visual style of hard-core as a distinct evolution of punk. This self-assessment was made all the more relevant as I started contemplating what I would write about, when I tried introducing a new girlfriend (who is originally from Vicksburg, Missis-sippi) to hardcore via Penelope Spheeris's iconic documentary *The Decline of Western Civilization* (filmed through 1979 and 1980; released in 1981). We didn't finish Black Flag's opening supersonic, angry performance before she asked, "You really like *this*?" "Yes," I affirmed without hesitation, "I really *do* like *this*."

That interaction instantly reminded me of hardcore's marginalized posi-tion in music history. She and I are both born in 1968, and although she had, of course, heard of punk, and had an inkling of what it "looked" like as a sartorial statement, it simply was never her music. (In fact, when we watched a new documentary on the Go-Go's released in 2020, she was surprised, perhaps even a little shocked, to learn that her favorite alt-pop girl band started out as a loud, angry, fast Los Angeles punk group.) Back when we were teenagers in 1980s America, you often still had to search in the dark for this music. One rarely came across it on television, let alone having access to a record store selling it, or a college radio station playing it. In smaller locales it was diffi-cult to even learn about its very existence, unless you dared to approach the "weirdos" marking themselves with band t-shirts and peculiar hairdos—that is, if you even had such people in your proximity. But why would you consider listening to a station "left of the dial," as Paul Westerberg of The Replacements aptly phrased it, unless you were intentionally determined to discover something outside the mainstream? Was there a Mississippi punk band from that era driving a beat-up van to sparsely attended gigs—be it a bar, basement or kid's backyard—on a Louisiana/Mississippi/Alabama touring circuit? Hell if I know. And she certainly would never have heard of them if they existed.

But even if she had a chance to make contact with punk/hardcore during those years, she would not have liked it anyway: too fast, too loud, too angry, the lyrics are unintelligible, all those negative assessments I heard from most of my friends throughout high school who were okay with a few bands labeled new wave—Devo, U2, maybe A Flock of Seagulls—but who just wouldn't cross that threshold into punk, let alone a musical style like hardcore that so self-consciously made itself into something unappealing to the general pop-consuming public. Hardcore even turned its back on its punk predecessors, casting them aside for wallowing in mere style: superficial, inauthentic, art-damaged. Hardcore birthed itself as an unruly progeny, an unhinged wild-eyed kid with a bloody nose who is screaming in your face in order to dissuade you from liking him. Super-fast, lo-fi, raw, messy, sweaty, ugly, and made by teenagers for the most part, hardcore is everything rock was supposed to be, rather than a lame soundtrack to aspirational desire fulfilled by doing drugs with bikini-clad women in a mansion.

This is, of course, already an overstatement, a broad generalization of hardcore's image that mirrors its over-the-top musical "stylings," an excess of speed and volume that stripped down music further than punk's attack of simplification and amateurism aimed at critiquing the bloated showmanship of prog rock. When it comes to depicting hardcore, I am as guilty as anyone of overly focusing on its problems with uniformity, the "exclusivity" of a closed system that chose to restrict its membership through codes of purity and sameness (MacLeod 96), eventually destroying itself by becoming a repetitive cliche; its original flatline aural attack, bordering on aesthetic avant-gardism, dissolving into sonic irrelevancy. This problem was critiqued at the time by plenty of bands labeled hardcore (Blush 42–44), and I see it as a functional metaphor for the scholarly method applied to the subject itself. Relistening to hardcore with a much closer ear than when I was 16 made me reevaluate my own dusty preconceptions and certainties about the genre. At its best this is what academic work in pop culture as a whole should do at the starting line.

In essence, this essay will keep to the path of my previous work's questioning of punk identity (cf. Traber "L.A.'s 'White Minority'"; *Whiteness, Otherness, and the Individualism Paradox*; "Locating the Punk Preppy"), yet tangentially because more focused on the music, while also touching on the identity of the punk rock scholar—three words that can speak to a research focus and/or a form of professional ethos—to build a bridge between scholarly practice and the more flexible post-hardcore musical code of self-guided heterodoxy which already existed within hardcore. Continuing my career-long critique of an essentialized punk identity, and now an essentialized scholarly one, willfully chooses to rub against the grain of the rules constituting authenticity and legitimacy, rebellion and nonconformity—be it an underground subculture in a dimly lit club or an above-ground academic performing in the daylight—so as to locate a liminal space in which assumed contradictory elements can be effectively juxtaposed and melded. The scholarly method, including a so-called elitist (because difficult to read) critical theory, seems antithetical to the spirit of punk, especially in its hardcore guise, as it takes a music so raw and straightforward in its style in order to "overthink" it, thereby potentially locking its subject matter in a box of totalized meaning simply by trying to figure out what it could "mean." I, however, see that as the moment for creative destruction on both sides, when guarded borderlines are circumvented so identity, *everyone's*, can cease to be restrained, controlled, limited by a shroud of transcendental subjectivity. I consider this part of the creed informing the initial promise of punk rock.

Heavy-Handed Aphorisms No One Asked For

Hate What You Love
Contaminate Your Authenticity
Burn Down Your Clubhouse
Murder Your Clique
Lionize the Poseur

More PoMo

Michelle Phillipov has censured punk studies for typically "focus[ing] on the cultural and political 'impact' of the movement rather than on the textures of punk as music . . . [thus,] punk's musical conventions are firmly anchored to questions of politics: that is, punk is often approached principally as an expression of youth rebellion and disenfranchisement, rather than as music per se" (384).[1] Surely, the scholarship (including my own contributions to that archive) focused on identity constructed through punk rock, hence the ever-evolving subculture that developed in conjunction with the music, succumbs to this tendency towards highlighting politics as it is rarely, if ever, not deployed as a key facet used to make punks into comprehensible subjects, knowable agents participating in a politicized culture industry. We force utility upon punk/hardcore to give it "worth" and "value" in the economy of applicable usefulness, as opposed to wasting time in pursuing the joy of just fooling around. Thus, it becomes a simultaneous defense of our own use of time—that vital investment we are told—which we can say is prudently spent by studying it. I hope to take Phillipov's admonition to heart in my thoughts on hardcore as a music worth learning something from as a form in its own right, furthermore with an embedded lesson for scholarly methodology, even when punk/hardcore is not the subject matter.

In a recent contribution to *The Oxford Handbook of Punk Rock*, I examine the alt-right's trend of referring to its brand of Trump-era conservatism as "the new punk rock." I make a case for rejecting this self-applied appellation, while also considering punk fans' angry negative response so as to question how punk ontology gets naturalized, concretized into a universal, transcendental form (i.e., a totalized notion of "Punk" as opposed to the more elastic "punk"); thereby discarding its earlier anti-foundational postmodern roots:

> As a method, postmodernism allows for a critique of patriarchy, racism, homophobia, and other discriminatory -isms favored by the alt-right as these positions are all buttressed by tradition, hierarchy, reason, et al., and depend upon a regulatory binary structure to maintain power by controlling what constitutes Truth. That is how Punk gets it wrong when it moves to lock down its subjectivity like an alt-right identitarian. Punk can be read as born from a postmodern sensibility that allowed for individual flexibility, a style of music and dress that sutured fragments drawn from multiple sources to invent new forms. This enabled new ways of thinking and being, all under the banner of a few shared characteristics given the *pliable* categorical name punk. But some people elide that history of diversity by promoting a singular authenticity to reduce the permissible strands of difference that might

---

1   For a musicological analysis of hardcore and an accompanying critique of postmodern theory see the article by Pearson in this book [the editors].

threaten the sameness of their idealized Punk Identity. . . . We need a way
to avoid imprisoning the spirit of punk—as music, as dress, and as a way of
moving through the world—in a transcendent realm while still being able
to point at something that can legitimately be called by that name, yet as
a flexible form. Wanting ontological closure, to conduct yourself as a Punk,
is the fatal flaw. (Traber, "You Ain't No Punk, You Punk")

The identitarian gesture happened early in punk's history as a fresh cultural
movement became a stifling trend in England, while in America a new sect of
compelled sincerity was developing that would come to be named hardcore,
and risk mutating unity into conformity.

Ryan Moore also connects punk to postmodern theories and artistic tactics, then turns to describing hardcore as an intentionally negative challenge
to those postmodern inflections:

Whereas the first response ["deconstructive" punk] to postmodernity appropriates signs, symbols, and style for the purposes of shock and semiotic
disruption, the second ["authentic" hardcore] attempts to go "underground"
and insulate punk subculture from the superficiality of postmodern culture.
. . . [Their] pursuit of purity has often led hard-core subcultures to enforce
a startling homogeneity of dress and sound, which effectively stifles artistic creativity and obstructs the participation of various types of "outsiders."
(307–08)

Moore continues:

Throughout the 1980s, the pages of *Maximum Rock 'n' Roll* and *Flipside*—including both regular articles and the letters sent by readers—were
overwhelmingly concerned with defining what punk is and what punk is
not, complaining about people who think they are punk but really are not,
distinguishing between true originators and "trendy" followers who just
"look cool," accusing certain bands of selling out or at least trying to sell
out, and so on. (321)

Regardless of the hardcore turn, neither approach ever gains complete reign
over the subculture during punk's multi-decade existence. My 2008 article on
the punk preppy has already walked over this cratered battleground of authenticity. That tension of co-existence accounts for why I raise the spectre of
postmodernism; namely, in order to raise the spectre of post-hardcore as "al-

ways already" present in hardcore proper, thus a challenge to allowing genre rigidity to infiltrate our thinking about hardcore as a cultural form.

The hardcore kids were engaged in the same language games as the early punks in choosing corporeal and sonic signifiers to represent their identity to the world. The difference is that too many wanted to close the circuit so as to lock it down into a monolithic, inflexible meaning, this included fans not preaching straight edge's doctrinaire mentality. Post-hardcore typically dates to the mid-1980s in connection to the Washington DC scene, with the growth of emo (or emocore, which was originally a dismissive word for emotional hardcore), as it developed with bands like Rites of Spring. This music maintained the intensity of hardcore but channeled it into songs more focused on giving expression to one's personal emotions. From there bands began to find more aesthetic freedom as well, especially as the influence of hardcore in its original form began to wane.

The aesthetic values of post-hardcore remind scholars to not get locked into the striated grooves (to use Deleuze and Guattari's term) of our own assumptions, paradigms, and theoretical frameworks, even our *memories* in the case of studying a fandom culture within which we participate(d). By extension, post-hardcore methodology can teach us to consider opening ourselves to pushing the boundaries of academic form in our own work. A post-hardcore scholarly practice would shy away from absolutist theoretical schools, be it Marxism or postmodernism or anything else; so also shying away from preordained critiques to better see how these ideological games function, and whether the players' master narratives unwittingly play against themselves.

Notes on 1980s Post-Hardcore Precursors (Incomplete and Random)

I hear pop-punk in the early Black Flag Keith Morris tracks of the *Nervous Breakdown* EP (1979). His voice modulates into something approaching melody rather than just speed-ranting the lines. Songs like "Nervous Breakdown" and "Wasted" are much faster than the Sex Pistols, yet still composed of catchy guitar riffs rather than monochrome notes designed simply to break the sound barrier. (Sometimes when you try to kill rock you just end up making it better.) Even on the *Damaged* LP (1981) there are honest chord changes and tempo shifts while Henry Rollins occasionally breaks with his rant-vocal style to slip into something like melody on "Depression" and "No More," alongside the wholly planned out artistry of "Damaged I" which presents emotion more than belched out lyrics over turbo drums and Guitar-For-Dummies chords. And, of course, there is the WTF moment in 1984, on side two of *My War*, when all preconceptions are decimated by Greg Ginn connecting into artsy heavy metal with slower, longer, *sludgier* guitar jams (also, the bass definitely keeps up its end in slaughtering hardcore's now outdated rules). Ginn goes the opposite direction of crossover thrash bands, like Houston's Dirty Rotten Imbeciles, who melded hardcore and metal with a faster metal guitar style.

Everyone correctly links pop-punk to the Descendents as they built their style on the "radical" element of melody and writing songs about wanting a girlfriend (and far too many about flatulence) rather than anti-Reagan diatribes. Previous 1970s bands like the Buzzcocks and Generation X had already offered a template for incorporating pop characteristics, however, the pop-punk designation wasn't a term at the time since they sounded so different from any pop music of their moment.

Hüsker Dü's 1984 *Zen Arcade* double LP: loud, fast, angry but also *intelligent* songs (e.g., "Indecision Time"), and the best (only?) punk rendition of the Bo Diddly riff on "Hare Krsna." They also showcased slower, contemplative acoustic songs; honest-to-god piano songs; psychedelia; politics and personal emotions (arguably setting a template for the birth of emo-punk) mixed with so many other challenges to the hegemonic punk/hardcore vernacular. They are already setting us up for their 1986 lunar-leap to a major label with *Candy Apple Gray*, revealing a roadmap to punk-rock musical maturity with less direct political lyrics as songs gained emotional depth, linked with fluctuations between hard rock assault and slower, mindful instrumentation.

Minutemen's 1984 *Double Nickels on the Dime* double LP: these 43 tracks are far more challenging and "weirder" than *Zen Arcade* (the bands were SST label mates), especially when taken as an artistic statement in toto, with its display of funk guitar, Spanish guitar, experimental bass lines, and thoughtful drumming (even bongos). The somewhat recognizably punk tunes are far outnumbered by idiosyncratic odd ones. There are political lyrics, sincere and personal lyrics, silly lyrics, smart lyrics: "So dig this big crux." All of which was preceded by the free jazz jam of "Dreams are Free, Motherfucker!" on the *Buzz or Howl Under the Influence of Heat* EP (1983).

Circle Jerks willfully deploy melody and have an intelligent, trained drummer who can do more than maintain a mono-rhythmic beat: "World Up My Ass."

The Exploited, sometimes, such as the melody and nearly discernible lyrics of "I Believe In Anarchy," and I still giggle at the melodious chanting, measured drumming, rollicking silliness of "Sex and Violence." (But when push comes to shove, the full tilt hardcore style of "Disorder" is still better than either of those songs.)

Flipper: "Shed No Tears," "Life," "The Game's Got a Price," "Sacrifice," "Ha Ha Ha." These songs are representative of how this band's early avant-garde instincts operated beyond the hardcore category as both genre and audience—which was always their desired endpoint. And if the saxophone-thick deranged funk of "Sex Bomb" doesn't make you grin, then you can go to hell. Thank goodness Flipper existed to explode the whole mystique of punk as instant musical rebellion, better than any No Wave performance of rehearsed haphazardness would do it. This is Art, in the holy-hush best sense of the word.

I am hardly the first to note how Minor Threat uses screaming melody, lyrics delving into emotional topics and solid rock guitar riffs rather than restricting itself to turbo-speed linear single notes, or at least what *sound* like the extremist minimalism of single notes. There is the periodic stop-and-start approach on "Screaming at a Wall;" the groovy rhythm section opening of "In My Eyes" with everything shifting to straight ahead hardcore when the chorus arrives. There is the dub style drum echo effect (showing the influence of The Clash and Bad Brains) after the intro on "Look Back and Laugh" which erupts into hardcore guitar and screaming lyrics. And if their cover of Paul Revere and the Raiders' 1966 garage-rock song "(I'm Not Your) Steppin' Stone" doesn't make you shimmy your shoulders, just a little, then you are dead inside; for even as a snarky joke on manufactured pop music, since the song is more famous as a Monkees number (one later covered by the Sex Pistols), it nonetheless sounds like the band enjoys playing the song. The foundations for what Ian MacKaye will do in Fugazi, his consciously post-hardcore outfit, in which he no longer had to feign disdain for exhibiting musical expertise and songwriting forethought, are already present.

Butthole Surfers' *Brown Reason to Live* EP (1983): instantly post-hardcore as some form of insane "acid" punk, these whacked out Texans use "Suicide" to play with the hardcore form but let "Wichita Cathedral" show real vision in using a funky bassline to make it actually danceable, *not* slamdancing, while the guitar emits enough sonic horror to keep it aesthetically interesting.

7 Seconds made their emo and/or pop-hardcore leap in 1986 with *New Wind*. The singing incorporated more melody and harmony yet still with a blitzing guitar, which it could be argued was really their original style all along, except on earlier releases like the straight forward hardcore sound of

"Fuck Your Amerika," their contribution to the 1982 *Not So Quiet on the Western Front* compilation. "Still Believe" is about the death of hardcore as a movement, which it wholly indicates by its more measured tempo of an actual instrumental intro—a church organ sound which reflects the theme of hardcore passing on, like a funeral for a dead religion—before blazing into the lyrics, but even then the bass is emphasized, making rhythm the prominent sonic note which is atypical in hardcore. The album closes with the seven-minute (an ironic play on seven seconds?) "Colour Blind Jam" that begins with another organ intro, followed by Kevin Seconds rapping the lyrics (maybe half-jokingly) over record scratching, dub echo and delay and other effects, ripping guitar riffs, and a closing homage to "World Destruction" (the brilliant Afrika Bambaataa/John Lydon song). However, the band had already shown these musical inclinations to unshackle themselves from generic chains. They do so on a fantastic cover of Nena's "99 Red Balloons," wherein the guitar actually gets a touch funky. Yet, I always found a proclivity for the melodic in their favoring the "whoa-whoaaaa" chant, which I take as a signal they wanted to do things a little differently. The chant occurs on my two favorite songs, which are more "traditionally" hardcore: "This Is the Angry Pt. 2" (from 1983's *The Crew*) and "We're Gonna Fight" on *Walk Together, Rock Together*, the same 1986 LP as "99 Red Balloons," which also uses the chant.

Finale

Post-hardcore's lessons for a scholarly methodology were present in the music from the beginning—always already. Punk initially appropriated fragments from the past to rebuild pop music, hardcore burned it all down in order to build no shrines to the past. And then it allowed itself to become formally derivative, yet that was a necessary process for post-hardcore to rise from those ashes and push the form in new directions. Few knew it would turn out that way, except those who were not afraid of the word "Art" and permitted themselves to enact the autonomy the clones wrote the same song about over and over.

Both punk and hardcore would come to box themselves within rules constituting musical authenticity and subcultural identity, rules about what makes you a sellout, rules about everything. The pluralism of post-hardcore, and the diversity of post-punk bands before it, remind the listener, including self-described scholars, that there are aesthetic and philosophical benefits to be gained from teetering on the liminal line between objectivity and subjectivity, theory and praxis. When is what sounds like a breakdown actually a breakthrough? The Jesus and Mary Chain unleashed squalls of sonic terrorism to walk the threshold edge of absolute noise by mixing white noise and feedback with the recognizably traditional elements of song writing—on their *first* album, to then keep building upon and progressing that form with every subsequent release. Ska-punk also teaches us that you can combine forms, juxtapose supposed paradoxes to create something different within a third-space (hybrid math: $1 + 1 = 3$), or even a fifth-space if that's what you need to get the job done.

In my own work, I usually place more emphasis on using a postmodern theoretical lens while remaining open to ideas that may not immediately seem a cohesive match with those epistemological paradigms. That may be to satisfy my own ideological preferences for making sense of the world, and sometimes my preferred aesthetic leanings toward border-crossing and fragmentation. Maybe it is because I turned 54 in 2022, so I'm just feeling ornery, but I think that approach enabled me to not be overly concerned with meeting an imagined overarching intellectual code. To state it another way, ultimately I just don't give a shit what you think about what I think. It is an attitude that is kind of punk, sort of hardcore, certainly the pose adopted by my sixteen-year-old self that still lurks within me nearly forty years later. Sometimes punk promised that being able to say "no" constitutes the most rudimentary level of individual freedom, that it signifies agency regardless of whether you can actually enact change outside yourself. Sometimes punk said "no" to your no by critiquing such a notion as granting only shadows of freedom and agency—another marketplace identity that affects nothing, achieves nothing significant. That dialectic dynamic is when punk—including all the bastard children to which it gave birth—is at its best, its most productive, in questioning not only its own Truths but seeing how that approach can extend beyond the music, clothing and posture. When I was 16, that moment of awakening made the earth shift beneath my feet.

Thanks, punk rock.

References

Blush, Steven. *American Hardcore: A Tribal History*. Feral House, 2001.

MacLeod, Dewar. *Kids of the Black Hole: Punk Rock in Postsuburban California*. University of Oklahoma Press, 2010.

Moore, Ryan. "Postmodernism and Punk Subculture: Cultures of Authenticity and Deconstruction." *The Communication Review* 7, 2004, pp. 305–27.

Phillipov, Michelle. "Haunted by the Spirit of '77: Punk Studies and the Persistence of Politics." *Continuum: Journal of Media & Cultural Studies* 20.3, 2006, pp. 383–93.

Traber, Daniel S. "L.A.'s 'White Minority': Punk and the Contradictions of Self-Marginalization." Cultural Critique 48, 2001, pp. 30–64.

Traber, Daniel S. "Locating the Punk Preppy (A Speculative Theory)." The Journal of Popular Culture 41.3, 2008, pp. 488–508.

Traber, Daniel S. *Whiteness, Otherness, and the Individualism Paradox from Huck to Punk*. Palgrave Macmillan, 2007.

Traber, Daniel S. "You Ain't No Punk, You Punk: On Semiotic Doxa, Postmodern Authenticity, Ontological Agency and the Goddamn Alt-Right." *The Oxford Handbook of Punk Rock*, edited by George McKay and Gina Arnold, Oxford University Press, 2021. Online. https://www.oxfordhandbooks.co m/view/10.1093/oxfordhb/9780190859565.001.0001/oxfordhb-9780190859 565-e-7. Accessed 30 May 2022.

"Have You Never Been Mellow?" – Joy and Ugliness in Punk and Hardcore Aesthetics

Maxwell Tremblay

> Faith is for the old world
> And hope is for the past.
> The new world is predictable
> Because everyone is dead.
> *Abi Yoyos, "All the Troubadours"*

> I don't want harmony, for love of
> mankind I don't want it.
> *Fyodor Dostoevsky,*
> *The Brothers Karamazov*

When I was 16, my band played a record release show at 924 Gilman Street.

Now, for my entire adult life one of my *a priori* principles has been that culture writing that starts with some personal anecdote about the author's salad days is a plague; this is particularly true for music writing, since the gambit is often meant to paper over a lack of aesthetic significance with emotional significance. However, let me reassure you that: i.) the anecdote is not really about me, and ii.) the band was bad—and not in that deflecting way that people say their bands were bad when they actually mean 'amateurish' and you find out years later they were in the Germs. I mean 'bad' as in we played emotional pop-punk with maximum earnestness, and I can say that objectively because I wrote nearly every song.

ANYWAY, that night I was standing around chatting with a friend—possibly about how hot tubs were in fact *not* straight edge—when another acquaintance walked up and handed us a flyer for a show the following weekend. My friend burst into wheezing hysterics, spraying some awful vegan cheese replacement into the atmosphere like the COVID transmission graphics we now all know so well. Between guffaws, all he could hoarsely say was "Too soon! Too soon!" It was Friday, September 14th, 2001, and our mutual friend had just handed us a flyer whose background, underneath the requisite list of bands, venue and time info, was an enormous picture of one of the World Trade Center towers collapsing in an orgy of smoke and flames.

As the popular tweet format goes, I probably think about this moment once a day. It contains a small, elegant kernel of that which makes punk and hardcore both enduringly delightful and also unlike other art forms or cultural phenomena.

While journal pages and anarchist book fair tables overflow with analyses of punk through the language of personal narrative, sociology, and cultural studies (I myself am guilty of the latter!), comparatively little has in fact been written about how punk and hardcore work—what makes them unique salvos in our history of making meaning. One could argue that they partake of camp, offensiveness, noise, collective rage—but anyone with more than a glancing understanding of them would readily admit that they are not reducible to any of those things. What we require, I argue—notwithstanding certain arid attempts to describe punk rock 'ethics'—is a philosophical approach to punk—and by extension hardcore—that takes it seriously as a singular phenomenon. And that's the reason I retell my opening story, because it illustrates beautifully the convoluted problem with pinning down punk/hardcore aesthetics in any meaningful way: i.) punk is usually not merely interested in offense *qua* offense, like a nine year-old saying "boobs" or Ricky Gervais joking about trans people, ii.) but punk is simultaneously not understandable *without* a pointed offensiveness that exceeds what polite society would allow, and finally iii.) that offensiveness is not reducible to any simplistic interpretive read one might try to give it (e.g., moral or political outrage, establishing some kind of community of sense-makers, etc.). Oh, and it's funny!

I should offer here a brief note on terminology, as I've been using the terms 'punk' and 'hardcore' roughly interchangeably. In aesthetic and, say, musicological or historical terms, 'hardcore' does have a particular meaning, which roughly cashes out as the harder, faster, and more aggressive version of punk exemplified by Bad Brains, Minor Threat, and others. But this 'hard'—ha!—and fast distinction has always seemed to me to obscure the more operative, colloquial meaning of 'hardcore,' which is, vulgarly, what punks call punk when they want to emphasize how different it is from the parts of punk one might consider lame: pop-punk, emo, overly arty shit, what have you. A small example that sticks in my mind: on my way to see the excellent Swedish band Terrible Feelings some years ago, I was making small talk with an acquaintance who referred to them as a hardcore band, and this wasn't the first time I'd seen that done. Now, Terrible Feelings sound like the Pretenders or The Knack at a Scandinavian Halloween party, which is great, but renders the simple aesthetic distinction meaningless, and the latter wouldn't be helpful without this additional social key. The impulse to 'hardcore' then can be read as an attempt, internal to punk itself, to further refine and describe that thing—that way of sounding or performing or making meaning happen—that only punk rock does. To that end, some slippage is appropriate.

Now, back to the 9/11 flyer: let me try to persuade you of my idiot friend's unwitting sophistication. In the first place, to use the picture of the burning towers before the NFL even had time to cancel any games is to, I think, transparently reveal interest in something beyond, say, simply trying to be gross for grossness' sake, or getting cheap kicks off of throwing minorities under the bus from a position of privilege. But it is pushing buttons, placing images of what was then extremely raw trauma in a seemingly trivializing context. And while it is potentially pushing those buttons with purpose—to, say, puncture the swiftly enveloping nationalistic atmosphere of those early post-9/11 days, anticipating the military adventurism that would be carried out in the name of that trauma—it's nowhere near as dour as all that. Indeed, as my cheese-spewing comrade could attest, it was funny as shit. Not only was it simply brazen, it was a hilarious meta-joke about punk itself: in normal times, punks just make flyers out of cool looking pictures, usually of death and stuff, and, well, we have some new material this week!

I'm not claiming that every single punk-related phenomenon operates in this mode, nor even that we can identify it in everything we call 'punk.' Indeed, plenty of punk bands are content to write shitty indie rock songs about how much they hate their ex-girlfriends. My point here is different: if we think that punk *is* anything, aesthetically speaking, we would have to concede that there must be something *only it can do*, that other styles, genres, or communities—say, psych, or rap, or poetry readings—can't. It's this sensibility, evident in my friend's 9/11 flyer, that I see as unique in punk and hardcore aesthetics both visual and musical. I emphasize in particular that this variety of punk abrasiveness doesn't neatly fit the most common scholarly and popular treatment of punk rock taboo-breaking, which is that it was primarily a matter of misappropriation of slurs by otherwise privileged people, and that it's primarily a thing of the past.[1] As such, it is twice as confusing to mainstream culture when it arises, and constantly in danger of passing from the world.

In what remains I'd like to try to clarify and refine this sensibility, tracking how it continues to make trouble when it encounters contemporary popular discourse, and trying to work out why punks do what they do. It should go without saying that I'm not trying to nail down this sensibility with any finality, just take a stab at what I think it is and why it matters, hopefully slightly advancing a discourse that hasn't progressed much beyond repeatedly worrying over punk's appropriation of the swastika.[2]

To that end, let's turn to another example of this sensibility in the wild, one that frustrates easily reducible meaning. In January 1986, the space shuttle *Challenger* blew up shortly after its launch, killing, among others, Christa McAuliffe, who was aboard as a part of the Reagan-era "Teacher in Space" program, a civilian accompanying experienced astronauts. Later that same year, an exceptional band from Arizona called Feederz—already notorious for involving bugs and dead animals in their live shows—released their second album. They called it *Teachers in Space*, and the accompanying cover was a grainy photograph of the *Challenger* exploding.

This is fucked up! You know it is, I know it is! It is, probably, one of the darker jokes I've seen ... and yet, I laugh every single time I think about it. And, I think, while it would probably get dismissed as merely awful, even by the counter-culturally minded, I'm persuaded it's more than that. While it's certainly uncomfortable, and absolutely insensitive, it's neither prurient (i.e., graphically violent), nor particularly mean-spirited. But it is designed to be the worst thing someone thinks about that day. And while it is potentially intended to puncture the way human interest stories like the civilian astronaut are used to paper over the horror of the march of technological advancement

---

1   See, for instance, Greil Marcus, who wrote that, in many LA punk records, "[c]ontempt for and a wish to exterminate the other is presented here as a rebellion against the smooth surface of American life, but it may be more truly a violent, spectacular accommodation to America's worst instincts" (81).

2   The Nazi kitsch gesture effectively has two versions, one smart and one dumb: the former a puckish attempt by primarily Jewish artists to puncture the sanctimony they grew up with surrounding the holocaust, the latter Sid Vicious wearing swastika shirts for kicks. See, for instance, Steven Lee Beeber's chapter, "Hotsy-Totsy Nazi Schatzes: Nazi Imagery and the Final Solution to the Final Solution," in *The Heebie Jeebies at CBGB's: A Secret History of Jewish Punk*, and Roger Sabin's essay, "'I Won't Let That Dago By': Rethinking Punk and Racism," in *Punk Rock: So What? The Cultural Legacy of Punk*.

in service to an arms race with the Soviets over the militarization of space—a constant concern of punk from the Reagan era—it's not doing so in a dour, didactic way. It is, in spite of its ugliness, smiling, and that smile at ugliness prevents it from being too self-satisfied in its worldview.

Why is this important? Because it carves out a seemingly unoccupyable space between two exhaustive options. Unlike, say, the song "Destroy the Handicapped" by Fang which uses the shock of picking on the most vulnerable to try to elicit groans and laughs, the shock of *Teachers in Space* can't be dismissed as cheap or bigoted. But on the other hand, unlike, to use a more contemporary example, the song "Trans Day of Revenge" by G.L.O.S.S. (Girls Living Outside Society's Shit), which imagines trans people enacting graphically violent retribution on a transphobic society, its target isn't so immediately irredeemable that its sense is merely literal and, thus, recoupable and easily forgotten. In other words, it punches neither up, nor down, and destabilizes reading cultural or artistic interventions in such grossly simplistic terms. That lingering awfulness and discomfort, the source of the laugh, is what keeps Feederz's work difficult and unrecoverable, and it does so without racism, misogyny, or homophobia *and* without creating easy villains to dunk on. By having fun with ugliness, Feederz make it impossible for their gesture to lapse into sanctimony, fatuousness, pomposity, or indulgence, and I struggle to think of another art form that does so—while also making songs that you want to listen to. It's what keeps punk aesthetically renewable and constitutively dissatisfied—appropriate for a band who began their first LP by tweaking Olivia Newton John lyrics to turn her song about chilling out into one about murder, and then screaming unhinged through a chorus of "HAVE YOU NEVER BEEN MELLOW???" The only answer, the one punk and hardcore demand, is "No."

I can hear the objection that I'm just pushing the "things were better back in the day" button for a cultural form that is well into its downward trajectory, all the way towards Jazz at Lincoln Center irrelevance. And that's fair! Especially considering that, at the present moment, the only people to publicly defend principled offensiveness have the absolute worst brains imaginable, and usually do so only to justify the money they continue to make shitting on, say, Muslims or queer people. I have two responses to this: first, I've tried to show that this idiosyncratic type of punk rock abrasiveness is not what people like Bill Maher do (not only because it's smart). Second, and I suppose more polemically, the unique contribution of punk rock aesthetics and sensibility, even at a more restrained scale, still causes significant trouble for more mainstream interpretations today. If you care at all about having a culture that *isn't* sanctimonious, vacuous, or indulgent—if you've never been mellow!—then that trouble might be a useful tool for preventing things from tending in that direction.

The winds, granted, are stiff, and when even whiffs of that sensibility do arise, they can quickly morph into something else. Take, for instance, the recent memoir by Laura Jane Grace of Against Me!, which she decided to call *Tranny*. Now, knowing that Grace came up through punk, what she's trying to do is immediately clear: she's taken an ugly word, one that she describes as constituting her own experiences of self-loathing as a trans person, and made people look at it. While there's certainly an element of reclamation in it, it's also, at least on my interpretation, something of a sly joke: her book is going to sit on the shelf in Barnes & Noble next to a hundred memoirs with self-serious subtitles like "A Life", and it is darkly funny that square consumers thumbing through Obama's ponderous tome will have to read the word "tranny," possibly over and over again if they've got a stack. It's not punching down—Grace is, after all, trans—but it's not easily interpretable as punching up either—it's more determinate than the Feederz example, but it's also not holding a sign that reads, "When I say this, I mean transphobia is bad." In other words, it retains a hint of that puckish determination to be abrasive I've described above. However, given how much pushback Grace received for her choice, so much so that she had to publish a long-ish blog post within days of the title's announcement explaining her rationale,[3] something like Feederz's gesture, or my acquaintance's 9/11 flyer, must surely remain almost unthinkable in a mainstream context, perhaps even more so today than when they first occurred, as our era calcifies further and further into mere earnestness.

Earnestness, to bring us full circle, sucks. As a wholly self-reinforcing system of justification, it provides cover not just for bad art—hundreds of boring bands excavating their feelings over third-rate Superchunk ripoffs—but the actual fucking system that continues to immiserate all of us to the benefit of

---

3   The biggest pushback, she describes, came not from the usual scolds but from trans people, who worried that it would contribute to a continuing anti-trans atmosphere of violence and hatred. Now, this isn't my conversation to have. But, insofar as this is in some way a matter of punk rock aesthetics versus the world, I would simply point out, how powerfully disruptive Grace's gesture—rooted in that unique sensibility of punk rock I've been trying to articulate here—was to even an ostensibly sympathetic audience (see Grace, "About That Title").

a disgusting few. Earnestness, in the form of the allegedly self-evident seriousness of national trauma, allowed many with otherwise left politics to be completely snowed by the nationalistic atmosphere of 9/11's immediate aftermath. That same impulse continues into the present, fractured and less obvious but pervasive, if not inescapable. I'm a lifelong stutterer, and it made me barf to see squishy liberals trumpet then-candidate Joe Biden's 'struggles' with stuttering, as if this evidence of his humanity justified his lackluster (to say the least) policy record or the crumbs he's going to throw a suffering population as president. Punk's ability to be pointedly insensitive—which, again, not all punk can do but *only* punk can do—is the constant disruption of any self-seriousness that might encroach on one's art and politics; it is one of the few things that can forestall the death-spiral of earnestness into which so much can be smuggled. It's occasionally ugly, but it is vastly preferable to the alternative.

I would close, then, by proposing what I think we can justifiably consider the two *a priori* principles of punk and hardcore aesthetics: i.) that being ugly is fun, funny, and, above all, *required*, because ii.) it is precisely that play with ugliness that prevents what you make from lapsing into mere earnestness, sanctimony, fatuousness, or sincerity. In other words, it is by having fun with ugliness that you know what sucks, and knowing what sucks is all we have.

References

Beeber, Steven Lee. *The Heebie Jeebies at CBGB's: A Secret History of Jewish Punk*. Chicago Review Press, 2006.

Grace, Laura Jane. "About That Title." *Noisey*. 28 March 2016, vice.com/en/article/65zedb/mandatory-happiness-about-that-title. Accessed 30 May 2022.

Grace, Laura Jane. *Tranny: Confessions of Punk Rock's Most Infamous Anarchist Sellout*. Hachette Books, 2016.

Marcus, Greil. "Crimes Against Nature." *White Riot: Punk Rock and the Politics of Race*, edited by Stephen Duncombe and Maxwell Tremblay, Verso, 2011, pp. 78–81.

Sabin, Roger. *Punk Rock: So What? The Cultural Legacy of Punk*. Routledge, 1999.

Queer-feminist Hardcore/Punk: Academic Research and Community Support in the Age of the Pandemic

Katharina Wiedlack

Queer-feminist politics have been part of North American hardcore/punk culture from the very beginning. At least since the mid-1980s different labels such as homocore, and later queercore, dykecore, and riot grrrl became frequently used to mark queer-feminist politics explicitly and create cultural and political affiliations. Using these labels, filling them with meanings and at the same time critically reflecting on issues of categorization, identification, and oppression, hardcore/punk culture contributed in significant ways to the very emergence of queer theory, especially antisocial queer theory—undoubtedly one of the most hardcore iterations of the academic field. Importantly, queer-feminist hardcore/punk theory is developed and distributed through musical and performed form. Moreover, it is intrinsically connected to the hardcore/punk community that gathers in concerts, festivals, street protests and on an everyday basis.

In my essay, I am trying to map how queer-feminist hardcore/punk answers to the contemporary moment that simultaneously asks to show up for each other in solidarity (against the conservative backlash, and in support of racialized minorities) and limits the possibilities to safely do so (due to the ongoing health crisis). I will ask how queer-feminist punks reacted to the backlash against queers, trans* and non-normatively gender individuals, and women* spearheaded by the Trump administration. What is their relationship to the Black Lives Matter movement? And what happens when showing up becomes a matter of risk under the current health crisis? How do queer-feminist punks sustain themselves and their communities during this pandemic that has affected the already marginalized to such a strong extent? What is left of hardcore/punk, when the mosh pit is not an option? When shouting is no longer a collective release, but a safety hazard? And what is the punk researcher left with, stuck at the home office?

I will take up these and other questions to argue that (queer-feminist) hardcore/punk does not only continue to thrive as a subculture and theory, but also that it is indeed a lot that the study of (queer-feminist) hardcore/punk can teach us today, especially in this moment of acute social and political crisis.

"We're Punk as Fuck and Fuck like Punks" (The Skinjobs)

One of the most important findings of my doctoral research and subsequent book was that queer-feminist punks show a high level of awareness and re-flection of the historic and epistemic overlaps and intersections between punk and queerness. This insight prompted me to use one of such reflections in the form of lyrics as the title for my dissertation *"We're Punk as Fuck and Fuck like Punks:" Queer-Feminist Counter-Cultures, Punk Music and the Antisocial Turn in Queer Theory.* The line "We're Punk as Fuck and Fuck like Punks" is borrowed from the song "Burn your Rainbow" by the Canadian queer-feminist punk band the Skinjobs on their 2003 album with the same name. Using this line for my academic thesis was both my reckoning with an exclusionary, racist, sexist and anti-queer academic system, and an attempt to highlight the community knowledge about the connection between queer sexuality and hardcore/punk rock. And while the academic system and my Alma Mater did not even bother to react much to my provocation, neither positive nor negative, members of the queer-feminist hardcore/punk community critically reflected on my aca-demic reading of their cultural productions and community. Especially those, whose most intense engagement with queer-feminist hardcore/punk cultures was in the past, often expressed that they appreciated the fact that someone valued the culture that had been or continued to be important and formative in their lives. No matter if they had been part of riot grrrl scenes, queercore, or dykecore, they appreciated being included in my research and provided me with their memories, anecdotes and a diverse array of cultural artifacts. I am forever indebted to the fantastic writer and former riot grrrl Nina Re-nata Aron, the queercore punk, label owner and hardcore/punk archivist Matt Wobensmith, the drummer Lee Frisari, the singer, comic artist, writer, and organizer Cristy Road and so so many others, who shared their views and histories of queer-feminist punk with me. The most beautiful and most grat-ifying moment was, when Mitch Fury, band member of the infamous Skinjobs, who I had never met before and only knew from the band's albums and through the works and words of other queer-feminist punks contacted me after the submission of my dissertation through a hand written letter, sending along some original Skinjobs pins and posters. The Skinjobs have long ceased to exist, but being remembered in my research apparently meant enough to Mitch to find my contact address and reach out. It is for these moments that I did my research, because I know that within academia, the topic of queer-feminist punk is not very highly valued. Interestingly, within the context of my home country Austria, it was never hardcore/punk or antisocial[1] theory that was criticized, but the queer aspects. Quite frequently I get to hear that I should not put myself in such a 'narrow niche' such as queer theory, because I will make myself unemployable. Quite often the reason for not choosing me for positions within the field of Gender Studies is that I have nothing else to show than queer research (which is not true, but I guess homophobia and queerphobia is still a legitimate reason to reject people). None of the reviewers or interviewers for academic positions, neither Gender nor American Studies has ever commented on the research field of hardcore/punk rock. Within punk and hardcore communities, in North America, Austria, Mexico, Germany or Australia, no one has ever asked why I would focus on such a narrow niche like queer-feminist politics. And although I have encountered latent homo- or queerphobia and sexism in these scenes, my queer research focus has never been questioned or dismissed in the way it was in academia.

It goes without saying that I was not the first or only one to reflect on the history of queer-feminist punk, or the connection between queerness and hardcore/punk, for that matter. Indeed, one important point that I make in my book is that queer-feminist punks themselves have at least since 1985 reflected on the epistemology of queer-feminist punk in writing.[2] In his recent article published on *afropunk.com*, Nathan Leigh argues that the "Queer Punk History" already started in 1575. He claims that punk was first used to signify "a sex worker in a 1575 song called 'Simon The Old Kinge'" and that "by

---

1   Antisocial in Lee Edelman's terms means a position that is outside of the symbolic order of meanings, an anti-meaning that disrupts the logic of meaning creation, hence can only lead into chaos and destruction, if acknowledged. In my book, I understand antisocial as outside of normative social structures as well as against the continuation of normative meaning production, which necessarily always signifies queerness as outside of the social.

2   G.B. Jones and Bruce LaBruce published their first edition of the queer-feminist punk zine *J.D.s* in Toronto in 1985.

1899 it was appearing in print as a description of amateurishly performed music" (Leigh). While Leigh's historic sources remain to be confirmed,[3] he makes the relevant point that the term punk was already used to signify the musical genre of queer, sexually and gender transgressive bands such as The New York Dolls, The Stooges or even The Velvet Underground, long before The Sex Pistols were born. The members of these bands embraced non-normative sexualities and gender performances. Most importantly the "[q]ueer men" in these bands, had previously "filtered through a prison system which criminalized homosexuality [and] emerged wearing 'punk' as a badge of pride," Leigh notes.

How much hardcore/punk and queer cultures are entangled shows the history of the term *queer* itself. According to Steve LaFreniere, a member of Toronto's queer-feminist punk community, queer-feminist punks started using the term queer in the mid-1980s when mainstream "[p]eople weren't saying 'queer' quite yet" (qtd. in Rathe 2). Digging through tons of punk zines, flyers and other prints, I found that punks were not just among the first to use queer in a critical and self-referential way, but discussed the definitions of the terms punk and queer in their intersections with each other. Craig Flanagin, for example, printed this dictionarylike note on the cover of the second issue of Homocore NYC from 1992: "Queer/'kwer/adj 1 a: fabulous; fierce (cf. fierce pussy); b: admirable; Homocore n 1: Queer Punk Rock; adj 1: punker than fuck; fucker than punk". The Canadian G.B. Jones and Bruce LaBruce provided a similar amalgamation of the terms queer and punk in a *Maximum Rocknroll* article from 1989. Much like Leigh, they emphasize its former use to describe homosexual prisoners in their article:

> [P]unk is also an archaic word for dried wood used as tinder, the original meaning of the word 'faggot' as well. Homosexuals, witches, criminals, all denounced as enemies of the state, were once burned at the stake. The word for the material used to set them on fire became another name for the victims themselves. (Jones and LaBruce, "Don't Be Gay")

Their ironic explanation of punk's etymology signifies queers and punks both as "enemies of the state" (Ciminelli and Knox 7), an aspect that continues to be important for many queer-feminist punks until today (Leigh). In contrast to James Chance's words in Don Letts's documentary *Punk: Attitude* as quoted

---

3   Leigh provides only the title of the songs and a date, but no details about the sources or information on their archival location etc.

by the scholar and queer theorist Tavia Nyong'o, LaBruce's and Jones' reference to the criminalized appears almost delicate. Chance said: "originally punk meant, [...] a guy in prison who got fucked up the ass. And that's still what it means to people in prisons" (Nyong'o, "Do You Want" 107).

Acknowledging that this queer meaning of punk(ed) is not necessarily dominant within mainstream culture, Nyong'o nevertheless insists that its discriminatory meanings never fully vanished. In specific contexts, for example in African American slang punk(ed) designates male homosexuality "associated with extreme forms of unfreedom [...] imprisonment, slavery and rape" (Nyong'o, "Punk'd Theory" 22). This surplus meaning of punk that connects male homosexuality to experiences or the threat of unfreedom and imprisonment is important. It hints to issues of racialization and racism that occupy the intersection of punk and queer, and are yet often ignored.

In his already mentioned short essay on the history of queer punk, Leigh emphasizes these racialized aspects by seemingly correcting the historic whitewashing and invisibilization or denial of queerness of punk rock history. Leigh argues that the first punk musician was Little Richard,

> [the] queer, Black man, who played his music loud and fast and with a defiantly masterful unpolish. Little Richard set the stage for everything that punk would become while inhabiting every sense of the word with pride. John Waters once declared Little Richard 'was the first punk.' Though he wasn't called punk in the contemporary press, that's only because the impolite professional journalism of Lester Bangs didn't exist yet. (Leigh)

Leigh further supports his case by quoting Little Richard himself, saying: "I went through a lot when I was a boy. They called me sissy, punk, freak..." (Little Richard qtd. in Leigh).

Leigh, much like contemporary queer-feminist anti-racist punk scholars such as Fiona I. B. Ngô and Elizabeth A. Stinson, Mimi T. Nguyen ("Riot Grrrl, Race, and Revival," and in the interview to Vaca), José Muñoz or Tavia Nyong'o, puts punks of color as well as politics around racialization and nonnormative genders, sexes, and sexualities at the heart of hardcore/punk rock. "[W]hile the straight white male bands may have gotten the press attention" (Leigh), queer-feminist punks of color were fostering communities through their music and writing even before the mainstream knew that hardcore/punk was a music genre. Moreover, the intersection between queer, punk and criminalization, unfreedom, and incarceration continues to be important to understand why Black people and queers and queers of Color find themselves drawn to hardcore/punk culture in today's America.

No Future

Before further analyzing some of the projects queer-feminist punks of color and others organized during 2020 to support each other and their communities, I want to look into the connection between hardcore/punk, queer, and death/No Future. In the book *Queer-feminist Punk: An Antisocial History*, I argue that antisocial queer theory is able to untangle the energy, formation and workings of queer-feminist hardcore/punk social bonds, and I think that the current moment makes this antisocial sociality even more visible and viable.

Hardcore/punk emerged as a powerful spit in the face of normative society from the position of its abjects. The white male heterosexual British Sex Pistols only appropriated the outsider status from Afro-Caribbean communities and with it the hardcore/punk signifier "No Future," as the first hardcore/punk researcher Dick Hebdige showed in his seminal analysis *Subculture: The Meaning of Style* (69-70). And while the Sex Pistols' appropriation offered hardcore/punk up for its further incorporation into racist cultures, the meaning of racialized (and sexual) otherness never fully vanished. Similar meanings of societal otherness stick to queerness. Antisocial queer theory, most famously represented by Lee Edelman, embraces this quality. Unsurprising to any queer-feminist punk, Edelman identified the hardcore/punk slogan *No Future* as appropriate signifier for the status of queerness within the social realm, using it as his book's title. Although he vehemently rejected any linkage between his theory and punk (cf. Halberstam 824), the analysis of queer-feminist hardcore/punk bands from the 1990s onwards shows that Edelman's antisocial queer theory had already been born and brought to use within the hardcore/punk underground more than ten years prior to his publication. Bands such as the New York City-based God Is My Co-Pilot produced antisocial discourses with their hardcore/punk lyrics. In their song "Queer Disco" God Is My Co-Pilot sing "We're here we're queer we're going to fuck your children." This rhetoric shows remarkable similarities to Lee Edelman's most famous expression from his book: "Fuck the social order and the Child in whose name we're collectively terrorized; fuck Annie; [...] fuck the poor innocent kid on the Net" (Edelman 29), which, by the way, would make a pretty good punk song.

Edelman as well as God Is My Co-Pilot address the conservative logic prevalent within US-American and all other so-called Western cultures before and during the 1990s that seemed to fear sexual desire to such an extent that they have to bind it to reproduction to cope with it. And although some things have changed in many places, it cannot be denied that heteronormativity and conservative ideas around sex as reproductive sex are still prevalent in many areas of public discourses. In his book *No Future: Queer Theory and the Death Drive* Edelman takes up the psychoanalytic assertion that the sexual instinct is a converging force towards destruction of the self, a death drive. To "save" the self from the destructing and irritating qualities of sexuality and integrate it into the symbolic order, sexuality has to become attached to the meaning and purpose of reproduction. This reproduction is signified through the imaginary Child with capital C. While some actual children might partly live up to this idea, if they are white, ablebodied and "sacred" enough, most children, and especially Black kids and kids of color, immigrant kids or kids with disabilities fall not into this category. And since queerness cannot be attached to reproduction, and the imaginary Child, it becomes assigned to the oppositional place within the symbolic order of meanings, according to Edelman, the opposite of creation and reproduction, "the place of the social order's death drive" (Edelman 3).

Tightly connected with the imaginary Child is the concept of the future and futurity. In fact, the future of society, according to Edelman, is always visualized through the imaginary "Child" (ibid.). Therefore, "the queer subject [...] has been bound epistemologically to negativity, to nonsense, to antiproduction, to unintelligibility [...]" (Halberstam 823).

While Edelman's theory remains in the abstract for most of his book, queer-feminist punks took it up with the right wing and other conservatives who, quite literally, wanted to safe their children by banning homosexuals and trans*gender people from the public sphere, or rather, letting them die in silence. Queer-feminist punks were among other queer activists of the late 1980s and early 1990s that reacted with anger and rage to the vilification of homosexuality and queerness within mainstream culture during the HIV/AIDS crisis. Public media and institutions pathologized and stigmatized gay men (cf. Padilla 39), creating a new wave of gay-hate rhetoric that had previously been restricted to conservative hardliners, while the "federal government inaction on that crisis dramatized the oppression of homosexuals" (ibid.). These punk musicians and activists were not interested in assimilationist gay politics that focused on "the rights of gays to fit in, shop, marry, and join the army" (Shepard 513). As Matt Wobensmith said in an interview to Punk Rock Academy:

> "[Punk] allows people truly on the outside—some women, queers, people of color, fat people, and on—to find a niche where they can feel accepted. They use its ideas and pretense to make an identity that includes them. It provides some relief for all people to escape from their horrible surroundings" (qtd. in Punk Rock Academy).

These queer-feminist punks embraced the social outsider status, fighting injustice and discrimination by fostering their communities with loud music.

Punk rock's negativity has always been and still is nurtured through inequality and oppression along the lines of race, class, gender and sexuality. In the late 1970s and 1980s unequal wealth distribution disadvantaged the Black and people of color population in the US-American city centers and privileged the white middle-class that had previously moved out to the suburbs. The poverty of urban – including Black and brown – youth still increased during the 1990s due to the criminalization of drug use and a no-tolerance policy against crime. A renewed US patriotism supported white hegemony, xenophobia and racism (Spade 2011: 34). Young people in urban centers became increasingly angry since they did not see a positive future for themselves and their peers as Alice Bag documents in her memoir (Armendariz 45).

Edelman disqualifies punks' expression of No Future "as crude and pedestrian", because they were driven by "material political concerns" and dismisses them "as already a part of the conjuring of futurity that his project must foreclose" (qtd. in Halberstam 824). Yet, scholars like Judith Jack Halberstam and José Muñoz embrace punk's negativity, the latter based on his own experience. Muñoz explains that "[p]unk made [his] own suburban quotidian existence radical and experimental,—so experimental that [he] could imagine and eventually act on queer desire" (*Cruising Utopia* 105).

Hardcore/punk's embrace of the outsider status intersected nicely with queer's rejection of a politics of victimization and of assimilation (cf. Driver 5). Most importantly, it offered practical methods to communicate political views: antiprofessionalism, DIY aesthetics, screaming, pogo dancing, and torturing the drums, among other things. As someone who is interested in social participation beyond the classroom or academic circles, I appreciate hardcore/punk subcultures' acceptance and even appreciation of unpolished forms and emotionality. Hardcore/punk's loudness, rhythm and immediacy pushes the political content to the fore. Most importantly, part of hardcore/punk politics is often the sustaining or support of its community, including those members that are most vulnerable.

Queer-feminist Anti-racist Punks

I realized that queer-feminist punks are crucially contributing to sustain marginalized communities beyond their inner circles when I was a visiting scholar at the University of California at Berkley, where I spent a year to finish my dissertation in 2011 and 2012. I lived in the adjoined city of Oakland, where, on October 10, 2011 people occupied Frank H. Ogawa Plaza in the center of downtown, forming a protest movement that would become known as Occupy Oakland. The protestors renamed the space Oscar Grant Plaza after a young Black man who had been killed by Bay Area Rapid Transit Police in 2009. The police cleared the protest encampment at Oscar Grant Plaza several times and forced the protesters to move the encampment to other locations over the months of October and November. After the last encampment was cleared on November 21, 2011, Occupy Oakland concentrated on other forms of protest such as strikes, street protests and community facilitating continuing until today. In contrast to other protests, for example those in New York City, Occupy Oakland was at its core about racist injustice in the USA, about the disregard of African Americans and about the unjust immigration system that criminalizes LatinX and other people of color. Moreover, it was spearheaded by Black activists and people of color protesters, including many queer-feminist punks of color.

My experience with the Occupy movement and its intersection with the flourishing hardcore/punk scenes significantly influenced the focus of my dissertation and subsequent book. Occupy Oakland and its sister protests throughout California where fights against police brutality and the disregard of Black and brown lives as well as against corporate greed and other forms of injustice. But in my experience, Occupy was most of all about caring for a community that the system – the state and neoliberal capitalism – continuously failed and that simply did not see a future in contemporary US America. The queer-feminist punk scenes did not simply join Occupy Oakland and other protests in the area but queer-feminist punk community members significantly contributed to the Occupy protests, shaping its goals and forms of protest.

The Occupy movement was accused of being disorganized because it refused to have a leader or a speaker and refused to name aims or goals or
strategies to reform the existing systems. Many dismissed the movement,
much like they dismiss punk for rejecting the current social system, without
offering a 'plan' to reform it. But I think this is the strength of both Occupy
as well as hardcore/punk. The articulation of anger, the rejection of normative society allows individuals who are constantly disregarded, minoritized
and oppressed to find social bonds that sustain them. The social bonds are
formed during concerts, or during street protests. Yet, showing up for one
another can also take other forms. One still ongoing punk initiative that is
connected to Occupy Oakland is Punks with Lunch (2021). The group provides food and basic necessities to the homeless and drug using community
of West Oakland. They offer needle exchange and Narcan Trainings.[4] They table at music shows and community events where they provide safer drug use
supplies, fentanyl drug testing, safer sex supplies, and Narcan.

Engaging with queer-feminist punks of color and community organizers in Oakland, Berkeley and Los Angeles, and meeting hardcore/punk icons,
such as the musician, author, educator and feminist archivist Alice Bag, who
had just published her memoir that focused on her membership in the Los
Angeles' hardcore/punk scene of the 1970s, I realized that North-American
hardcore/punk rock had always been about queer, feminist and anti-racist
struggles long before Bruce LaBruce and G.B. Jones came up with the term
homocore or before the term Afro-punk was created. Moreover, and most importantly, I saw that queer-feminist punks of color use hardcore/punk's d.i.y.
culture to facilitate and support their communities beyond strictly defined
cultural, class or other borders. One hardcore/punk performer who has been
a stable member of and prolific contributor to the hardcore/punk and queer
community of Oakland is Brontez Purnell.[5] I saw him first perform in the
band Gravy Train at some point in the 2010s. My favorite cultural production
by Purnell, however, is a music video with his band The Younger Lovers. The
video and song are called "Keeps on Falling Down," yet there is no falling happening. On the contrary, in the video Purnell performs dance moves together
with a varying group or crowd of people, with every move being announced by
a sheet of paper, containing the move's name. This community of queers and

---

4   Narcan or Naloxone is a drug used in cases of acute opioid-overdoses (https://www.dr
     ugs.com/monograph/naloxone.html#)

5   https://brontezpurnellartjock.com/

punks and queer punks of color dance together in different locations such as a downtown Oakland street, in front of a fast food restaurant or in a basement or garage space. The video creates the idea of a community of diverse people that care for each other and enjoy being and dancing together. Purnell and the Younger Lovers have done many videos since then, and Purnell has also cofounded the experimental dance group the Brontez Purnell Dance Company, has created the zine *Fag School*, has directed several short films and the documentary *Unstoppable Feat: The Dances of Ed Mock*. Moreover, he has created a graphic novel, a novella, and a children's book, written the novel *Since I Laid My Burden Down* and published his recent book *100 Boyfriends*.

Yet, in the year 2020, and sitting at home in my two-room apartment that dubbed as office, classroom, studio etc. with no one but my partner to engage, or share a live and physical (not virtual) space with, the video "Keeps on Falling Down" was my go-to leisure time activity. It is not the angriest hardcore/punk song, and has almost a pop feel to it. But in this moment it was hardcore/punk, because it showed me mutual and collective care and support and enjoyment of each other that allowed me to relate to. This experience of relationality, which frequently occurs at queer-feminist hardcore/punk concerts, was always radical or hardcore in the sense that it was empowering and including those who were meant to be excluded by normative communities. Yet, in the moment of heightened societal divide and individual isolation, the pop-punk song and video became hardcore because it showed solidarity, and mutual care across differently racialized populations, generations and species and created feelings of belonging that were so strikingly absent in mainstream society.

The kind of solidarity and care for each other that the Younger Lovers' video shows are needed more than ever in 2021. The year 2020 has brought many ugly truths to the surface. The pandemic and a populist administration that encouraged white supremacy, brutal and racist capitalism, and racist violence has highlighted and amplified the inequalities among US Americans. It has shown that Black communities and other communities of color are, due to systemic oppression and marginalization, more vulnerable to the Corona virus (Eyes on Discrimination Centre; Soucheray). These communities have suffered more losses, while at the same time carrying much of the burden of providing and caring for the sick as essential workers in low paid jobs or as family members and friends. While hit hardest by the pandemic, systemic state violence and police brutality have continuously or even increasingly targeted Black communities and other communities of color. No Future is the grim reality for many who chose to march in protest with the Black Lives Matter movement rather than dying in silence.

Queer-feminist punks of color such as the above-mentioned Purnell or the New York-based artist Cristy Road[6] and her band Choked Up[7] showed up for the Black community with their social commentary, by providing music, writing and art, and organizing fundraisers etc. Event organizers such as Punk Black[8] have continued to support their community with virtual venues for the streaming of live concerts from their living rooms and basements. There are countless examples out there of how hardcore/punks employ punk music and art to support each other and the BLM movement. One very recent one is the *No Silence: Sounds of the Underground* album released by the Oakland-based label Psychic Eye in December 2020. The album consists of two CDs with over 40 tracks of music from US bands that support the Black Lives Matter movement and abolition of I.C.E. According to their bandcamp page, "[a]ll proceeds are split between Black Lives Matter Louisville and The Florence Project, an organization that provides legal support to migrant detainees in U.S. concentration camps."[9] These and other queer-punks of color have supported the homeless in different parts of the US through online fundraisers, for example in support of the homeless resource center GRACE in Gainesville and Alachua County.[10]

Putting Theory into Practice

Queer-feminist punks continue to not only engage with queer and feminist politics as well as with academic theory but also produce queer-feminist political theory. Purnell, Road and co. are writing in a "Black organic intellectual tradition" (Harris; also cf. Weiss-Meyer;). They speak back to white privilege, analyze, explain and counter oppressive social structures. In their writing, on their social media sites, in their music and art, we can find valuable knowledge. Their queer-feminist hardcore/punk politics address the rampant sexism, misogyny, trans*phobia, anti-Muslim and anti-Black racism present in

6   https://www.croadcore.org/
7   https://chokedup.bandcamp.com/track/home-2
8   https://www.facebook.com/wearepunkblack/
9   https://psychiceye.bandcamp.com/album/no-silence-sounds-of-the-underground
10   https://grace.rallyup.com/FEST2020

contemporary America. But they also address in nuanced ways the participation in racialized, sexualized and anti-queer structures of the neoliberal mainstream. Such queer-feminist hardcore/punk activists are in a dialogue with academic writing and contribute through their art practices to academic discourse that seek social justice through art as well as law and other means (Stardust et al.). Authors such as Nguyen (*Evolution of a Race Riot*; *Race Riot II.*), Osa Atoe ("Feminist Power") or Helen Luu (*How to Stage a Coup*) brought and bring queer-feminist theory into the hardcore/punk communities through their widely distributed zines. Some of these hardcore/punk writers hold academic positions themselves,[11] and together with former and current hardcore/punk community members,[12] these scholars and educators bring hardcore/punk aesthetics, theory and hardcore/punk research practice into the universities. Importantly, they encourage and mentor younger generations of queer-feminist punks to engage with hardcore/punk research inside and outside the universities.

Queer-feminist punks continue to participate in movements for social justice such as the Black Live Matter movement. They find alliances with different groups of queer, feminist, anti-racist and decolonial thinkers and activists. Many fabulous queer-feminist and anti-racist hardcore/punk initiatives and projects reacted to the dire need of its community members during the last months; I have shown how queer-feminist punks more than ever use hardcore/punk music and theory to connect to and support each other. Living, working and collaborating within queer-feminist hardcore/punk communities has prepared queer-feminist punks for the current moment. Due to their DIY ethos as well as the solid analytical tools developed to analyze social, gendered, sexual, racialized and ableist inequalities, queer-feminist anti-racist punks were not only able to identify the social and political injustices amplified by the Corona crisis but also to sustain and add to the existing support structures as well as to continue their anti-racist queer and feminist work till today.

If the year 2020 has shown me anything useful, it is that queer-feminist punks continue to apply queer, feminist and decolonizing politics, activist strategies and social analysis to fight the racialized discrimination, misogyny, homophobia, ableism and transphobia of contemporary US-American

---

11   Mimi Thi Nguyen, for example, is Associate Professor of Gender and Women's Studies and Asian American Studies at the University of Illinois, Urbana-Champaign.

12   Among them was the late José Muñoz.

culture on all societal levels. They combine anti-racist, decolonial and feminist accounts with their specific hardcore/punk philosophy of antisocial queerness or queer negativity through their art. Thereby, they have created a collective and freely available oeuvre of work—videos, writing, drawing, music, photography, installations, paintings, dances—that negotiates, translates and appropriates academic approaches but also produces negative and politicized queer-feminist theories without any direct inspiration from academic discourses. Hence, queer-feminist punk communities accomplish what academic queer theory often does not achieve: They transform their radically antisocial queer positions into livable activism. Moreover, they maintain social bonds and keep caring for each other. While the sound of their musical productions might not always be fast, loud and restricted to three chords, their rootedness in punk structures and queer-feminist politics and ethics makes them hardcore.

References

Armendariz Velasquez, Alicia (Alice Bag). *Violence Girl: East L.A. Rage to Hollywood Stage, a Chicana Punk Story*. Feral House, 2011.

Atoe, Osa. "Feminist Power." *Maximum Rocknroll* 327, August 2010.

Ciminelli, David, and Ken Knox. *Homocore: The Loud and Raucous Rise of Queer Rock*. Alyson Books, 2005.

Driver, Susan. *Queer Youth Cultures*. State University of New York Press, 2008.

Eyes on Discrimination Centre. "Why are black Americans suffering more from coronavirus?" TRT World. 9 April 2020, trtworld.com/magazine/why-are-black-americans-suffering-more-from-coronavirus-35270. Accessed 27 May 2022.

God is my Co-Pilot. "Queer Disco Anthem." *The Best of God Is My Co-Pilot*. Atlantic, 1996.

Halberstam, Judith. "The Politics of Negativity in Recent Queer Theory." *Publication of the Modern Language Association of America* 121.3, May 2006, pp. 823–5.

Harris, Christopher. "The Black Organic Intellectual Tradition and the Challenges of Educating and Developing Organic Intellectuals in the 21st Century." *The Journal of Intersectionality* 2.1, 2018, pp. 51–107.

Hebdige, Dick. *Subculture: The Meaning of Style*. 1979. Routledge, 2001.

Jones, G.B., and Bruce LaBruce. "Don't Be Gay: Or How I Learned to Stop Worrying and Fuck Punk up the Ass." *Maximum Rocknroll* 69, February 1989.

Leigh, Nathan (June 22nd, 2020). "Queer Punk History: 1575 – Present." *Afropunk.* 22 June 2020, afropunk.com/2020/06/queer-punk-history-1575-present/. Acccessed 27 May 2022.

Luu, Helen., editor. *How to Stage a Coup: An Insurrection of the Underground Liberation Army.* 2000.

Marinucci, Mimi. *Feminism is Queer: The Intimate Connection between Queer and Feminist Theory.* Zed Books, 2010.

Muñoz, José. *Cruising Utopia: The Then and There of Queer Futurity.* New York University Press, 2009.

Muñoz, José. *Disidentifications: Queers of Color and the Performance of Politics.* University of Minnesota Press, 1999.

Muñoz, José. "Forum: Conference Debates: The Antisocial Thesis in Queer Theory." *Publication of the Modern Language Association of America* 121.3, May 2006, pp. 819–28.

Ngô, Fiona I., and Elizabeth A. Stinson. "Introduction: Threads and Omissions." *Punk Anteriors.* Special issue of Women & Performance: A Journal of Feminist Theory 22.2, 2012, pp. 165–71.

Nguyen, Mimi T. "Aesthetics, Access, Intimacy, or Race, Riot Grrrl, Bad Feelings." Sarah Lawrence College. 2010. Oral presentation.

Nguyen, Mimi T., editor. *Evolution of a Race Riot.* The editor, 1997.

Nguyen, Mimi T. "How to Stage a Coup: Interview with Helen Luu." *Race Riot II,* edited by Mimi Thi Nguyen, The editor, 2002, pp. 36–40.

Nguyen, Mimi T. "It's (Not) a White World: Looking for Race in Punk." (reprint from *Punk Planet* 28. November/December 1998) *White Riot: Punk Rock and the Politics of Race,* edited by Stephen Duncombe and Maxwell Tremblay, Verso, 2011, pp. 257–77.

Nguyen, Mimi T. "Race, Riot Grrrls, Bad Feelings." *Thread & Circuits: An Archive of Wayward Youth* 3, 28 March 2010, threadandcircuits.wordpress.com/2010/03/28/58/. Accessed 27 May 2022.

Nguyen, Mimi T., editor. *Race Riot II.* The editor, 2002.

Nguyen, Mimi T. "Riot Grrrl, Race, and Revival." *Women & Performance: A Journal of Feminist Theory* 22.2–3, 2012, pp. 173–96.

No Silence: Sounds of the Underground. Psychic Eye, 2020.

Nyong'o, Tavia. "Do You Want Queer Theory (or Do You Want the Truth)? Intersections of Punk and Queer in the 1970s." *Radical History Review* 100, 2008, pp. 103–19.

Nyong'o, Tavia. "Punk'd Theory." *Social Text* 84/85, 2005, pp. 19–36.

Padilla, Yolanda. *Gay and Lesbian Rights Organizing: Community-Based Strategies.* Harrington Park Press, 2004.

Punk Rock Academy. "Interview with Matt Wobensmith." *Punk Rock Academy*, 26 March 2008, punkrockacademy.com/stm/int/mw.html. Accessed 27 May 2022.

Punks! Punks! Punks! "Punks Occupy." 27 December 2011, https://www.punk spunkspunks.com/wordpress/tag/punks-occupy. Accessed 22 May 2012.

Punks With Lunch. Official Website. 27 January 2021, punkswithlunch.org. Accessed 27 May 2022.

Rathe, Adam. "Queer to the Core: Gay Punk Comes out with a Vengeance. An Oral History of the Movement That Changed the World (Whether You Knew It or Not)." *Out.* April 2012, out.com. Accessed 30 April 2012.

Road, Cristy. "Freedom is subjective." *Facebook.* 8 November 2020, face-book.com/croad. Accessed 27 May 2022.

Shepard, Benjamin. "Bridging the Divide between Queer Theory." *Sexualities* 13, 2010, pp. 511–27.

Soucheray, Stephanie. "US blacks 3 times more likely than whites to get COVID-19." *Center for Infectious Disease Research and Policy*, University of Minnesota. 14 August 2020, https://www.cidrap.umn.edu/news-pers pective/2020/08/us-blacks-3-times-more-likely-whites-get-covid-19. Accessed 27 May 2022.

Spade, Dean. *Normal Life: Administrative Violence, Critical Trans Politics, and the Limits of Law.* South End Press, 2011.

Stardust, Zahra, Roslyn M. Satchel, Afsaneh Rigot, Kendra Albert, and Micaela Mantegna. "Movement Lawyering for Alternative Futures: Social Movements & the Limits of the Law." *Berkam Klein Center for Internet and Society at Harvard University.* 4 January 2021, medium.com/berkman-klein-center/movement-lawyering-for-alternative-futures-404ba2010bf2. Accessed 27 May 2022.

The Skinjobs. "Burn Your Rainbow." *Burn Your Rainbow.* Bongo Beat Records, 2003.

"The Younger Lovers – Keeps on Falling Down." *YouTube*, uploaded by Gary Fembot, 26 August 2011, youtube.com/watch?v=DHau4cOdgpo&t=103s.

Vaca, Chantal. "Profile: A political punk's path to a PhD and tenure." *The Daily Illini.* 29 June 2020, dailyillini.com/longform/2020/06/29/profile-a-political-punks-path-to-a-phd-and-tenure. Accessed 27 May 2022.

Weiss-Meyer, Amy. "What Novelists Can Learn From Playwrights: Brontez Purnell on writing fiction from a theater background." *The Atlantic.* 21 January 2021, theatlantic.com/books/archive/2021/01/brontez-purnell-talks-about-his-new-short-story-early-retirement/617395. Accessed 27 May 2022.

Contributors

In addition to handing in short biography notes, all contributors were asked to fill out a short questionnaire and list 1.) their most important publications on hardcore/punk, 2.) three records that shaped their interest in hardcore/punk, 3.) three theoretical books that are important for them, and 4.) the first hardcore/punk show as well as 5.) the first academic conference they attended. The individual information not only provides interesting insights into the personal and academic backgrounds of the respective author, but also inspiration for further reading, hearing, and looking into the subcultural and academic discourses that underlie and pervade the articles in *Hardcore Research*.

Gerfried Ambrosch is an independent researcher, writer, and musician based in Munich, Germany. He received his PhD in English and American Studies from the University of Graz in 2015. His publications include *The Poetry of Punk: The Meaning behind Punk Rock and Hardcore Lyrics* (Routledge 2018) and various papers on related topics.

List your most important academic publications on hardcore/punk:
Ambrosch, Gerfried. *The Poetry of Punk: The Meaning behind Punk Rock and Hardcore Lyrics*. Routledge, 2018.
Ambrosch, Gerfried. "'Guilty of Being White': Punk's Ambivalent Relationship with Race and Racism." *The Journal of Popular Culture* 51.4, 2018, pp. 902–22.
Ambrosch, Gerfried. "'Refusing to Be a Man': Gender, Feminism, and Queer Identity in the Punk Culture." *Punk and Post-Punk* 5.3, 2016, pp. 247–64.

Name three records that shaped your interest in hardcore/punk:
1. Catharsis. *Passion*
2. Tragedy. *Vengeance*
3. Propagandhi. *Less Talk, More Rock*

Name three theoretical books that are important for you:
1. Lars Eckstein. *Reading Song Lyrics.*
2. Simon Frith. *Performing Rites: Evaluating Popular Music.*
3. Dick Hebdige. *Subculture: The Meaning of Style.*

Name the first hardcore/punk show you attended:
local band NUFO (Nuclear Fallout)

Name the first academic conference you attended:
AAUTE (Austrian Association for University Teachers of English) 2016

Ellen M. Bernhard is an assistant professor of Digital Communication at Georgian Court University in Lakewood, New Jersey. Her research focuses on punk rock scenes and their relationship with social media, popular culture, and technology. Her book, *Contemporary Punk Rock Communities: Scenes of Inclusion and Dedication* was published by Lexington in 2019.

List your most important academic publications on hardcore/punk:
Bernhard, Ellen. *Contemporary Punk Rock Communities: Scenes of Inclusion and Dedication.* Lexington Books, 2019.
Bernhard, Ellen. "'I thought it was a very punk rock thing to say': NOFX's (sort-of) public apology and (in)civility in defining contemporary punk rock in online spaces.", *Punk & Post-Punk* 9.1, 2020, pp. 7–22.
Bernhard, Ellen. "Bad Religion and the Burlesque: Framing Extremist Rhetoric in 'The Kids are Alt-Right.'" *Rock Music Studies*, 2022, DOI: 10.1080/19401159.2022.2110768.

Name three records that shaped your interest in hardcore/punk:
1. Bad Religion. *The Empire Strikes First*
2. Pennywise. *Land of the Free?*
3. Anti-Flag. *The Terror State*

Name three theoretical books that are important for you:
1. David Muggleton and Rupert Weinzierl (eds.). *The Post-Subcultures Reader.*
2. Joseph Heath and Andrew Potter. *Nation of Rebels: Why Counterculture Became Consumer Culture.*
3. Stacy Thompson. *Punk Productions: Unfinished Business.*

Name the first hardcore/punk show you attended:
Stadium show: blink-182 & New Found Glory, Allentown Fairgrounds, Sep. 2001;
small venue show: Thrice, Midtown, the Movielife, Face to Face, Trocadero, Philadelphia, April 2002.

Name the first academic conference you attended:
PCA/ACA (Popular Culture Association/ American Culture Association), Boston, 2012

Russ Bestley is Reader in Graphic Design & Subcultures at the London College of Communication. He is lead editor of the journal *Punk & Post-Punk*, series editor of the *Global Punk* book series published by Intellect Books and a member of the Punk Scholars Network. His research archive can be accessed at www.hitsvilleuk.com.

List your most important academic publications on hardcore/punk:
Bestley, Russ, Mike Dines, Alastair Gordon, and Paula Guerra (eds.). *Trans-Global Punk Scenes: The Punk Reader Vol. 2*. Intellect Books, 2021.
Bestley, Russ (as consultant editor), Adrian Shaughnessy, and Tony Brook (eds.). *Action Time Vision: Punk & Post Punk 7" Record Sleeves From the Collections of Russ Bestley and Tony Brook*. Unit Editions, 2016.
Bestley, Russ, and Alex Ogg. *The Art of Punk*. Omnibus Press (UK), 2012.

Name three records that shaped your interest in hardcore/punk:
1. The Stranglers. *Rattus Norvegicus*
2. Killing Joke. *What's THIS For...*
3. Wire. *Pink Flag*

Name three theoretical books that are important for you:
1. Daniel C Dennett. *Darwin's Dangerous Idea: Evolution and the Meanings of Life*.
2. John Carey. *The Intellectuals and the Masses: Pride and Prejudice Among the Literary Intelligentsia, 1880-1939*.
3. Sadie Plant. *The Situationist International in a Postmodern Age*.

Name the first hardcore/punk show you attended:
Stranglers, Clash, Ramones etc. (1978-80), Dead Kennedys, Black Flag, Killing
Joke etc. (1980-81)

Name the first academic conference you attended:
Design Beyond Design, Maastricht 1998

Konstantin Butz is a researcher and lecturer at the Academy of Media Arts
Cologne, Germany. He has studied American Studies and Cultural Studies at
the University of Bremen and at Dickinson College in Carlisle, Pennsylvania.
He holds a doctorate degree in American Studies from the University of
Cologne. His research interests include subcultures, youth cultures, and (un-)
popular literature and music. Despite (or because of...?) being completely
talentless, he has been playing in crappy hardcore/punk bands for more than
25 years.

List your most important academic publications on hardcore/punk:
Butz, Konstantin. *Grinding California: Culture and Corporeality in American Skate
Punk*. transcript, 2012.
Butz, Konstantin. "Backyard Drifters: Mobility and Skate Punk in Suburban
Southern California." *Pirates, Drifters, Fugitives: Figures of Mobility in the US
and Beyond*, edited by Heike Paul, Alexandra Ganser, and Katharina Gerund.
Winter Verlag, 2012, pp. 175–94.
Butz, Konstantin. "The Authenticity of a T-shirt: Ryan Gosling, Roddy Dan-
gerblood, and the Rebellious Genealogy of Thrasher Magazine." *Rock Music
Studies* 4.1, 2017, pp. 47–56.

Name three records that shaped your interest in hardcore/punk:
1. Surf Nazis Must Die. *Anti-Everything E.P.*
2. Refused. *The Shape of Punk to Come*
3. From Ashes Rise. *Nightmares*

Name three theoretical books that are important for you:
1. Jack Halberstam. *The Queer Art of Failure.*
2. Iain Borden. *Skateboarding, Space and the City: Architecture and the Body.*
3. Hans Ulrich Gumbrecht. *Production of Presence: What Meaning Cannot Convey.*

Name the first hardcore/punk show you attended:
Besides the dubious appearances of my friends' local band Am Bodenwälzen it was a show by No Fun at All at JZ Kamp in Bielefeld, Germany, 1997.

Name the first academic conference you attended:
Post-Graduate-Forum of the German Association of American Studies at Friedrich-Alexander-Universität Erlangen-Nürnberg. 2007.

Marcus Clayton is a PhD candidate in English Literature and Creative Writing at the University of Southern California. While primarily practicing creative Nonfiction, his scholarship locates the various bridges between Black and Latinx literature, genre-bending media, and how people of color use punk rock as a decolonial praxis.

List your most important academic publications on hardcore/punk:
Clayton, Marcus. "Guilty of Not Being White: On the Visibility and Othering of Black Punk." *The Oxford Handbook of Punk Rock*, edited by George McKay and Gina Arnold. Online edition, Oxford Academic, 2020.

Name three records that shaped your interest in hardcore/punk:
1. At The Drive-In. *Relationship of Command*
2. Black Flag. *Jealous Again EP*
3. Bad Brains. *Bad Brains*

Name three theoretical books that are important for you:
1. Frantz Fanon. *The Wretched of the Earth*.
2. José Esteban Muñoz. *Dissidentifications: Queers of Color and the Performance of Politics*.
3. Stephen Duncombe and Maxwell Tremblay (eds.). *White Riot: Punk Rock and the Politics of Race*.

Name the first hardcore/punk show you attended:
I cannot remember the bands who played, but I was in my late-teens and it was a backyard show in Downey, CA with a few local bands. Broken up by cops within a couple hours.

Name the first academic conference you attended:
UC Riverside Punk Conference, 2019

Brian Cogan is an associate professor in the Department of Communications at Molloy College. He is the author, co-author and co-editor of ten books and dozens of articles and anthologies on popular culture, music, and the media. His most recent works are two books on Monty Python's Flying Circus.

List your most important academic publications on hardcore/punk:
Cogan, Brian. *The Encyclopedia of Punk Music and Culture*. Sterling, 2006.

Name three records that shaped your interest in hardcore/punk:
1. Descendents. *Milo Goes to College*
2. Bad Religion. *Against the Grain*
3. Adolescents. *S/T* (Blue Record)

Name three theoretical books that are important for you:
1. Mark Andersen and Mark Jenkins. *Dance of Days: Two Decades of Punk in the Nation's Capital*.
2. Greil Marcus. *Lipstick Traces: A Secret History of the Twentieth Century*.
3. Jon Savage. *England's Dreaming: The Sex Pistols and Punk Rock*.

Name the first hardcore/punk show you attended:
Black Flag, City Gardens, New Jersey, 1985

Name the first academic conference you attended:
New York State Communication conference

Shaun Cullen is an independent writer and researcher in Los Angeles, who has recently taught at Woodbury University and Middle Tennessee State University. He has published articles on Black Flag in *Criticism*, and Kanye West and Taylor Swift in the *Journal of Popular Music Studies*. His current research interests include genre stratification in post-Nirvana U.S. rock music, the songwriter Elliott Smith, and the evolution of analog and digital recording studios.

List your most important academic publications on hardcore/punk:
Cullen, Shaun. "White Skin, Black Flag: Hardcore Punk and the Racialization of Sound in Southern California." *Criticism* 58.1, 2016, pp. 59–85.

Name three records that shaped your interest in hardcore/punk:
1. Ramones. *All the Stuff (And More) Volume One*
2. Stiff Little Fingers. *Alternative Ulster* (7")
3. Black Flag. *Damaged*

Name three theoretical books that are important for you:
1. Dick Hebdige. *Subculture: The Meaning of Style.*
2. Greil Marcus. *Lipstick Traces: A Secret History of the Twentieth Century.*
3. Frantz Fanon. *The Wretched of the Earth.*

Name the first hardcore/punk show you attended:
Depends on your definition of punk. I saw the Ramones on their last tour at the Electric Factory in Philadelphia on 2/16/1996. I was a sophomore in high school. The year before I had seen Fugazi with Make-Up opening and Ween at the Trocadero, also in Philadelphia. Some might call Fugazi hardcore. I consider Ween punk, especially during that phase.

Name the first academic conference you attended:
The annual conference of the Midwest Popular Culture Association in Indianapolis in 2006.

Ms. Bob Davis, founder of Louise Lawrence Transgender Archive, received an MFA in Electronic Music from Mills College Center for Contemporary Music and engineered sound for two tours of Laurie Anderson's *United States, Parts I-IV*. She served two terms on the GLBT Historical Society Board of Directors and has taught American music for over 40 years.

List your most important academic publications on hardcore/punk:
Belsito, Peter, Davis, Bob, and Marian Kester. *Street Art: The Punk Poster in San Francisco 1977-1981.* Last Gasp of San Francisco, 1981.
Belsito, Peter, and Bob Davis. *Hardcore California – A History of Punk and New Wave.* The Last Gasp of San Francisco, 1983.

Name three records that shaped your interest in hardcore/punk:
1. *The Threepenny Opera (Die Dreigroschenoper)* by Bertolt Brecht, music by Kurt Weill, original New York cast
2. The Velvet Underground. *The Velvet Underground & Nico*
3. Carl Orff. *Carmina Burana*

Name three theoretical books that are important for you:
Lou Harrison. *Lou Harrison's Music Primer.*
John Blacking. *How Musical is Man?*
Manly P. Hall. *The Therapeutic Value of Music Including the Philosophy of Music.*

Name the first hardcore/punk show you attended:
Some show at Tool & Die in San Francisco, 1980

Name the first academic conference you attended:
A world music conference at University of California, Berkeley in the late 1970s. I don't recall the name of the presenting organization.

Mike Dines is Co-Pathway Leader for Popular Music at Middlesex University, and is co-founder and chair of the Punk Scholars Network. As a scholar he has written widely on subcultures and popular music, including the co-editing of *The Aesthetics of Our Anger: Anarcho-Punk, Politics, Music* (2016), *Punk Pedagogies: Music, Culture and Learning* (2017), *The Punk Reader: Research Transmissions from the Local and the Global* (2019), *Punk Now!! Contemporary Perspectives on Punk* (2020), *Trans-Global Punk Scenes: The Punk Reader Vol. 2* (2021) and *Punk Identities, Punk Utopias: Global Punk and Media* (2021). His current writing takes him in the direction of popular music and spirituality with the co-edited collection *Exploring the Spiritual in Popular Music: Beatified Beats* (2021).

List your most important academic publications on hardcore/punk:
Dines, Mike. *Tales From the Punkside.* Itchy Monkey Press, 2014.
Dines, Mike, and Matt Worley (eds.). *The Aesthetics of Our Anger: Anarcho-Punk, Politics, Music.* Autonomedia/Minor Compositions, 2016.
Dines, Mike, Gareth Dylan Smith, and Tom Parkinson (eds.). *Punk Pedagogies: Music, Culture and* Learning. Routledge, 2017.
Dines, Mike, Russ Bestley, Alastair Gordon, and Paula Guerra (eds.). *The Punk Reader: Research Transmissions from the Local and the Global.* Intellect Press, 2019.

Name three records that shaped your interest in hardcore/punk:
1. Culture Shock. *Onwards and Upwards*
2. Crass. *Yes Sir, I Will*
3. Electro Hippies. *The Only Good Punk...*

Name three theoretical books that are important for you:
1. Paul Willis. *Learning to Labour: How Working Class Kids Get Working Class Jobs.*
2. Theodor W. Adorno. *Negative Dialectics.*
3. *The Bhagavad-Gita.*

Name the first hardcore/punk show you attended:
UK Subs, 1987.

Name the first academic conference you attended:
Salford University, 2000.

Kevin Dunn is a professor of international relations at Hobart and William Smith Colleges. A regular contributor to *Razorcake* magazine, he also runs a small DIY punk label, and plays in several active bands, including The Sriracha-chas, What About Now, and World Heroes.

List your most important academic publications on hardcore/punk:
Dunn, Kevin. *Global Punk: Resistance and Rebellion in Everyday Life.* Bloomsbury, 2016.

Name three records that shaped your interest in hardcore/punk:
1. Bad Brains. *Rock For Life*
2. The Clash. *London Calling*
3. Naked Raygun. *All Rise*

Name three theoretical books that are important for you:
1. Antonio Gramsci. *The Prison Notebooks.*
2. Frantz Fanon. *The Wretched of the Earth.*
3. Stuart Hall

Name the first hardcore/punk show you attended:
Stevie Stiletto and the Switchblades, Jacksonville, FL, 1983

Name the first academic conference you attended:
International Studies Association

David Ensminger is an instructor at Lee College in Baytown, TX, where he teaches English, Humanities, and Folklore. He received his M.A. at City College of New York City, with a focus on short fiction and poetry, and received his M.S. in the Folklore Program at the University of Oregon, where he specialized in punk visual culture. His research includes multiple areas of subcultural studies, including street art, DIY archiving, vernacular spaces, underground media productions, and more.

List your most important academic publications on hardcore/punk:
Ensminger, David. *Punk Women*. Microcosm Press, 2021.
Ensminger, David. *The Politics of Punk*. Rowman and Littlefield, 2016.
Ensminger, David. *Visual Vitriol: The Street Art and Subcultures of the Punk and Hardcore Generation*. University Press of Mississippi, 2011.

Name three records that shaped your interest in hardcore/punk:
1. Buzzcocks. *Singles Going Steady*
2. Minor Threat. *Minor Threat*
3. The Clash. *The Clash*

Name three theoretical books that are important for you:
1. Dick Hebdige. *Subculture: The Meaning of Style*.
2. Craig O'hara. *The Philosophy of Punk*.
3. Jon Savage. *England's Dreaming: The Sex Pistols and Punk Rock*.

Name the first hardcore/punk show you attended:
Black Flag, 1986

Name the first academic conference you attended:
Society for Ethnomusicology, University of British Columbia, 2008

Shayna Maskell is an assistant professor in the School of Integrative studies at George Mason University. She received her PhD in American Studies from the University of Maryland. Her book *Politics as Sound: The Washington,*

DC, *Hardcore Scene, 1978-1983* (2021) explores how and why cultural forms, such as music, produce and resist politics and power. Her areas of research include youth culture, popular culture, and social justice.

List your most important academic publications on hardcore/punk:
Maskell, Shayna. *Politics as Sound: The Washington, DC, Hardcore Scene, 1978-1983.* University of Illinois Press, 2021.
Maskell, Shayna. "We're Just a Minor Threat: Minor Threat and the Intersectionality of Sound." *The Oxford Handbook of Punk Rock*, edited by George McKay and Gina Arnold. Online edition, Oxford Academic, 2020.
Maskell, Shayna. "Performing Punk: Bad Brains and the Construction of Identity." *Journal of Popular Music Studies* 21.4, 2009, pp. 411–26.

Name three records that shaped your interest in hardcore/punk:
1. Minor Threat. *Minor Threat*
2. Bad Brains. *Bad Brains*
3. Minor Threat. *In My Eyes*

Name three theoretical books that are important for you:
1. Pierre Bourdieu. *Distinction: A Social Critique of the Judgement of Taste.*
2. Dick Hebdige. *Subculture: The Meaning of Style.*
3. Michel Foucault. *The History of Sexuality.*

Name the first hardcore/punk show you attended:
Fugazi

Name the first academic conference you attended:
Southwestern Popular Culture Association

Alain Müller holds an assistant professorship in cultural anthropology and gender studies at the Institute of cultural anthropology and European ethnology in Basel, Switzerland—a position he shares with Marion Schulze. In 2019, he authored the book *Construire le monde du hardcore*, in which he examines the translocal distribution of hardcore punk. His current work focuses on knowledges, materialities and ontologies in diverse practices.

List your most important academic publications on hardcore/punk:
Müller, Alain, and Marion Schulze. "Le Hardcore (punk) entre distribution quasi globale et géohistoire localisée et localisante: à propos d'une tension instituante." *Circulations musicales transatlantiques au XXe siècle: Des Beatles au hardcore punk*, edited by Philippe Poirrier and Lucas Le Texier. Editions Universitaires de Dijon (Musiques), 2021, pp. 263–79.
Müller, Alain. *Construire le monde du hardcore*. Seismo (Terrains des sciences sociales), 2019.
Müller, Alain. "Beyond Ethnographic Scriptocentrism: Modelling Multi-Scalar Processes, Networks, and Relationships." *Anthropological Theory* 16.1, 2016, pp. 98–130.

Name three records that shaped your interest in hardcore/punk:
1. Suicidal Tendencies. *Lights... Camera... Revolution!*
2. Sick of It All. *Scratch the Surface*
3. Earth Crisis. *Gomorrah's Season Ends*

Name three theoretical books that are important for you:
1. Bruno Latour. *Reassembling the Social: An Introduction to Actor-Network-Theory.*
2. Howard S. Becker. *Art Worlds.*
3. Michel Serres and Bruno Latour. *Conversations on Science, Culture, and Time.*

Name the first hardcore/punk show you attended:
Besides local shows, this was probably Biohazard, Dog Eat Dog, and Downset in Fribourg, Switzerland in 1994. Earth Crisis (Geneva, 1999) left a strong impression on me, and I see it as the real beginning of my hardcore career.

Name the first academic conference you attended:
The IASPM-US annual conference "Don't Fence Me In: Borders, Frontiers, and Diasporas" at the University of California San Diego, USA, May 30, 2009, where I presented a paper entitled *Constructing and Performing "Otherness" and "Sameness": Group's Boundary Making Processes in the Tokyo Hardcore Scene.*

Alan Parkes is a PhD candidate studying US history at the University of Delaware. His research focuses on understanding the relationship between music scenes and policymaking in US cities at the end of the twentieth century.

List your most important academic publications on hardcore/punk:
Parkes, Alan. "Don't Forget the Streets: New York City Hardcore Punk and the Struggle for Inclusive Space." *sITA–studii de Istoria și Teoria Arhitecturii* 3, 2015, pp. 133–48.
Parkes, Alan. "Discriminate me: Racial exclusivity and neoliberalism's subcultural influence on New York hardcore." *Punk & Post-Punk* 6.1, 2017, pp. 81–96.

Name three records that shaped your interest in hardcore/punk:
1. Minor Threat. *Complete Discography*
2. Instead. *What We Believe*
3. Unbroken. *Life. Love. Regret.*

Name three theoretical books that are important for you:
1. Stuart Hall and Tony Jefferson (eds). *Resistance Through Rituals: Youth Subcultures in Post-war Britain.*
2. George Lipsitz. *Dangerous Crossroads: Popular Music, Postmodernism, and the Poetics of Place.*
3. Raymond Williams. *Culture and Materialism.*

Name the first hardcore/punk show you attended:
7 Seconds in 2004 in Fresno, California.

Name the first academic conference you attended:
The One Century of Record Labels Conference for the International Association for the Study of Popular Music at Newcastle University, UK, in November of 2014. I presented a paper titled "Leaving A Mark: Hardcore Punk's DIY Labels," which wasn't very good.

David Pearson is a music historian, teacher, saxophonist, and composer. His book, *Rebel Music in the Triumphant Empire: Punk Rock in the 1990s United States*, was published by Oxford University Press in 2021. His music can be found at https://fearsomepearson.bandcamp.com. He holds a PhD in musicology from CUNY Graduate Center and is an adjunct associate professor at Lehman College.

List your most important academic publications on hardcore/punk:
Pearson, David. *Rebel Music in the Triumphant Empire: Punk Rock in the 1990s United States.* Oxford University Press, 2021.

Name three records that shaped your interest in hardcore/punk:
1. Aus-Rotten. *The System Works… For Them*
2. NOFX. *Punk in Drublic*
3. Subhumans. *The Day the Country Died*

Name three theoretical books that are important for you:
1. Samuel Floyd. *The Power of Black Music: Interpreting Its History from Africa to the United States.*
2. Susan McClary. *Feminine Endings: Music, Gender, and Sexuality.*
3. Amiri Baraka. *Blues People: Negro Music in White America.*

Name the first hardcore/punk show you attended:
Hmmm … if we're talking hardcore specifically, then DFL? Integrity? We should probably go with Integrity so that Cleveland is proudly represented.

Name the first academic conference you attended:
International Association of Popular Music Studies (US)

Stacy Russo (stacy-russo.com), librarian/associate professor at Santa Ana College in Southern California, is a writer and artist who is committed to creating books and art for a more peaceful world. She is currently pursuing her PhD at California Institute of Integral Studies. Stacy always takes her coffee black and eats chocolate every morning.

List your most important academic publications on hardcore/punk:
Russo, Stacy. *We Were Going to Change the World: Interviews with Women from the 1970s & 1980s Southern California Punk Rock Scene.* Santa Monica Press, 2017.

Name three records that shaped your interest in hardcore/punk:
1. Dead Kennedys. *In God We Trust, Inc.*
2. Conflict. *Increase the Pressure*
3. Minor Threat. *Minor Threat*

Name three theoretical books that are important for you:
1. Clarissa Pinkola Estés. *Women Who Run with the Wolves: Myths and Stories of the Wild Woman Archetype.*
2. bell hooks. *Communion: The Female Search for Love.*
3. bell hooks. *Teaching Community: A Pedagogy of Hope.*

Name the first hardcore/punk show you attended:
Social Distortion/TSOL, Fender's, Long Beach, California, 1985

Name the first academic conference you attended:
Berkshire Conference on the History of Women, Claremont, California, June 2005

Marion Schulze holds an assistant professorship in gender studies and cultural anthropology at the Center for Gender Studies at the University of Basel, Switzerland—a position shared with Alain Müller. Author of the book *Hardcore & Gender*, Schulze still publishes on hardcore from time to time and currently works on and with praxeological approaches to gender.

List your most important academic publications on hardcore/punk:
Müller, Alain, and Marion Schulze. "Hardcore-Punk als Weltwerdung. Eine Erprobung des Konzepts der Konvention." *Musik und Konventionen – Qualitätslogiken, Strukturen und Prozesse in Musikwelten*, edited by Rainer Diaz-Bone and Guy Schwegler. Springer VS (Soziologie der Konventionen), forthcoming.
Schulze, Marion. *Hardcore & Gender. Soziologische Einblicke in eine globale Subkultur.* transcript, 2015.
Schulze, Marion. *Harsh Forms.* Hardcore-punk Layout Series, blog, harshforms.com/series-hardcore-punk-layout, ongoing since 2011.

Name three records that shaped your interest in hardcore/punk:
1. Sick of It All. *Scratch the Surface*
2. Uniform Choice. *Screaming for Change*
3. All Out War. *For Those Who Were Crucified*

Name three theoretical books that are important for you:
1. Norbert Elias. *The Civilizing Process*.
2. Howard S. Becker. *Art Worlds*.
3. Virginia Woolf. *A Room of One's Own*.

Name the first hardcore/punk show you attended:
I consider a Sick of It All show in Bielefeld, Germany, at JZ Kamp on June 15, 1995, my first hardcore show because I made friends there for a hardcore lifetime.

Name the first academic conference you attended:
The first conference where I presented was "Unbeschreiblich weiblich? Mädchen und junge Frauen in Jugendkulturen" in Weimar, Germany, in 2007. I was asked by an audience member to demonstrate how people dance in hardcore and I felt mortified. From the very beginning of my academic career, I thus realized that most people would not be interested in my theoretical arguments but in hardcore as a curiosity (me included).

Francis Stewart is the Implicit Religion Post-Doctoral Research Fellow and lectures in the theology department at Bishop Grosseteste University (BGU). She gained a Masters in Theology from the University of Glasgow and completed her PhD at the University of Stirling. Her PhD thesis was the first ever sociological overview of the UK Straight Edge punk scene and the first ever exploration of the connections between religion and Straight Edge punk. Prior to joining BGU, Francis was a teaching fellow at the University of Stirling, and a high school teacher of Religious Studies before that. Her research interests include punk and anarchy subcultures in Northern Ireland; Straight Edge punk; Sound and Noise; Curation and Memorialization; Marginalisation; and Animal Activism. Francis is a steering group member of the Punk Scholars Network and editorial board member for the Intellect journal *Punk & Post-Punk*.

List your most important academic publications on hardcore/punk:
Stewart, Francis. *Punk Rock is my Religion: Straight Edge Punk and Hardcore 'Religion'*. Routledge, 2017.
Stewart, Francis. "No More Heroes Anymore: Marginalized Identities in Punk Memorialization and Curation." *Punk & Post-Punk* 8.2, June 2019, pp. 209–26.

Stewart, Francis. "From Belfast with Love: The Women and Female Presenting Punks of Northern Ireland and their 'Subculture.'" *Punk Identities, Punk Utopias*, edited by Russ Bestley et al. Intellect, 2022, pp. 19–38.
Stewart, Francis, and Laura Way (eds.) *Punk Pedagogies in Practice: Disruptions and Connections*. Intellect, forthcoming, 2023.

Name three records that shaped your interest in hardcore/punk:
1. Minor Threat. *Complete Discography*
2. Sick of It All. *Blood Sweat and No Tears*
3. Stiff Little Fingers. *Inflammable Material*

Name three theoretical books that are important for you:
1. Salomé Voegelin. *The Political Possibilities of Sound*.
2. Stuart Hall. *Encoding and Decoding in the Television Discourse*.
3. Robert Beckford. *Documentary as Exorcism: Resisting the Bewitchment of Colonial Christianity*.

Name the first hardcore/punk show you attended:
Stiff Little Fingers, Belfast, 1992

Name the first academic conference you attended:
Socrel (Sociology of Religion), Birmingham, 2008

Daniel S. Traber is a professor of English at Texas A&M University at Galveston. He is the author of *Culturcide and Non-Identity across American Culture* (Lexington, 2017) and *Whiteness, Otherness, and the Individualism Paradox from Huck to Punk* (Palgrave, 2007). His work has appeared in journals such as *Cultural Critique, The Journal of Popular Culture, American Studies, Popular Music and Society*, and *Critical Studies in Men's Fashion*. He is also an invited contributor to the recent essay collection *The Oxford Handbook of Punk Rock*.

List your most important academic publications on hardcore/punk:
Traber, Daniel S. "L.A.'s 'White Minority': Punk and the Contradictions of Self-Marginalization." *Cultural Critique* 48, 2001, pp. 30–64.
Traber, Daniel S. "Locating the Punk Preppy (A Speculative Theory)." *The Journal of Popular Culture* 41.3, 2008, pp. 488–508.
Traber, Daniel S. "You Ain't No Punk, You Punk: On Semiotic Doxa, Postmod-

ern Authenticity, Ontological Agency and the Goddamn Alt-Right." *The Oxford Handbook of Punk Rock*, edited by George McKay and Gina Arnold. Online edition, Oxford Academic, 2020.

Name three records that shaped your interest in hardcore/punk:
1. Sex Pistols. *Never Mind the Bollocks …*
2. Dead Kennedys. *In God We Trust, Inc.*
3. Hüsker Dü. *Zen Arcade*

Name three theoretical books that are important for you:
1. Gilles Deleuze and Félix Guattari. *A Thousand Plateaus.*
2. Jean-Luc Nancy. *The Inoperative Community.*
3. William E. Connolly. *Identity/Difference: Democratic Negotiations of Political Paradox.*

Name the first hardcore/punk show you attended:
Public Image Ltd. (technically John Lydon's post-punk band but they played Sex Pistols songs).

Name the first academic conference you attended:
Southwest Popular Culture Association (1996)

Maxwell Tremblay received his PhD in Philosophy from the New School for Social Research, where his dissertation focused on Frantz Fanon and anti-colonial thought. He is the co-editor of *White Riot: Punk Rock and the Politics of Race*, and plays drums in Sleepies.

List your most important academic publications on hardcore/punk:
Duncombe, Stephen, and Maxwell Tremblay (eds.). *White Riot: Punk Rock and the Politics of Race.* Verso, 2011.

Name three records that shaped your interest in hardcore/punk:
1. Blatz/Filth. *The Shit Split*
2. Turbonegro. *Ass Cobra*
3. Feederz. *Ever Feel Like Killing Your Boss?*

Name three theoretical books that are important for you:
1. Immanuel Kant. *Critique of Judgment*.
2. Frantz Fanon. *The Wretched of the Earth*.
3. Susan Buck-Morss. *Hegel, Haiti and Universal History*.

Name the first hardcore/punk show you attended:
Groovie Ghoulies at Bottom of the Hill in San Francisco, CA

Name the first academic conference you attended:
"Rethinking Subjectivity," the graduate conference at the New School for Social Research Philosophy Department.

Katharina Wiedlack is a post-doctoral scholar of American Studies at the University of Vienna. She has published extensively in the fields of Feminist, Queer, Punk and Cultural Studies, most notably in her monograph *Queer-Feminist Punk: An Antisocial History* (Zaglossus, 2015). Currently, her research focuses on transnational American Studies, particularly on historic Russian American cultural exchange.

List your most important academic publications on hardcore/punk:
Wiedlack, Katharina. *Queer-Feminist Punk: An Antisocial History*. Zaglossus, 2015 (Open Access available at: https://e-book.fwf.ac.at/detail/o:774#?q=Wiedlack &page=1&pagesize=10).
Wiedlack, Katharina. "Pussy Riot and the Western Gaze: Punk Music, Solidarity and the Production of Similarity and Difference." *Popular Music and Society* 39.4, 2015, pp. 410–22.
Wiedlack, Katharina. "Loud, rude, and with an attitude. Queer-Feminist Punk Form, Meaning and Affect." *Perverse Assemblages*, edited by Ina Beyer, Barbara Paul, and Josh Hoehnes. Revolver, 2017, pp. 124–38.

Name three records that shaped your interest in hardcore/punk:
1. X-Ray Spex. *Germfree Adolescents*
2. Petro, Muriel & Esther. *The White to Be Angry*
3. The Skinjobs. *Burn Your Rainbow*

Name three theoretical books that are important for you:
1. José Muñoz. *Disidentifications: Queers of Color and the Performance of Politics.*
2. Gloria E. Anzaldúa. *Borderlands/La Frontera: The New Mestiza.*
3. Lee Edelman. *No Future: Queer Theory and the Death Drive.*

Name the first hardcore/punk show you attended:
I don't remember. But the most amazing and life-changing show I ever attended was a Stag Bitten, NighTraiN, My Parade, and Kusikia concert at the feminist bookstore In Other Words in Portland, on 28 August 2010.

Name the first academic conference you attended:
Probably, the Lesbian Lives Conference in Dublin in 2004, or 2005... really don't remember...

Robert A. Winkler is a postdoctoral researcher and lecturer at the Paris Lodron University of Salzburg in Austria. He received his PhD from the *International Graduate Centre for the Study of Culture* (GCSC) at Justus Liebig University Giessen in 2019 with a dissertation on race and gender in US hardcore. Robert published on topics as diverse as hardcore/punk; whiteness; ecocriticism; or the philosophy of Martin Heidegger. He bugs his colleagues with loud music emanating from his office.

List your most important academic publications on hardcore/punk:
Winkler, Robert A. *Generation Reagan Youth: Representing and Resisting White Neoliberal Forms of Life in the U.S. Hardcore Punk Scene (1979-1999).* WVT, 2021.
Winkler, Robert A. "Was John Wayne a Nazi? The Racial Politics of Taste in 1980s US Hardcore Punk." *Punk & Post-Punk* 5.2, 2016, pp. 131–46.
Grebe, Justus, and Robert A.Winkler. "Putting the 'Punk' Back into Pop-Punk: Analysing Presentations of Deviance in Pop-Punk Music Videos." *Punk & Post-Punk* 10.1,2021, pp. 15–27.

Name three records that shaped your interest in hardcore/punk:
1. NOFX. *The War on Errorism*
2. Reagan Youth. *Youth Anthems for the New Order*
3. Minor Threat. *Complete Discography*

Name three theoretical books that are important for you:
1. Martin Heidegger. *Sein und Zeit.*
2. Friedrich A. Kittler. *The Truth of the Technological World: Essays on the Genealogy of Presence.*
3. Hans Ulrich Gumbrecht. *Production of Presence: What Meaning Cannot Convey.*

Name the first hardcore/punk show you attended:
Speaking of punk: Beatsteaks at the Taubertal Openair 2004 in my beloved hometown Rothenburg ob der Tauber; speaking of hardcore: Agnostic Front at the Backstage in Munich in 2010 or 2011

Name the first academic conference you attended:
As a young student assistant at the Annual Meeting of the Historians of the DGfA in Tutzing in 2010 or 2011.

Acknowledgements

We would like to thank Farrah Skeiky for providing the great photograph that became the cover of this anthology. Check out her work at farrahskeiky.com! A great many thanks and high-five go to Alex Butz who created the cover design and perfectly expressed our ideal conception of hardcore research: Just as Alex visually weaved the letters into the audience depicted in Farrah's photograph and thus made the book title—almost organically—grow out of an active hardcore crowd, we conceive of hardcore research as particularly strong when it emerges from and is conducted, presented, articulated or inspired by the people who are involved and immersed in the respective hardcore/punk scenes. We owe you, Alex! Furthermore, we would like to thank Benjamin Brendel, Moritz Ingwersen, Philipp Meinert, Simon Ottersbach, Susana Sepulveda, Karl Siebengartner, Audrey Silvestre, Christoph Straub, Paul Vickers, Nico Völker, and Anne Wheeler.

Cultural Studies

Gabriele Klein
Pina Bausch's Dance Theater
Company, Artistic Practices and Reception

2020, 440 p., pb., col. ill.
29,99 € (DE), 978-3-8376-5055-6
E-Book:
PDF: 29,99 € (DE), ISBN 978-3-8394-5055-0

Markus Gabriel, Christoph Horn, Anna Katsman, Wilhelm Krull,
Anna Luisa Lippold, Corine Pelluchon, Ingo Venzke
**Towards a New Enlightenment –
The Case for Future-Oriented Humanities**

October 2022, 80 p., pb.
18,00 € (DE), 978-3-8376-6570-3
E-Book: available as free open access publication
PDF: ISBN 978-3-8394-6570-7
ISBN 978-3-7328-6570-3

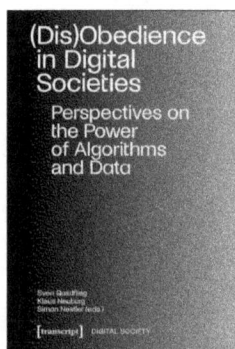

Sven Quadflieg, Klaus Neuburg, Simon Nestler (eds.)
(Dis)Obedience in Digital Societies
Perspectives on the Power of Algorithms and Data

March 2022, 380 p., pb., ill.
29,00 € (DE), 978-3-8376-5763-0
E-Book: available as free open access publication
PDF: ISBN 978-3-8394-5763-4
ISBN 978-3-7328-5763-0

Cultural Studies

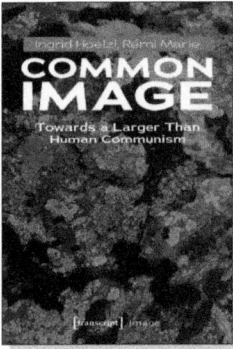

Ingrid Hoelzl, Rémi Marie
Common Image
Towards a Larger Than Human Communism

2021, 156 p., pb., ill.
29,50 € (DE), 978-3-8376-5939-9
E-Book:
PDF: 26,99 € (DE), ISBN 978-3-8394-5939-3

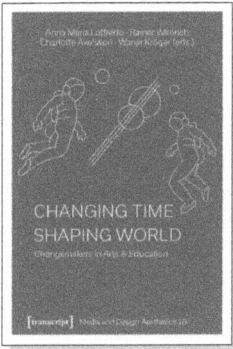

Anna Maria Loffredo, Rainer Wenrich,
Charlotte Axelsson, Wanja Kröger (eds.)
Changing Time – Shaping World
Changemakers in Arts & Education

September 2022, 310 p., pb., col. ill.
45,00 € (DE), 978-3-8376-6135-4
E-Book: available as free open access publication
PDF: ISBN 978-3-8394-6135-8

Olga Moskatova, Anna Polze, Ramón Reichert (eds.)
Digital Culture & Society (DCS)
Vol. 7, Issue 2/2021 –
Networked Images in Surveillance Capitalism

August 2022, 336 p., pb., col. ill.
29,99 € (DE), 978-3-8376-5388-5
E-Book:
PDF: 27,99 € (DE), ISBN 978-3-8394-5388-9

**All print, e-book and open access versions of the titles in our list
are available in our online shop www.transcript-publishing.com**

GPSR Authorized Representative: Easy Access System Europe, Mustamäe tee
50, 10621 Tallinn, Estonia, gpsr.requests@easproject.com